Praise for *Civil Rights Baby*

"This book is a lesson for any person with astronomical goals. Like athletes, Nita beat the odds!"
— **Everson Walls**, *Super Bowl winner and kidney donor*

"A must-read that will help other people find out where their strengths lie."
— **LaToya Gibson**, *founder and CEO, Texas Tutors*

"Nita is a tour de force of a human being and has so much experience and knowledge to offer."
— **Todd Brown, PhD**, *Founder, The Inspire Project*

"To me, it was her calming but confident interviewing style that made her one of the most trusted news reporters in our area back then."
— **Russell Maryland**, *three-time Super Bowl champion, Dallas Cowboys*

"This is a real guidebook for tapping into excellence in the broadcasting field."
— **Amal Shah**, *author and SiriusXM radio host*

"You can't imagine how moved I was when she said, 'If you don't feel represented, then go for it and represent yourself.'"
— **Lydia Toukal**, *student, Sciences Po Toulouse (France)*

"It's a profound book with important messages and a lot of good stories. I recommend it."
— **Jack Canfield**, *best-selling author and* Chicken Soup for the Soul *series co-creator*

"Civil Rights Baby has given me more heartache than I care to endure. In the face of the passage about the hotel towels, I suddenly burst into tears. This passage reminds me of Ralph Ellison's *Invisible Man* and Franz Kafka's *Metamorphosis* . . . as I have friends who are also facing the challenges Nita has faced."
> – **Angela Shaw**, *former staff attorney for the FCC and the NAACP*

"Nita Wiggins taught us that we can do anything we put our minds to despite the obstacles or unfair treatment that may come our way."
> – **Carmesha Blackmon**, *student, Bennett College, Greensboro, North Carolina*

"It's more than a book. It's a confessional."
> – **Charly Mérinos Liatou**, *journalist, Paris, France*

"Nita shares her saga with a light hand, never indulging in self-pity or mean-spiritedness. Civil Rights Baby spurred captivating conversations in my book club."
> – **Christina Howell**, *Founder of Memoir Mentors*

"We need this kind of testimony. It is a story of resilience, like with many African Americans. She had a triple threat: racism and sexism, and it caused an illness. She managed to heal, so it's enriching to read. When we have black skin, this is a reality."
> – **Falila Gbadamassi**, *journalist,* Franceinfo

"It was remarkable hearing Nita's personal and professional experiences."
> – **Ricardo Bravo**, *Rotary Club of Martinez-Evans (Georgia)*

"I really appreciate the stories of brave women who managed to change their lives. That shows us that we can fulfill our dreams, not being afraid to have big ones."
> – **Perrine Scheer**, *former student, L'École Supérieure de Journalisme de Paris (ESJ Paris)*

Civil Rights Baby

Civil Rights Baby

My Story of Race, Sports, and Breaking Barriers
in American Journalism

NITA WIGGINS

Ordering Information:
Special discounts are available on quantity purchases by educators, associa-
tions, or corporations. For details, contact nita@nitawiggins.com.

Edited by J.M. Walker
Book design by Christy Day, Constellation Book Design
Publishing guidance by Martha Bullen, Bullen Publishing Services
Author photo on book cover by Wade Livingston
Author photo on About the Author page by Lucie Cervantes
Author baby photo by Hollywood Studio in Macon, Georgia

ISBN 978-1-7375805-0-8 (paperback)
ISBN 978-1-7375805-1-5 (ebook)

Printed in the United States of America

Dedicated to my supportive family members and to barrier-breaking journalist Alice Dunnigan (1906–1983). Her autobiography, *Alone Atop the Hill*, gave me a clear path to follow in retelling the events of my career with journalistic objectivity.

CONTENTS

A Word to the Reader

I am guided by a desire to create empathy by showing the sameness of people at their most human level. The same journalistic integrity that I took into the job of telling the stories of other people's lives I employed as the author of this book.

I do not intend this to be an Afrocentric perspective in competition with a Eurocentric perspective. Rather, I intend to deliver an honest, personal view at a time when women's stories and black women's stories are being recognized as a missing element in explaining a place or a time period. More than one year has passed since the abominable, videotaped police murder of George Floyd committed by then-officer Derek Michael Chauvin in Minneapolis in the U.S. It is nearly four years since Me Too statements exposed the crushing domination of (mostly) women by higher-placed men in the movie and television industries around the world. *Civil Rights Baby* inspires a necessary contemplation of the accompanying paradigm shifts.

A reader from Uganda says that this story mirrors "what most of us women experience." For that reason, I repeatedly use the generic descriptor "white male." Some readers may interpret that as a sign of resentment, but most readers would recognize the need to know the race and gender of the person who pulls the strings of power in different settings in this narrative. I use race descriptors for most people in my story (except sports figures, celebrities, scholars, doctors, and my family members).

In addition, I use race descriptors because the default race in my America is the white race. Most written narratives in our country do not identify a character's race when that character is white. That assumes white is the norm. The parallel in the internet age would be comparing what we call the "white race" to the Google search engine—something so all-encompassing and ever-present that we must point out when it is not present. However, that premise is not accurate. Not all readers, American or otherwise, envision white as the default. So, other than the exceptions listed above, throughout this book I note when the person is white just as I do when the person is not white.

More directly, an early reader mistakenly believed a heroic person in my story to be white, while picturing an uninspired medical technician in my story to be black. The reverse is the truth. Regardless of which person is heroic and which is uninspired, I am presenting for you my life and the people who affected me in the truest distillation that my writing will allow.

Nita Wiggins
Paris, July 2021

Preface

Broadcast journalism's coveted positions in front of the camera need a warning label. Something blunt like *Hazardous to Your Health*. That's straightforward and clear. *Pitfalls Ahead* also works.

My gynecologist told me I had fibroid tumors in 2006. I had three growths of various sizes in my uterus. One, detected initially as the size of a golf ball, had grown to grapefruit size by the time I underwent invasive surgery to have them all pulverized and extracted in December 2008. I escaped the debilitating side effects, but some women suffer pelvic and back pain, bladder discomfort, menstrual irregularities, and intestinal-tract disruptions. I did, however, have a daily reminder of my fibroids. Before surgery, my bloated belly gave the impression of a sixteen-week pregnancy.

No need for alarm, my doctor cautioned during the initial exam. Three out of four women of color experience the same non-cancerous growths, she told me. As a forty-two-year-old black woman, I was typical, she said.

"What's behind the tumors? Why do I have them?" I asked her. Though the tumors were not life-threatening, I needed to know the prognosis for my long-term health. *Three out of four women of color?* With such a pervasive occurrence, surely the medical community could tell me more.

"No reason. It just happens. It's one of those things" came the nonchalant reply.

Her answer did not satisfy me. For some reason, it made me feel like a statistic, a throwaway patient, even though I was in a first-rate medical facility with insurance provided by my corporate media employer in Dallas, Texas. I received a little more information weeks later, during my follow-up exam. "I have had them myself," said the white imaging technician who was performing an ultrasound probe of my uterus. "Having tumors does not affect being able to become a mother. I have three children. Some women choose to do nothing about them. But we will monitor them."

Eleven years passed before I finally heard something more than a cursory or dismissive explanation about the cause of my fibroids. I was attending a conference in the United States, where a doctor on a panel said that research linked certain social environments with the formation of fibroid tumors. One of those conditions, she pointed out, was a workplace setting in which a woman endured sustained levels of high stress and opposition.

The news was troubling.

Had my career choice made me sick?

Of course, when my tumors were diagnosed, I had no idea of their cause. They were simply an added challenge to my already-challenging quest to succeed in a non-traditional field. Whenever the camera captured me in a full-body shot, I was acutely aware of the pregnancy look of my belly. News like that—*TV broadcaster expecting child*—could excite the viewers and increase a journalist's following, but in my case, it would be a never-ending pregnancy with no payoff to viewers who loyally watched me through the "gestation." And, as an unmarried woman, it would not be an acceptable image for the conservative television managers of Dallas, Texas. All of it becomes a losing ticket for a female journalist who strives for longevity in front of the camera.

I thought I was coping well within the oppressive work environments at my TV stations, but I now know that my body was out of balance. While outwardly I masked my unease, I failed to convince my insides. And I was not alone. Several of my broadcasting contemporaries, black women who worked together under one white male news director, encountered so much job stress that they all suffered from the medical condition called *amenorrhea*, an interruption of the menstrual cycle. This seems to support the panel doctor's assertion that unhealthy social environments can create physical disruptions in the most intimate part of a woman's body.

True, all journalists live with stress—it is an inherent part of the job. I actually enjoyed defeating the routine stresses in my line of work. But I am referring to the *unnecessary* stress I endured because of someone else's refusal to fully accept my presence in the newsroom. You see, I set out on my career journey believing in the protections of the Civil Rights Act of 1964, which was passed the year I was born. The laws, as written, were supposed to obliterate the sources of biased-induced stress that could come my way.

My experience convinces me of the opposite. Women in broadcasting—especially those in my specialty, sports broadcasting—can find themselves standing toe-to-toe with a special set of circumstances and expectations unknown to their male counterparts. In addition to causing physical harm, this being singled out for special *mistreatment* becomes an emotional burden. At one point, the weight of it grew so great I came heart-poundingly close to a decision that would have thrown away my respected professional standing and all the blessings in my life.

I want to expose the detrimental effects that my career in television exacted on me. I want workplace mistreatment to stop for people in all traditionally marginalized communities. I mean, specifically, mistreatment based on "race, color, religion, sex, or national origin," the words engraved into American law.[1] This is why I write.

I write, too, in the hopes that young Marley Dias and her generation can add my name to a group that is distressingly small: black female protagonists for whom readers can root. Impassioned by books, the eleven-year-old African American girl in New Jersey pleaded for school reading assignments that did not focus only on "white boys and their dogs."[2] I agree with Marley. Young readers in

---

1. Protections as listed in the Civil Rights Act of 1964.
2. Marley Dias' quote from an episode of Comedy Central's *The Nightly Show with Larry Wilmore*, 2016.

a wonderfully diverse country deserve curricula rich in ethnically diverse points of view.

Civil Rights Baby illustrates how I, as a female person of color, confronted an entrenched system and attempted to manage my emotions and actions against daunting odds. I conducted deep introspection to decide what price I would pay to insert myself into a world—broadcast journalism—that held the most appeal for me.

This is my story of what unfolded in America's Land of Opportunity.

Nita Wiggins
Paris, March 2019

Introduction

Fighting the Invisible

I look for the good in all people. I approach others in the workplace believing they will see in me what I look for in them: merit. While I must allude often to racism as I tell my story, I do not believe it motivates every unpleasant act or outcome. I know that sometimes a person of color doesn't get a promotion or a contract simply because the person doesn't deserve it. I am aware, too, that I might not receive respectful treatment at work simply because someone else is unprofessional, resentful, or unhappy.

But.

The fact remains that most of the resistance I received during my twenty-one years on American television came from white men. Some used underhanded, malicious tactics to prevent me from advancing in my field. Even when I complained to superiors about the practices and presented what I believed to be proof, I continued to receive the mistreatment. The same happened to other African American female reporters in my circle, including those who worked in other cities and states. In some cases, the bosses perpetrated these actions and seemed to operate with one goal: to block the path of black females in their world.

I wish such injustices were not part of my life's story, but as we say in the U.S., *It is what it is.*

The elusive nature of racism makes mine a hard story to tell—or, rather, a hard case to prove. How do you describe it to someone who does not receive it? How do you prove its presence in another's heart? After all, you can't *see* a motive.

You can, however, feel the effects of a motive. Professional minority women across all industries often must fight for more than job promotions. They must fight for job *survival*. White women, too, fight a battle in professional settings. Though they may usually escape racial resistance, many would admit they routinely face patriarchal and sexist foes.

Return of the Noose

Even with federal laws mandating racial and gender equality in hiring, devious people in the workplace still maneuver to chop the knees out from under the "other" (members of traditionally marginalized groups). The actions of these attackers seem to be an expression of discontent at being forced to work alongside individuals who are not members of the attackers' groups. Is this the same motivation lynchers harbored decades ago in the United States?

Dictionaries employ stark language to define "lynching," using expressions such as "extrajudicial mob action" or "execution without legal authority," and even "informal public execution, usually by hanging." But dictionaries do not explain the reasons for lynching. My research points to race-based terrorism as the root of the more than 4,000 lynchings of black people, post-slavery, in the United States. The work of the Equal Justice Initiative reveals that race-based lynchings occurred, in many instances, because a respectable black person had achieved a measure of success—and someone was jealous of that success.[3]

Of course, in my career experience, no one tried to execute me. Instead, at more than one television station between the years 1986 and 2009, someone tried to kill my dreams. Someone executed judgment against me without first finding out what I knew and what I was capable of doing in my field. Not a literal lynching, true, but an act I believe was born of the same type of jealousy that inspired this shameful legacy.

---

3. "The lynching of African Americans was terrorism, a widely supported campaign to enforce racial subordination and segregation. *Lynching in America* documents more than 4,400 racial terror lynchings in the United States during the period between Reconstruction (1877) and World War II (1939-1945)." (See www.eji.org.)

Hence, an *economic* lynching.

In private torment, even as I presented a professional and pleasant face to the world, I endured the effects of the jealousy, or whatever was the dark motive that drove my tormenters.

For years, I was afraid to speak out about this nightmare. Not anymore. When I began writing this book in 2014, I had arrived at a peaceful and powerful new stage in my life. I had found the courage to write about my experience.

I began finding my courage that year in Paris, France. Doctoral student Doria Dee Johnson, an African American from the University of Wisconsin-Madison, was a guest speaker at Dorothy's Gallery, an American-culture oasis located in Paris' 11th *arrondissement*. I was present when Ms. Johnson transported her audience, about one hundred people, back to a detestable place and time in America's race-relations history. Ms. Johnson focused on a crime that had occurred some one hundred years earlier. She began:

> "I am the great-great-granddaughter of Anthony and Tebby Crawford, the great granddaughter of George and Annabelle Crawford, the granddaughter of Joseph and Fannie Crawford Brooks, and the daughter of Dr. Charles and Helen Brooks Johnson. My story is about my great-great-grandfather's lynching in 1916 in Abbeville, South Carolina."[4]

After this intriguing opening, Ms. Johnson began a gripping enumeration. Because her speech took place on September 26, she read the names of those who had been lynched in American history on the date of September 26.

"Charles Mack, lynched, Swainsboro, Georgia, September 26, 1891.

---

4. Historical accounts report that on Saturday, October 21, 1916, in Abbeville, South Carolina, a white mob lynched black businessman and community leader Anthony Crawford. According to the Equal Justice Initiative (www.eji.org), the murder, though committed openly, did not lead to prosecution or conviction for any members of the mob.

"One unidentified black man, lynched, Lincoln, Oklahoma, September 26, 1894.

"Felician Francis, lynched, New Orleans, Louisiana, September 26, 1895."

Grimaces etched the faces of members of the lecture's audience—French citizens, Americans, people from other countries.

Pausing after each name as if to punctuate the slain one's humanity, Ms. Johnson continued:

"Raymond Bushrod . . . lynched. Hainesville, Kentucky, September 26, 1897.

"John Williams . . . lynched. Mountain City, Tennessee, September 26, 1898.

"One unidentified black man . . . lynched. South Pittsburg, Tennessee, September 26, 1900.

"Charles Anderson . . . lynched. Perry, Florida, September 26, 1909."

The audience had fallen into silence. I imagined Ms. Johnson's delivery pierced each listener to the core, as it was doing to me. But something else happened to me as I listened. An otherworldly, out-of-body quasi-consciousness overtook me. I felt as if I were hovering above each raging historical mob that was carrying out its act of bloody injustice.

"The United States allowed this to go on?" a shocked someone in the Dorothy's Gallery audience uttered softly.[5] No one in the audience answered the question; Doria Dee Johnson's litany of names was answer enough.

"Peter Hudson . . . lynched. Cuthbert, Georgia, September 26, 1916.

"Elijah Sturgis . . . lynched. Cuthbert, Georgia, September 26, 1916.

---

5. According to *Lynching in America: Confronting the Legacy of Racial Terror* (2015), released by the Equal Justice Initiative (www.eji.org), the U.S. government and state governments, by not prosecuting the guilty parties, allowed black citizens to be terrorized for decades by the possibility of being lynched.

"John White . . . lynched. Opelousas, Louisiana, September 26, 1933 . . ."

Many in the audience squirmed and contorted their faces with pity and disgust, and even with indignation. Still others covered their mouths and gasped as Ms. Johnson showed photos of tortured victims, including men, women, and children—and of smiling white onlookers, dressed in their Sunday best for the occasion.

Ms. Johnson admitted that her family initially felt humiliated because of the lynching. So did other families who lost loved ones to these executions. She had come to realize, she said, that "the shame goes to the lyncher and his society." Sadly, her family did not realize that fact soon enough. Her bereaved ancestors uprooted themselves from their home, leaving behind a wealth of property. They not only felt stained by the violent death but feared for their lives. (See Endnotes.)

Decades later, Ms. Johnson recaptured territory. On that autumn night in 2014 in France, not far from where Parisians had stormed the Bastille in protest against their monarchy, Ms. Johnson claimed ownership of her great-great-grandfather's dignity. She mesmerized the audience. She forced her listeners to ponder the idea that the shame of lynching belongs to the one who commits the crime, not to the person whose breath is stolen, nor to that one's family.

Doria Dee Johnson's speech ignited my pen. When she shared the sobering sample of the names of lynch victims, I knew that I needed to come forward with the fact that while literal lynching had gone underground, a symbolic version of it was still alive and well in the country of my birth. And if such a comparison seems an exaggeration, I know it is safe to say that the dark motives that spawned historical lynching are still alive and actively damaging American souls today.

Because of this grim reality, I am determined to help effect a change. I know that silence on the part of the mistreated only emboldens those who mistreat. Therefore, with this book, I am no longer silent.

PART I

The Strongest Voices

CHAPTER 1

With the Grace of Grandmothers

"Nita and Daddy will watch tomato cans box!" my brother Ronald, a teenager at the time, playfully pointed out. Three years younger than I, Ronald was not ridiculing my father and me and our shared activity; he was simply stating a fact.

In boxing terminology, a "tomato can" is an unskilled or not-yet-developed boxer. Observers of the sport expect a tomato can to lose to the hot boxer who is on his way to a title shot. At the root of the expression is the belief that it's easy to knock over a tomato can. As my younger brother's teasing remark revealed, my father and I would spend many hours watching these lesser fighters on television.

Ronald himself liked sports. He played basketball and baseball on teams that our dad coached at the Warren Road recreation center near our home in Augusta, Georgia. Ron watched football, basketball, some golf, and a few other sports on TV, even boxing. But he drew the line at tomato cans.

That gave me an open shot at my dad's time and attention. I capitalized on this opportunity during my formative years, using sports as the glue. As a six-year-old, I sat at his elbow nearly eight hours on Sundays during football season, watching NFL games. He asked me to predict the winners and explain my reasons. No matter what I said—whether I named player injuries, team inexperience, or coaching changes as the basis for my reason—he allowed me to state my views and support them. He would listen intently and then would offer his own ideas—sometimes, the same ones I had expressed, but in grown-up words. I would use those words in my next go-round.

Another wonderful thing my dad did was give me a role in Ronald's baseball games.

"Keep count of the balls and strikes. OK?" Dad said when he gave me my new assignment.

In 1975, a girl usually could get no closer than the bleacher seats for a boys' baseball game. To fulfill the role Daddy had given me, I was still confined to the bleachers, but I had a choice location—the area directly behind home plate, where I could clearly monitor the umpire and catcher.

Better than my location on the field, though, was the instrument I held in my hands to carry out Daddy's order. I remember the first time he handed me the piece of molded black plastic. A pitch score counter!—maybe a Spalding or Franklin brand. It was small, tiny enough to fit snugly inside my eleven-year-old hand. It felt like gold. Unblinkingly, I would watch the pitches thrown and use my plastic palm mechanism to click *ball* or *strike* as signaled by the umpire.

Truthfully, my assignment served no real purpose, as far as the game was concerned, though I did not know it at the time. I kept myself ready to yell out the pitch count in case the coach—my daddy!—looked to me, needing reliable information in a split-second. My job linked me to Dad during the games. Linked us symbolically. The wire fence along the first and third baselines, and the sport's gender-based rules, physically separated us. The man-made barriers kept me from being where I wanted to be during the games: at my father's elbow.

My father's hands-on mentoring was the greatest factor that shaped me, but later in life I realized the important role my hard-working, churchgoing grandmothers played in forming the woman I had become. I gained this appreciation for my grandmothers, and for all such early-20th-century black women, because of a career perk that I deeply enjoyed.

National Football League teams negotiate attractive hotel group rates for players, coaches, and the traveling media members who cover road games. This meant that when I covered an NFL team as a Fox-affiliate reporter, I often flew on the team's chartered plane and slept in the finest hotels. Philadelphia's French-themed Sofitel was my favorite, but I also enjoyed assorted Radissons, Westins, and Ritz-Carltons. With the one-thousand-thread-count Egyptian cotton sheets and the goose-feather down pillows, I always felt like I was sleeping on a cloud.

As the luxurious Saturday nights spent in America's fine hotels became commonplace for me, I absorbed and felt gratitude for the divine grace that had smiled on the women of my generation. What fortunate creatures we were, to be able to sleep in settings fit for queens. But even as I relished the luxury, in the hallways of the hotels I would occasionally encounter the women who cleaned the beautifully appointed suites.

The women who cleaned the rooms but likely could not afford to sleep in them.

In the last two or three years of my American career, I took on the habit of carefully tidying up after myself before leaving the hotels to return home. I threw away all newspapers and scribbled notes, as well as the sales tags from purchases I had made. I finished by wiping down the marble bathroom sinks. I added these practices to what I had already done for years when I stayed in hotels: using just one towel and one washcloth, with the objective of cutting down on unnecessary laundering and water use. The other towels remained untouched so that no work was required to ready them for the next guest. If I stayed for several nights on a road trip, I would leave the *Do Not Disturb* sign hanging outside until I closed the door behind me for the last time. I did not want any servicing done to the room because I was trying to lighten the load for the woman who would eventually come in to clean the room.

I had a private reason for doing so.

At the time, I was a central figure in a world that, to outsiders, must have seemed glamorous. A world of bright studio lights and television cameras and celebrity athletes. A world in which I moved within a privileged entourage in and out of the lobbies of elegant hotels. A world in which deferring bellhops quickly relieved us of our luggage, and room cleaners readily supplied us with practical comforts. To these hotel staffers, I must have seemed worlds removed from their life experience.

But the reality was that my grandmothers had earned money by cleaning up behind other people.

As I became increasingly sensitive to the vast differences between my life and that of my dear foremothers, I began to see the hotel cleaning ladies as modern-day versions of my industrious grandmothers.

Malinda Lott, my maternal grandmother, was born in 1916 and worked for wealthy white families in Macon, Georgia. She chose to work because she wanted her own spending money, something separate from my grandfather's construction salary. On the other hand, my paternal grandmother, Bernice Wiggins, whom we called "Boo Mama," had to work. She cleaned motel rooms in Pensacola, Florida, after she and my grandfather divorced. She was born in 1913.

My grandmothers' employment options were limited largely because of the times in which they lived. During the first half of the 20th century, most working black women in the United States were laborers or servers. Though I have black friends whose grandparents attended college, mine did not.

My grandfather James Lott built homes, and my other grandfather, Walter Wiggins, worked in railroad construction. Their jobs paid well enough for them to provide financial security for their families, but the work was hard. They died at ages fifty-six and fifty-three, respectively, while my grandmothers lived nearly forty years longer.

My maternal grandmother, whom I called "Grandmama," lived long enough to see a black man inaugurated as president of the United States in January 2009. She noted Senator Barack Obama's victory with pride because, living her entire life in the Southern part of the country, she had seen her share of racial subjugation. Despite this, Grandmama found joy with her family, her friends, and her church. In true Southern-grandmother fashion, she cooked a sumptuous and generous turkey dinner for the family at Thanksgiving and at Christmas. She doted on me even after I became an adult.

When I worked at WMGT in Macon, where Grandmama resided, I enjoyed Sunday dinners with her from the spring of 1986 to the autumn of 1987. She beamed happily whenever I drove her to church in my low-riding Mustang. I would stay to listen to the sermons, but mostly I watched her. Seated in the front row as a leader in the church, she would glance back to see if I were following the message.

Every time I attended church with her, Grandmama would insist I submit a visitor's card so that the preacher could call on me to stand and receive the greeting of the churchgoers. After the service, Grandmama would introduce me to her church friends as her granddaughter *and* the woman on WMGT—in that order. The people I met said that my TV station would be the one they would watch in their homes from that point on.

Those were good times in Grandmama's church. I was in my first job as a television reporter; I had not yet faced having my aspirations cast aside by those who challenged my ability to perform my role. I felt my grandmother's unconditional love for me and the satisfaction of knowing that she was proud of what I had become at age twenty-two. And I felt the approval of her congregation friends. Later, when the going got tough in my career, part of what kept me burning to succeed was the memory of the people in Grandmama's church. So many good-hearted, solid, sincere, and well-meaning people who were happy that someone they knew had touched a dream that was previously inaccessible for black people.

With a foundation that sturdy, the strength of Southern black people and their altruistic hopes, I was fortified to face the on-the-job discrimination that was coming my way. I did not know it at the time, but like my grandmother's determination, I would need a resolve that could not be bent.

CHAPTER 2

Noisy Neighbors, Media Icons, and Martyrs

I grew up in a remarkable era in American history. At the time of my birth in 1964, the medium we call television was only thirty-seven years old. Though still a novelty, it was beginning to release its force as a developer of media icons.

By the time I came along, television watching had become a nightly ritual for black and white families across the country. However, unlike white television viewers, black people often did not see depictions of themselves on this intriguing new entertainment platform that Americans called *TV*. "Negroes do not exist," the acclaimed playwright and intellectual Lorraine Hansberry observed in 1963.[6]

Hansberry was right. Compared to the presence of white performers on television, black faces were virtually missing. I vividly remember witnessing collective joy when one black person would announce to another that someone black was going to be on television. Someone! It didn't matter *which* black person would appear before national viewing audiences on ABC, CBS, or NBC, the only network options available on the TV dial at that time. It didn't matter which black star—as long as the person was black.

---

6. "America as Seen Through the Eye of the TV Tube," a brief commentary from January 1, 1963, from Lorraine Hansberry and Robert Nemiroff, *To Be Young, Gifted and Black: A Portrait of Lorraine Hansberry In Her Own Words* (New York: Vintage Books, 1995).

Many black people held this sentiment during the decade of my birth. I believe theirs was a reaction to a long history of suppression and to white resistance to black progress. According to Mississippi-born author Joseph Reiff,[7] this resistance peaked from 1962 to 1964. Fortunately, it soon met with an even greater force, the Civil Rights Act of 1964, which outlawed various forms of discrimination. The act became law on July 2, a mere fifty-six days after my birth.

However, the unwillingness of many whites to follow the new law and to relinquish social customs meant that blacks still had to fight for positions of mainstream respect and high visibility. No medium offered such instant regard as did television. That is why the appearance on TV of *one* black person represented a triumph of acknowledgement for *all* of us. In my developing mind, if a person appeared on this alluring medium, this meant the American power structure recognized that he or she had something worthy to say to the world. Maybe that is why I decided, as a child, that I would one day add my face to the television landscape.

Dr. Martin Luther King Jr. appeared often on television and captured my attention during my preschool days. I did not fully comprehend the intricacies of his message, but he grabbed me with the passion he exuded. The reverberation of his voice in every setting, the way he moved purposefully across the screen on his way to a destination, the way people fell in step with him—all of this enthralled me. I would install myself in front of our floor-model console to absorb the images of this man. I would anticipate his next TV appearance. And his next...

Finally, there came the news bulletin on April 4, 1968. I was watching TV while seated on the floor just inches away from the screen. After I absorbed the announcement of King's assassination

---

7. Joseph T. Reiff, *Born of Conviction: White Methodists and Mississippi's Closed Society* (New York: Oxford University Press, 2016).

in Memphis, Tennessee, my family says that I turned away from the television and, with the clear-hearted impulse of a four-year-old, said, "I love Dr. King."

An act of outright and calculated violence had silenced my first media icon.

⁓

I watched TV news as soon as I could toddle. Still, as a child, I did not know that Democrat Carl Sanders held the post of governor for my home state, Georgia, from 1963 to 1967. In contrast, I knew very well the governor of the neighboring state from the same period.

On June 11, 1963, Alabama Governor George Wallace stood in the doorway of Foster Auditorium at the University of Alabama in Tuscaloosa to block black students from entering. In doing so, he defied the U.S. Supreme Court ruling in the precedent-setting *Brown v. Board of Education of Topeka* case. The order meant that the time had come to desegregate the Alabama university.[8]

I had not been born at the time of the showdown between the governor and President John F. Kennedy. However, through the magic medium of television, images from that dramatic day were burned into my thoughts from as early as I can remember. In a nationally televised address the evening of June 11, President Kennedy advised the wayward governor to "admit two clearly qualified, young Alabama residents who happened to be born Negro." Kennedy added, "I hope that every American, regardless of where he lives, will stop and examine his conscience about this and other related incidents."[9]

Black-and-white film footage of the Stand in the Schoolhouse Door introduced to me that watershed moment of rebellion. Even as a toddler, I came to understand the intractable nature of some people—the absolute determination to not break from doing things as they had always been done. Such recalcitrance is evident in the

---

8. UA was founded in 1831. According to the school's website, in the year 2014, the student body was 12 percent African American, 3 percent Hispanic American, and 2 percent Asian American.

9. President John F. Kennedy, "Report to the American People on Civil Rights," June 11, 1963.

following words Mr. Wallace spoke during his gubernatorial inauguration address:

> It is very appropriate that from this Cradle of the Confederacy, this very Heart of the Great Anglo-Saxon Southland . . . in the name of the greatest people that have ever trod this earth, I draw the line in the dust and toss the gauntlet before the feet of tyranny. I say, "Segregation now, segregation tomorrow, and segregation forever!"[10]

Despite his rousing speech and flinty resolve, Wallace lost the battle to block Vivian Malone and James Hood from becoming the first two black students at the University of Alabama.

The governor parlayed his segregationist position into a run for president of the United States in 1968. Governor Wallace and vice presidential candidate Curtis LeMay received the votes of more than 9.4 million people, or 12.9 percent of the popular vote.[11] The winning ticket of former Vice President Richard Nixon and Maryland Governor Spiro Agnew captured 31.7 million votes (43.4 percent). The Republican candidates defeated Senators Hubert Humphrey and Edmund Muskie, Democrats who collected 31 million votes, (42.3 percent).

These political doings emboldened people resistant to the racial tides of change. Their champions sat in high places across the United States. Simultaneously, voices on the other side of the battle were falling silent from assassins' gunshots. Civil rights combatant Medgar Evers died on June 12, 1963, in Jackson, Mississippi. He succumbed to his wounds during the early-morning hours after Kennedy's directive to Wallace. (See Endnotes.)

On November 22, 1963, President Kennedy was assassinated in Dallas, Texas. This happened five months after Evers' death, and five months after Kennedy ordered Wallace to follow the law of the

---

10. Quote transcribed by the author from video archives. Accessed Nov. 4, 2017, at digital. archives.alabama.gov/cdm/singleitem/collection/voices/id/2952/rec/

11. From *presidentelect.org*: Gov. Wallace (from Alabama) and Gen. LeMay (from Ohio) represented the American Independent Party.

land. Six months after the president's assassination, I was born in Macon, Georgia.

The distinct and bloody battle lines of these iconic media events served as the foundation of my understanding of the world as a TV-watching toddler. I saw the virulent backlash, including the assassinations of a sitting U.S. president and of the most prominent black American of the time.

In my own life, a version of Alabama Governor George Wallace would attempt to stop me in my tracks twenty years after I initially watched his famous standoff. Before I faced my doorstep opponent, however, I would have to navigate through the obstacles of elementary school.

CHAPTER 3

Starry-Eyed, then Bleary-Eyed

When a close female relative told me, when I was five, that I should become a nurse or a school teacher, my spirit rebelled. In the 1970s, American women of color could follow those paths without facing much friction, but I rejected the suggestion because even at that young age, I knew that a person did not have to follow expected paths. I believe I felt this from the beginning of my conscious thought. For one thing, I had witnessed Dr. Martin Luther King Jr. on television, full of emotion, having become a mature communicator at the ages of 37 and 38. He spoke boldly and punctuated his well-written messages with facial expressions—the latter lingered in my mind's eye. I was gripped. I wanted to know how it felt to stamp an impression on people in the way that he did.

Unabashedly, at the young age of eight, I envisioned my own glorious future. The year was 1972, and the dreams of my deepest inner child were set in motion. I decided I would not live my entire life in Georgia. Though I adored my family, I steeled my heart, knowing that my choices would take me away from my home base. I accepted that I would see my relatives during visits from the cities where I would make my way as a journalist.

I pointed my compass toward Dallas, Texas, and resolved to become a celebrated reporter covering the men I considered to be the kings of sports: the venerated Dallas Cowboys.

Why sports reporting? Why the Cowboys?

When I watched TV broadcasts that featured professional and international sports, I became the enthralled spectator. Waves of sensations and emotions drenched me. I don't know if it were skillful pitchman writing or my own innate curiosity that fascinated me, but phrases such as "the agony of defeat" and "tomorrow's champions" enticed me to follow the human drama that accompanied the competitions. I wanted to know not just who had won the trophy, but who the person was on the inside. What unseen obstacles had he overcome to reach the all-or-nothing outcome? Even as a child, I yearned to know the struggle the athlete had faced before his moment on center stage.

As if to satisfy my lust for sports drama, fate delivered to me the made-for-TV Cowboys franchise. In marketing appeal, it was unrivaled by the other National Football League organizations. The sports and business worlds nicknamed it "America's Team." In my young mind, it became my team from the moment I saw the first image on the TV in our family room in Augusta.

Everything about the Dallas presentation dazzled me. I recall, as early as age six, witnessing this display of athleticism, precision, and choreography. I'm not referring to the sideline jazz dancing of the gorgeous globetrotting Dallas Cowboys Cheerleaders, who debuted in the fall of 1972. Instead, I have in mind each fit and focused male player. Their performances on the field elevated football to a high art for me, and it started before kickoff.

Sporting the pearlized white jersey emblazoned with blue numbers, each player carried out his role in a choreographed pregame entrance. The players would trot onto the field in a line precise enough to make a discipline-minded primary school teacher jealous. At just the right moment, each man would crisply turn the corner at the appointed yard-line.

And the killer final detail: Each man held his helmet at his side, seemingly attached at the belt. The pose afforded the player his moment to be captured by the television cameras, a chance for his clean-shaven face, his hair, and his gritty game-day expression to get beamed across the country and preserved in the archives of NFL Films. As a child, I imagined what stories each player would tell me and my microphone. *One day, I'll find out,* I vowed. *I know I will.*

Coach Tom Landry had created the impressive team formation. It added a special ingredient to the football on offer in Dallas and so far away from Augusta, Georgia. Years later, Rayfield Wright and "Mr. Cowboy" Bob Lilly, two Pro Football Hall of Famers, would both tell me that they detested the run-out that I absolutely adored.

In seasons when the Cowboys were eliminated short of winning the Super Bowl's Lombardi Trophy, I felt as abandoned and lonely as a girl whose best friend had moved away. It was more than a pining for an absent crush; I missed the inspiring on-screen excellence that distinguished talent. The undeniable rewards for those who prepare. The rich accolades at the center of the sports universe.

And that is where I was going.

I viewed my elementary-school days as my springboard to journalism, so I took seriously the job of going to school—and getting home promptly to review the lessons and do homework. I would zip along on my blue bike with its white banana seat and high-rise chopper handlebars. Multicolor plastic streamers hanging from the handlebars would catch the wind as I pedaled. Focus straight ahead! From third grade on, I couldn't wait to return to our new home on Thread Needle Road in the mostly white Montclair neighborhood. I'd reach home between two thirty and three p.m., thanks to the easy bike ride on the sidewalks of the subdivision.

After a snack of buttered and maple-syrup-soaked cornbread, it was down to business on the seven hours of studying I would put in on a typical day. I would log three-and-a-half hours before dinner, and another three-and-a-half after the family meal. On the evenings when it was my turn to perform dishwashing duty, I would be delayed a bit, but I would still meet my study goals. The Formica kitchen table provided ample space for me to arrange within my grasp the stacks of notebooks and assorted pens and colored pencils I needed for the task.

Social studies or history was first. I concentrated on the new terms I learned from the reading assignment. For science or biology class,

I drew plants and, when I was older, practiced the chemical-reaction equations from the periodic table. Simply put, whatever we studied in the classroom became my afternoon and evening entertainment.

"I don't remember ever having to tell you to do your homework," my daddy has said to me. "And I didn't have to check it because I knew it was done right."

When I had completed the day's assigned exercises, I would work ahead. On one occasion, I was so engrossed in the information in the health textbook that I was running four chapters ahead of the classroom work. I reined myself in, though, and waited for the class lectures to catch up to me. I loved drawing and coloring the detailed illustrations of human anatomy.

I wanted to always have the correct answer when called on in class. During third and fourth grades, I was one of only two black students at my neighborhood school, Warren Road Elementary. I did not want to stand out any more than I already did, with my brown skin and textured hair, which, after I used a straightening comb on it, I wore in two pigtails, and sometimes with bangs, like Olympic gymnast Nadia Comaneci.[12] I reasoned that if my classmates took note of the physical differences between themselves and me, at least I could attribute their notice to my studiousness.

In that setting at Warren Road school, I suffered a painful and bewildering moment in sixth grade. The culprit, not a peer—the kids were never unkind to me—but the white music teacher. A woman in her early thirties, who wore a cocoa-colored, chin-length pageboy hairstyle, came to teach us once a week. We students would sit in a semicircle, facing her. She would call out a page number, and we would turn to the song in our music book. However, one day, I sensed something was about to go wrong. I spied the words *Negro Spiritual* on the page in the righthand corner above the first bars of music. Knowing that my birth certificate proclaimed me a "Negro" baby, the label on the song made me instantly self-conscious and alarmed.

---

12. As a 14-year-old from Romania in the 1976 Olympics in Montreal, Canada, Nadia Comaneci earned the perfect score of 10 seven times. She captured three gold medals, one bronze, and one silver. Young girls copied her bouncy bangs.

"Nita's going to show us how it's done," said the teacher to everyone.

The gazes of more than a dozen young pairs of eyes turned away from her and landed on me. I was mortified.

Negro spiritual? What do I know about that?

I had always been a dancer, someone who uses the body for expression, but I was not a singer at all. And while my nuclear family enjoyed many different interests, music was not one of the top.

"Come on," the teacher coaxed, her lips curled in a close-lipped smile. But her eyes were not smiling.

I wanted to vanish, to vaporize, to do anything other than sit there and perform for the group of my schoolmates. I sat frozen and mute.

Finally, the teacher leaned over from her seated position and placed the arm of her record player on a vinyl disc that rested on the device's turntable. She had brought not only a record player but also the record, which made me wonder why she thought it necessary to ask me to demonstrate the song's delivery.

As the music played, I tried to follow the printed lyrics but could not focus; my eyes were bleary. Nor could I catch on to the rhythm coming from the record player. The teacher's request had made me feel isolated, attacked, challenged, powerless. I felt unprotected in my own school—abused by this employee of the school system.

The rest of the school day is lost to me.

Today, my family says I recounted the event at home—but with a twist.

"You told us you blew it out of the water."

Not likely. I still cannot carry a tune. It's more likely I created a fiction that made me the hero. A fiction sweeping and bold, to mask the turmoil I had felt in class.

No matter the story I told my family, I formulated my retaliation before the next music class. I would not let the music teacher get away with using her position of authority to have fun at my expense.

So, I plotted.

Each week, the students could bring a hit song for the teacher to play at the end of the music lesson. We would vote on which song it would be, and we would enjoy it as a group. We first had to earn

the reward by singing enthusiastically the songs in the program that
the teacher had prepared.

The week after the incident involving the Negro spiritual, I told
my friends, "We have to do a good job in music today." They did not
know it, but I was laying the groundwork for payback. "And then vote
to play my record at the end of the lesson, OK?" I asked. They agreed.

I selected a song that I knew would make a point. Not one of my
classmates knew Carly Simon's "Dishonest Modesty," but I promised
them that playing it would get a memorable reaction from the teacher.
"It has dirty lyrics," I informed the eleven- and twelve-year-olds. "It
uses the words 'bitch' and 'screw.' So, vote for my song and we can
have some fun with the teacher."

Even kids who enjoyed the weekly break for the arts and who liked
the teacher aligned with me for the potential fireworks. Their reasons
were not the same as mine, but I successfully enlisted them in the prank.

During the lesson that day, we sang our hearts out on every song.
The teacher seemed overwhelmed with satisfaction that she had
converted this usually mediocre group into impassioned songbirds.
*My, oh my! How well I have gotten this group to appreciate the power
of music!* she probably thought.

Little did she know what the power of music had in store for her.

At the end of class, she asked what popular song we would like to
play. I nominated the Simon song. No one offered any other songs,
falling in line with my plan.

Because the song was not a chart-topper, the teacher did not know
about the sexually potent words that obviously did not belong in a
primary-school setting. She turned the record player on, causing
the *Another Passenger* long-play album to begin its rotation on the
turntable. We students held our collective breath as she carefully
positioned the record-player needle before the tenth song.

As Carly Simon began to sing, I held my breath through the first
verse and the refrain. At the 1:09 mark of the three-minute song,
sweet vengeance arrived—scorching hot.

The inappropriate words rolled off the singer's lips and into the
classroom of sixth-graders. We burst into laughter, squeals, snorts,

and hoots. No one tried to contain it. We deserved the release after the force we had put into singing the teacher's songs.

The teacher had been nodding her head in rhythm and enjoying the music, but the obscene lyrics caught her off guard. She realized she did hear what she thought she heard. With the lightning speed of a javelin, she lunged toward the record player. She tried to grab the arm of the device before more inappropriate words bounced off the walls. She stopped the music with a violent drag of the needle across the vinyl, creating the resulting unpleasant screech.

Flushing red in the face and most likely feeling battered by the waves of student laughter, the teacher shut the record-player case with a thud and hastily shoved her teaching materials into her satchel. She barely looked up at the roaring preteens. I hoped she felt, as I had felt the week before, the isolation and powerlessness she had visited upon me.

That was the last I saw of the music teacher. The following week, the homeroom teacher announced that our music program was over for the year. We students thought that the music teacher had been fired.

⟶🐎

Now, when I reflect on my display of revenge, I don't feel the satisfaction I felt that day. At the time, I enjoyed making the teacher as uncomfortable as she had made me. I liked watching her become the person in the room who was different from the others and whose difference had been singled out for what I perceived, then, to be an attack.

Now, I realize something: If the music teacher had lost her job, then I affected the financial health of her family. She could have been a contributor to her family's financial bottom line, as wife, as mother, or possibly the chief breadwinner. I am ashamed that innocents, my young classmates and the teacher's family, may have been harmed when I sought tit-for-tat revenge.

Yes, I could argue that as a stealthy effective aggressor, I had redressed the imbalance of power and defended myself. But the ugly truth is that I was guilty of acting against my tormentor—of striking out at the *other* in a group. Such was not my normal way of behaving. The unsettling music-class experience had transformed me from my usual demeanor at school. Handwritten commentary from my seventh-grade homeroom teacher, recorded at the end of the academic year in May 1977, confirms the fact that I was a docile, obedient, well-adjusted thirteen-year-old student. She writes:

> *Dear Nita,*
>
> *You're the sweetest one! Thank you for being my friend this year.*
>
> *I hope that life will bring you the best of everything always. May all your best dreams come true!*
>
> *With love,*
> *Miss Hayes*

Miss Hayes was partially right; I wasn't "sweet," but I usually maintained pleasant relationships with teachers. It was a natural thing for me to do, but I also had another reason: I earned pocket money from a grades-for-pay deal I had negotiated with my parents. They did not believe in giving an allowance, the spending money that most of my white classmates and friends received freely from their parents. My black friends also did not receive allowances. In my circle, black parents regarded an allowance as cash just for *being* and refused to pay it.

This taught me early in life to monetize information.

The classes of written and oral English, reading comprehension, spelling, penmanship, and health became my gold mines. Each A-plus (a 95 to 100 average) on my six-week report card put one dollar in my pocket. Each A (90 to 94) paid seventy-five cents. I don't recall the payout for B and below because, always aiming for an A, I usually got it.

Every six weeks during the school year, I could earn as much as nine dollars—enough to keep a twelve- or thirteen-year-old satisfied in the mid-1970s. In addition to my highest-paying courses, I loved the way Mrs. Asserson, an older white teacher, taught social studies. The class focused on ancient civilizations in Mesopotamia, far away in time and location from my home state of Georgia. It fascinated me greatly. How did people live? Eat? Survive? Play?

The gray-haired, bespectacled Mrs. Asserson would fill up the green chalkboard with beautiful cursive handwriting, drawn in yellow or white, as she asked those questions. I would copy the questions in my own flowery cursive handwriting, leaving ample space to fill in detailed answers gleaned from the reading assignment.

In addition to my beloved letters classes and enriching social studies, I performed well in math throughout junior high and high school. I earned solid enough grades in geometry, algebra, and beginning trigonometry, but the study of people and the truthful historical records of their lives intrigued me more.

I used my hard-earned cash to finance my guilty pleasure of buying *Tiger Beat* magazine, with its pictures of John Travolta, the two actors from *Starsky & Hutch*, and the Jackson 5. However, the thing that crystalized for me the necessity of having my own money was a yearning I had for an item of clothing. I fancied having a pair of the trendy denim bellbottoms that all the fashionable girls were wearing in junior high.

"Can we go shopping this weekend?" I asked my parents one afternoon. It was not necessary to explain to them why I wanted to shop; I had been dropping the hint for days.

The resounding answer of *No*, and the repetition of it no matter how I restructured my appeal, stung me to the core.

"What do I have to do?" I exclaimed. "All I'm asking for is a four-teen-dollar pair of jeans!"

My explosion of anger caught me off guard, but I was frustrated. Wasn't I justified in asking for something so small? Didn't I deserve to look as fashion-forward as the other girls? *If I wait too long to buy the jeans, I'll be lagging behind the hot style!* said a hysterical voice in my head.

"That's not fair!" I continued, throwing out the phrase American teenaged girls carry in their back pockets for easy deployment. "I don't do anything wrong. I make good grades! I don't think it's fair that I ask for *one thing*—and the answer is no!"

The discussion, which never reached the discussion level, had ended. While I did not get the jeans, I walked away from my outburst with a valuable personal trait: a vow to be self-sufficient. That day in 1978, at age fourteen, was the last time I ever asked anyone to give me money.

I could draw, freehand, the celebrities my friends and I adored, including the rock band KISS, disco kings the Bee Gees, and disco queen Donna Summer. Luckily, my classmate and friend Bubba fanatically followed KISS and would pay my charge of fifty cents per drawing. (Remember: These were the days before one could instantly summon up images on a handheld electronic device.) Others bought Charlie's Angels and Rolling Stones drawings.

"What did you draw?" Bubba and a few others would ask enthusiastically on Monday mornings when greeting me before the first school bell sounded.

"It's my turn to pick!" someone would say, as three or four classmates positioned themselves around me to view the pencil drawings.

With the income streams from the drawings and good grades, I was flush with money in my early years. The only financial pinch I ever felt came later, during my pursuit of self-actualizing as a television journalist. Those days and years of low funds, however, would never force me off my path.

CHAPTER 4

Meritocracy, But Not on
Any Given Saturday

With television as my tutor, I soon began to understand that every journalist at the heart of the big stories had groomed himself to be at the hub of what was happening.

I said "himself," but the one who initially touched me through the sports broadcasts I saw on my TV screen was Phyllis George, the lone female on the NFL broadcasts on CBS. (She joined the cast of *The NFL Today* in 1975.) I wanted to be in Phyllis George's place in the same way that kids have longed to be in the skins of sports icons they have followed: Michael Jordan for basketball, Lionel Messi for soccer, Tiger Woods for golf.

When twenty-seven-year-old Jayne Kennedy replaced Ms. George in 1978, America and my young eyes witnessed a first: an African American woman in a coveted seat on a trendsetting sports broadcast. Seeing her, I was sold on my future.

I was aware that the rarity of being a female in sports reporting could elicit from others a microscopic scrutiny of the journalist. I knew that if I fell down, in some way, while reporting sports, others would immediately notice my mistake. So, I vowed to never be lacking in preparation and to never let a fear of undue scrutiny cow me. I deeply desired to train the spotlight on people at the height of their perfection—those who prepared themselves for Game Day, the showdown, the all-or-bust competition, their personal excellence.

I admire the meritocracy of sports. Each participant contributes something of value and has likely overcome an obstacle before arriving for the day's game. Still, each shows up, ready to add his or her unique set of experiences to the whole. Diversity among players, when channeled the right way, creates unity on a team. The human parts fit together to form a machine that is built for the task. The boys my father coached in basketball and baseball were real-world examples of this noble idea. As a child, I adored watching their working together, despite racial and socioeconomic and academic differences, to develop their skills from novice level to game-day precision.

Any Given Saturday: Not Interested

During the school year in junior high, and even in high school, I rarely invited my friends, Debbie, Jennie, Terri, Alyssa, and Robin (black and white girls from my grade), over to my house. I had my studies, first and foremost; my Pekingese dog, Lady, and her puppy, Velvet; and television. When I watched for fun instead of career training, I chose the sitcoms *Happy Days*, *Good Times*, and *Welcome Back, Kotter*, and the Saturday-morning dance show *American Bandstand*.

On *Bandstand*, I saw the debut of two singers who would later explode into worldwide fame: Prince and John Cougar (who later added his family name Mellencamp to his stage name). I knew about Don Cornelius' *Soul Train* but watched it less often than *Bandstand* because I preferred danceable rock and roll music over soul.

Unfortunately, my satisfying Saturday-afternoon music fix eventually devolved into a long-running disappointment because of the changing landscape of weekend television programming. One could call it college-football *creep*, the gradual encroachment of something upon something else.

Here is what happened.

Television broadcast managers began hitching themselves to the money-making machine of college football games. And why not? Stadiums such as those used by the University of Southern

California and the Michigan Wolverines held upwards of one hundred thousand fans in the early 1970s. Broadcasters correctly assessed that some people who would like to see the game might not be able to go. So, those broadcasters usurped the airwaves of my Saturday early-afternoon viewing and dropped in football games. Naturally, they followed the profit margin, knowing that the real money in sports comes with broadcast deals.

Therefore, on some Saturdays, as I prepared to catch Dick Clark's introduction of a rising star, I landed on ABC network's replacement programming. I did not like the low hum of the stadium crowd, a constant distraction under the voices of the broadcasters. The sound reminded me of an electric fan that is putting out annoying noise more than it is circulating cool air. Also, when I looked at the images the broadcasts showed, the sweater-wearing cheerleaders and the oversized tiger and bear mascots, nothing enticed me.

One might find it surprising to read that I, a born lover of competition, found annoying this intrusion into my Saturday TV-viewing schedule. There were two reasons for my annoyance. The first: I looked forward to the normal preteen and teenager pastime of listening to new musicians. I wanted to be in the know about the next great star. The second reason for my annoyance is because of what I did *not* see on my TV screen during those intruding sports broadcasts.

Though I did not have the vernacular, at age eleven, to say "long-running plantation system in college football," the images I saw on screen said it for me. I noted the pattern, week after week, when the teams and their white coaches trotted onto the field. Though the players were helmeted, I could eventually see that black athletes and white athletes (and surely a few members of other ethnic groups) were playing together—but were being led by white men only.

Having no black coaches in charge of rosters looked wrong to my preteen eyes. And I felt profoundly confused. How could it be that not one black person possessed enough leadership acumen to command a team?

I had watched my dad coach black and white boys in basketball and baseball. They respected him; they respected his rules. They matured as athletes. I knew from my father's example that a black person could develop strategy and teach plays. And win.

Because I did not see black men in the spectrum of roles that exist in college sports, I began to ignore the games. I felt shut out of that world; it disdained men who were like my father and brother and grandfathers. The dearth took me back—with a tinge of pain—to the days of one black person's announcing to another that someone black was going to be on television. "We get society's crumbs in sports, too?" I mused.

Obviously, blocking and tackling weren't happening only on the field.

In full color, college football pageantry, even college basketball's pageantry of the same era, illustrated discriminatory barriers that existed and that needed to be broken down.[13]

I wanted no part of reporting on high-profile college sports when, at the age of thirteen, I began preparing in earnest to become a journalist. In self-guided fashion, I diverted from my schoolbooks some of my verve for learning and began to attentively study the journalists who cut the mustard well enough to make it to television.

Thankfully, the diversity that was missing from college-football sidelines I found in an impressive place: the national news-anchor chair. The emergence, if almost by magical means, of female news anchors and one black anchorman, Max Robinson (ABC News, 1978), gave me visual references to determine how I would look and sound and uncover stories. These new journalists brought a conversational speaking style to their news broadcasts. The change in tone made me think, *Hey, the news affects me. This is my news.*

Before the faces of news messengers started changing, the most

---

13. When the author covered the Southeastern Conference at WREG-TV in Memphis (from 1993 to 1995), the University of Mississippi had only recently hired Rob Evans as its first black head coach of a major sports team. The Oxford, Mississippi, school had played its first organized basketball game 83 years earlier, in 1909.

I had felt about the broadcasts was, simply, *This is what I need to know.* I had always operated with the belief that an educated person seeks to be informed, but I had never felt that I was a stakeholder in the news. The presenters (though award-winning, accomplished, credible journalists) always seemed to be talking *at* me, instead of *with* me or for my benefit.

But then, the wonderful change happened.

National broadcasters began putting forth racially and gender-inclusive news teams by adding presenters who were not white males. That signaled to me that everyone in our American fabric of ethnicities could find, report, and affect the news. *News is not something that happens* to *you. News is something* you make *happen when you are accurately informed,* I began to believe. With that, I became convinced of the importance of my role in the information game.

⁓🐎⁓

It was Walter Cronkite whose announcement on CBS of Dr. King's assassination I watched in 1968. He was the newscaster most often on my television during my childhood. But Jessica Savitch (NBC, 1977), Connie Chung (NBC, 1983), and Robinson became the anchors I sought when choices were available. Even more, I preferred the approach of Peter Jennings (foreign desk anchor for ABC's *World News Tonight*, 1978).

A white male born in Toronto, Canada, Jennings illustrated that diversity did not begin or end with skin color. His diversity in perspective and in story selection set him apart from his contemporaries. He included people whose ideas sat outside the mainstream narrative. As a journalist-in-training, I admired that Jennings handed a microphone and the amplifying power of a national television newscast to ignored voices.[14]

---

14. Jennings produced ABC network specials titled "Palestine: New State of Mind" (1970); "Guantanamo," "LAPD [Los Angeles Police Department]," and "War and Power: The Rise of Syria" (all in 1984); "Hiroshima: Why We Dropped the Bomb" (1995); and "Unfinished Business: The CIA and Saddam Hussein" (1997). Source: *Peter Jennings: A Reporter's Life*, edited by Kate Darnton, Kayce Freed Jennings, and Lynn Scherr (New York: Public Affairs, 2007).

His international leanings in the topics he covered appealed to my belief that one should go beyond what is familiar—not staying too close to home. In addition to his professional standards, I found charming Jennings' personal attributes. His Canadian accent slipped through on occasion, especially on the word "about," which he pronounced "a-boot." That he was handsome, with dark hair swept most often to the right, and an oblong, clean-shaven face, attracted me all the more.

During this period when I watched the local and nightly news nearly every night, my first sports articles began appearing in the Tutt Junior High newspaper. I reveled in being a teenaged sports journalist during eighth grade. I never paused to consider how odd my chosen assignment must have seemed to observers. Imagine a buck-toothed shy girl who must ask the football coach about losses. When our Tutt Dragons stumbled, I was that person with the notebook, the pen, and the questions.

I groomed myself to make respectful inquiries, to not judge the answers, to accept the perspective of the person who was speaking. I followed up the interviewee's honest responses with even more interesting questions. I learned how to draw out answers from a sports person who is in the throes of a bad season or a failing season. Tutt Coach Tom Tarpley wrote in my 1978 yearbook: "I have enjoyed teaching you this year. You are an excellent student and I appreciate your desire to learn in any class. May you get all that you desire in life."

Later, defying the stay-behind-the-scenes personality of my youth, I volunteered for the position of sports editor during my senior year at Westside High School. Yes, I enjoyed working in the background as a sportswriter. However, to ensure that I could write the articles I wanted to write, I knew I would have to be more than just a member of the student staff. So, I became sports editor.

In what might be considered a revolutionary move, I selected a girl as assistant sports editor for our *Westside Story* newspaper. Kathy Johnson, a student I knew from staff meetings, impressed me to the max at a football game between our Patriots and another team. I overheard her explain to someone what options the team faced on third-down. In her insightful discussion, she recounted the play-calling tendencies of our team in that situation, and she correctly predicted the coach's move.

Kathy kept informed everyone around her, including the newly minted sports editor. I capitalized on her knowledge and was glad that, in my first stab at media management, I chose a person based on merit. No cronyism. No favoritism based on gender. My resolve has never wavered about the importance of meritocracy in sports and journalism.

CHAPTER 5

Say the Right Thing

Being greeted as "our Miss America" by a college official in my hometown offended me in the fall of 1983. At the time, I was a serious nineteen-year-old college student and a clothes model for the fashion board of a regional department store. My school's president, Dr. George Christenberry, thought he was complimenting me by comparing me to another female African American college student and model, twenty-year-old Vanessa Williams.

Ms. Williams' win of the 1984 Miss America title (on September 17, 1983) proved that a woman of color could be crowned "the fairest of them all" in a head-to-head beauty pageant with white women.[15]

But I wanted to be valued for more than my appearance.

At the time of Dr. Christenberry's comment, I was a sophomore at Augusta College. The school had a student body of twenty-five hundred, and minorities were less than 5 percent of that number. I was an incoming member of the executive board of AC's Student Government Association. My fight for the coveted role began the year before, when I was a freshman and ran for the campus-wide office of SGA secretary. Though others warned me that a freshman would be too new to the college landscape and would lack the campus connections to win, I disregarded the naysayers and threw my all into the goal.

---

15. With her triumph, Vanessa Lynn Williams became the first black woman to win the annual Miss America Pageant, a competition which began in 1921. In 1970, Cheryl Adrienne Browne, a New Yorker who was Miss Iowa, became the first African American contestant. (missamerica.org)

The position paid a full scholarship, an attractive prospect along with that of playing with the big guys on campus the following year. Craig Stanley, as presidential hopeful (and rising senior), Faye Lyons, as vice president (rising junior), and Ted Everett, as treasurer (rising junior), had already noticed my efforts as a student senator for the history department. The trio of upper-class students selected me—over a rising senior who had also decided to run for secretary—to round out the ticket. The TASK Party (Together Achieving Student Knowledge) would win or lose as a group.

We won.

The college election meant much to me. It carried with it a place on the SGA's standing executive committee, which had the honor of presenting ideas to campus movers and shakers—to have a seat at the table when it came to creating campus policy. In fact, I was literally taking my seat at the table of discussion when the college president's "compliment" sounded. I was one of maybe five students in the room—surely, the youngest. SGA vice president Faye and I were the only black students in the meeting.

A great sense of accomplishment and, admittedly, much nervousness had accompanied me into my first meeting with the school's administration. But the president's choice of words made the occasion worse for me. His introduction shifted the focus in the room away from what I wanted people to notice: the reputation I was building as a studious, active, community-minded scholar and leader.

At the time of my matriculation, from August 1982 to March 1986, Augusta College,[16] which locals referred to as Harvard on the Hill, was known for presenting an academically tough row to hoe. In some circles, it seemed a requirement to jut out one's chin and point the nose skyward, to signal "snob," when talking about any experience at the school. That explains the "Harvard" in the nickname.

Though the school was located only ten miles from my family's home, I did not picture it in my future until I was in my senior year of

---

16. Through expansions and acquisitions, the school from which the author earned a Bachelor of Arts in 1986 became Augusta University in 2015.

high school. The college had begun its communications department one year earlier. My parents decided that AC is where I would study, taking advantage of the in-state tuition cost of two hundred fifty dollars a semester. When I arrived at Augusta's Harvard, I devoured everything placed before me in the fields of communications and journalism. My general-studies minor included advertising and West African history. I loved taking tests, but not because it gave me the chance to mark progression toward a degree; no, I simply loved listening, learning, processing, and applying the material.

I did not know how roundly I had succeeded in my coursework until three years after graduation, when I was sending my college transcript to Marshall University for a political-science graduate class. I had earned a perfect 4.0 in the courses related to my communications major. Twice, I received *Who's Who in American Colleges and Universities* honors (1984-85 and 1985-86 editions). In 1986, I was one of twelve finalists for a National Association of Black Journalists paid internship.

After finishing my bachelor's degree at Augusta College in March of 1986, I began working full-time in the advertising department of the J. B. White retail chain. I had worked at the store since age seventeen, on the teen fashion board, on the sales floor, in gift wrapping, and in the executive offices as a switchboard operator. With my studies out of the way, I signed on as a full-time advertising copywriter, layout designer, and TV-commercials creator. I did not start looking for a broadcast-journalism job in March because I wanted to bide my time in Augusta until the degree ceremony in May. Besides, I was testing advertising as a career option.

Soon, however, I began to feel frustrated with the sameness of each workday. There was too much certainty in working a predictable schedule of Monday through Friday, eight thirty a.m. to five thirty p.m. I also sorely missed the reward of encountering new people and turning over stones to find untold stories, as I had done in my roles as student journalist and paid contributor to weekly newspapers. So, I told my manager, Kiel Aldersen, that I would be looking for other work. My affable and fair white male supervisor nodded and said he appreciated being notified.

Leaving Kiel would mean leaving behind a prestigious office job that paid fourteen thousand five hundred dollars a year—not a bad salary for a college-educated twenty-one-year-old in 1986. True, it was not the thirty-seven thousand dollars my father earned at the time as a signal instructor for the U.S. Army at Fort Gordon, but with fourteen thousand five hundred, I was on financial easy street. My rent was only three hundred fifty dollars a month. I had no college loans to repay, and no car payments. (As a sophomore, I had bought a Dodge Duster muscle car with seven hundred dollars of my own savings.) Because of my comfortable income and the potential for career growth, I knew that my post in the advertising division offered me a charmed career-launching opportunity.

But.

My inner child's voice would not let me cash in my chips so soon. *A victory that is easy is cheap*, we say in sports. And this was too easy. I had transitioned into advertising directly from the store's telephone switchboard. Besides, I yearned to work in television reporting in a setting where each day differed markedly from the last.

As I progressed from one job to the next at J.B. White, the president of the retail group noticed. I considered Randall Burnett to be the ultimate professional. I admired immensely the superbly dressed, lanky, gregarious white exec, a man who enjoyed talking about the University of South Carolina's football team. I appreciated his enthusiasm for the sport, though I did not share it.

From Mr. Burnett's respectful and always appropriate interactions with his management team, I could see that he valued productive, people-oriented employees. It seemed of little concern to him how the outside packaging looked. There were numerous women in prestigious buying and assistant-buyer positions in his store. They often worked as team captains, with men in support roles.

My position as switchboard operator put me in close quarters and regular contact with these women. I loved seeing talented and likeable people leading the stores. However, the sad fact is that as I look back over my five years at the store, I can recall seeing only one black person ascend to the highly paid circle of the store's management team, including the advertising executives. I am jarred now that it did not jar me at the time. Perhaps the only effect it had on me was a reassuring one: Seeing one minority professional break through reinforced the notion that a black candidate could access higher terrain by putting forth extraordinary effort.

That is exactly what happened for me at the store. I produced a college assignment about the creator of the J. B. White business, James Brice White. I shared my history project with chain president Mr. Burnett, who remarked that my work gave him information he did not know and that it was a well-done, polished document.

In short order, Mr. Burnett elevated me from the comfortable confines of the switchboard job and offered me a paid internship as a worker for Joyce Ducker, director of broadcast advertising. The internship blossomed into a permanent job, one that provided me with my own desk and phone extension in the copy-and-layout-design room. However, despite my nice new role, in only a matter of months my journalist's heart told me to walk away from the security blanket of J.B. White.

I contacted the supervisor in charge of my earlier internship at WAGT-TV, the NBC television affiliate in Augusta. The Thursday-afternoon phone call to Reggie Cofer, the black assistant manager in the production department, led to an interview with another station two days later. On Saturday, I drove the two-and-a-half hours from Augusta to Macon because WMGT-TV news director John Gimlin needed a reporter right away.

During the interview, John tried to intimidate me with his manner and a test question. I guess he thought I would scare easily. It would have been a safe bet, for I was twenty-two years old at the time, in June 1986. He was a crusty veteran newsman, white, twice my age, and a smoker who growled when he spoke. "What is news?" he asked.

"News is what the news director says it is," I volleyed without hesitation. I had anticipated that exact question.

Pretending to be unimpressed, he asked whether I was prepared to read a script. I wrote one from the wire copy he pulled from the wire-service printer. Seated beside Gimlin in a dark corner of the empty newsroom, I read it.

I resigned my position in advertising two days later.

Kiel, my supervisor back in Augusta, said he had never heard of anyone's starting a job search on a Thursday, actually finding one, and resigning the following Monday. That was the case, however, and it began my pattern of bucking tradition as a journalist.

Before jumping into my first TV job, I had to say goodbye to my *de facto* mentor, store president Burnett. He asked if I had a Plan B. I told him I did not have one. As a veteran of business, Mr. Burnett smiled warmly as he complimented me for not having a Plan B. Having a backup allows one to shoot for goals in a cautious way, he said. Too much caution can stifle passion and limit the boldness needed to take giant steps. Risk-taking advances one's career, he said. I appreciated his advice and, thus assured, walked away from my good-paying and secure cushion.

I would forfeit more than four thousand dollars a year in pay when I took the job at Channel 41 in Macon, located in central Georgia. Not a surprising decrease, considering the station's reputation in the city's journalistic circles. In the years before I arrived at the station, some witty employees began calling WCWB-TV (the station's previous call letters) the We-Can't-We're-Broke station.

Employees embraced the biting nickname because they derided the low pay and the overworking of staff. The station had only eight full-time positions in the news department, which produced news updates during the national early-morning *Today* show and followed with noon, six p.m., and eleven p.m. full newscasts. The broken-down and aging equipment in every corner of the building proved that the station definitely was not the leader in a competitive field.

By the time of my hiring, WCWB had rebranded itself WMGT, proudly proclaiming to be Middle Georgia Television. Although WMGT was an NBC affiliate in the era of Tom Brokaw's domination of the six thirty p.m. national ratings, the station cast neither fortune nor local fame upon me.

One must start somewhere.

Wilted Magnolias

A one-woman (or one-man) band is a journalist who shoots the interviews and the support video, asks the questions during interviews, and edits the material into a story. In 1986, the position involved taking video from three-quarter-inch-wide, professional-grade tapes and physically editing the clips onto a master tape. (Now, virtual or nonlinear editing is the process, with the material from the field being captured on video cards and manipulated on a computer.) In those older days, carrying the Ikegami camera, the shoulder-slung recording deck, the bulky and heavy tripod, the lighting kit, the microphone, and assorted cables presented numerous challenges. The full complement of gear to perform a day's work must have weighed twenty-five to thirty pounds.

Added to that burden was another pressure on broadcast journalists. With just a few channels on the television dial, most on-camera presenters dressed up to impress TV executives and viewers alike. Women with sights set on advancing tried to avoid slacks; they were appropriate only for dress-down days or nasty weather. Denim jeans—even dark, fitted designer jeans—were unheard of. Coordinated suit pieces of the same fabric—usually, a skirt suit, not a pantsuit—ruled the day. On days when the Southern heat threatened to make us all wilt like magnolias under a heat lamp, one could discard the jacket and slide by with just a blouse.

Dressing like a lady and lugging around equipment like a man were two inescapable requirements of my new role of one-woman band. I happily accepted the tasks because I was now able to spend my workday on the move. Already seduced by politics, I relished covering Macon's city-government meetings, especially the ones in which the highest levels of leadership would participate. And working alone meant that I could drive the station's white Subaru wagon wherever I wanted. Thus, I would explore parts of the viewing area that I would never have seen without the shield of a marked TV news vehicle.

With my own eyes, I saw that the quality of life in neighborhoods where mostly people of color lived differed from the neighborhoods of mostly white populations. As an outsider whizzing by the homes, schools, corner stores, churches, and community centers, I noticed the terrible condition of the roads in the poorer neighborhoods. Dangerous railroad crossings were sometimes not marked, leaving an unsuspecting driver vulnerable to collision with a passing train. The roughly finished tracks in the black parts of town could damage a person's car unless she first saw the tracks and inched across them.

I learned the hard way.

I suffered *the* scare of my WMGT-TV career when I drove too fast over unmarked railroad tracks. I was totally at fault as I coasted down a hill at a pretty good speed and spotted, at the last moment, the tracks running across the road. "It's not my car," I selfishly thought. "No need to put on the brakes. It's too late, anyway!"

Wrong answer.

The sturdy four-wheel-drive car hit the tracks hard. Doing my best imitation of a Hollywood stunt driver, I gripped the steering wheel tightly as the car and I went airborne. A few harrowing seconds later, my news vehicle, with me inside, landed with a thud and with absolutely no bounce, like a gymnast who perfectly sticks a dismount from the parallel bars. The seatbelt had cinched while I was in the air and held me in place. The tires' traction grabbed the asphalt upon landing, and the wheels resumed rolling, but the impact had thrown the stick shift out of gear. The engine died.

Panicking, I slipped the car into neutral and turned the key to restart the ignition. Nothing. Still rolling and fortunately alone on the two-lane roadway, I tried again. The engine responded, so I was able to go on as if nothing had happened.

But something had happened: I had seen the reality of the dire living conditions in the city. The sobering knowledge stayed with me.

Grim Nativity

I claim Augusta, Georgia, as my home because my family moved there when I was two years old. But the fact is, I was born at Macon Hospital on Hemlock Street in the heart of Macon, Georgia. My

1964 birth certificate identifies me as a "Negro" baby, the acceptable racial term of the time.

My father worked as an instructor at Warner Robbins Air Force Base, providing for our family a comfortable beginning on Macon's Forest Avenue. My family lived in a black neighborhood (naturally) in a shotgun house, or a shotgun cottage. This early-20th-century style is distinguished by its rectangular shape and a simple floorplan in which the entrances and exits of every room fall along the same spatial line. With this plan, theoretically a person could stand on the front porch and fire a shotgun through the front door. The bullet would exit out the back door without hitting a wall. My family left Macon for Augusta because my father accepted a job as a signal instructor (U.S. Army communications) at Fort Gordon.

When I returned to Macon in 1986 as a twenty-two-year-old TV journalist, I had some remembrances of the neighborhoods I saw as a toddler. (Even as a toddler I took in details in a manner like that of an older child.) I discovered that housing divisions persisted along racial lines, as did differences in the overall quality of life. Substandard living conditions swept up poor white people, too. I saw the depressingly downtrodden areas during the sightseeing afternoons I spent in my news vehicle. I found astonishingly dilapidated houses, especially on streets near the nine-thousand-seat Macon Coliseum, built in 1968.

In interviews with me, a white Macon city-council member decried the building of the coliseum. The project claimed his childhood neighborhood, he said, and displaced poor families who had still had the misfortune of living there. He talked about the eminent-domain clause, which the government utilized to uproot people and bulldoze their lives and memories. As a cub reporter (someone with less than three years on the job), I was not yet skilled in compartmentalizing my emotions. I took home with me the pain of his story.

I yearned to tell the stories of those suffering despair amidst the wealth of others. I yearned to show the living conditions of people who could not establish firm foundations for their lives.

Thus awakened, I launched my first television report of substance. I proposed and produced a three-part series about substandard housing. While newsroom managers routinely look for prostitute- and drug-related angles during the Sweeps months (times of the year when TV ratings are recorded to set future advertising rates), I wanted to jolt audiences in another way. I wanted to reveal the disturbing and subhuman conditions in which some Macon citizens lived.

Over several days I knocked on the doors of homes that were, in some respects, literally falling down. I asked residents if I could shoot video inside. Then I went for the most powerful interview: the mayor's.

George Israel was an unusually charismatic political personality. He served as Macon's mayor from 1979 to 1987. That Mayor Israel had become only the second Republican since 1833 to hold the city's top post speaks to his charm. For the current assignment, I told him about the miserable living conditions I had captured on video. I invited him to comment. Because of my regular appearances at City Hall and the intelligent questions I had been asking, Mayor Israel respected my interest in the topic. He even visited one home with me and appeared in the video. In my report, he acknowledged the problems that existed in some neighborhoods.

WMGT promoted my multipart series. News director John Gimlin proudly introduced the segments from his anchor chair. The smugness of his expression seemed to say to the viewers and to the competing stations, "Look at the reporter I hired! You can expect more from Nita Wiggins!"

Tracking Oprah's Trail

As I was getting started in a small Southern market in the mid-1980s, I saw the rise of charismatic African American journalist Oprah Winfrey as a national television phenomenon. I followed in her reporting footsteps for the first time when I went to Forsyth County, Georgia, located north of Atlanta and a ninety-minute drive from Macon. Oprah had taped a show about the all-white county, a place she described as a "hotbed of racism" and a community where not one black person had lived for seventy-five years.[17] (Forsyth the county, however, is not to be confused with Forsyth, Georgia, the *city* north of Macon.)

In one of Oprah's February 1987 broadcasts about Forsyth County, a white female audience member, who appeared to be under the age of thirty, explained: "They [black people] have the right to live wherever they want to, but we have the right to choose if we want a white community, also. That's why we moved here." In video from the show, two white men carry a banner that proclaims *Racial purity is Forsyth's security.*

Great fortune for my news career to have this "hotbed of racism" a quick drive away. Into the news car I went so that I could see it. I interviewed several of the county's white residents about being on the negative end of national reports. Each person called the attention unwarranted. Each reassured me that racial peace had been established. Not one of the white respondents acted uncivil or disrespectful to me, a black woman working alone. The most fortunate aspects of my time in the segregated community were the Channel 41 television camera on my shoulder and the daylight hours that together offered me a healthy measure of protection.

I do not recall finding anyone black to interview during my one hour on the ground, and as Oprah and her production team had done, I left before sundown.[18]

---

17. Patrick Phillips explains the history of the community in *Blood at the Root: A Racial Cleansing in America* (New York: W.W. Norton & Company, 2016).

18. James W. Loewen discusses all-white communities in *Sundown Towns: A Hidden Dimension of American Racism* (New York: Touchstone, 2006).

CHAPTER 6

Top Gunn: The Shooting Match

The assignment editor, also called an assignment manager, holds everything together in the newsroom. This team member connects reporters to information, sources, equipment, driving directions, and even orders from the upstairs executive offices. The assignment editor knows how the reporters and anchors and photographers can stay on the good side of the news director. For anyone working on a news team, having the assignment editor as an ally means the stint at the station will be as good as gold.

Our assignment editor Jerry Gunn carried added gravitas because he had served as a media witness at the execution of an inmate in the Georgia correctional system—a gruesome and news-heavy thing to experience. That told me that Jerry had seen more of the world than I had seen—and more than I thought I would ever want to see. A tough customer in the journalism business, even his name evoked steeliness: Gunn.

Remember that I had not been frightened by John Gimlin's feigned toughness during my job interview, but this guy, Jerry Gunn—tough enough to watch the State execute someone. Impressive.

Truth be told, Jerry, a fortyish white male guided by nervous energy, supported me and accepted my lack of knowledge about many things in my new profession. How trying his job must have been, training one newcomer after another. Such is the turnover in a media starter market like Macon, ranked higher than No. 100 by

Nielsen in 1986. (The higher the number, the smaller the market. Nielsen uses population size to determine ranking, so New York City is, of course, Nielsen's No. 1 market.)

Jerry set me up to win every time. Sweating, and often going about with the top three buttons of his shirt undone because of the Georgia heat, Jerry would lay out all the information I needed. He would explain it to me with the patience of a Sunday School teacher.

He stressed the importance of making beat calls to law-enforcement agencies. It is keenly important, he said, to get the police-blotter news at the beginning of the work shift. If there had been any crime committed overnight, that might lead the newscast. He would harp on and on about using the tripod to shoot all the video, to avoid unsteady images. White-balance the camera, carry enough tapes, wear the beeper, call in after finishing the shoot at each location. And did you read the wire, rip the stories, and file them by category?

It was unremitting work to get us, the rookies, ready. His job required him to both train and coddle us.

Drawing Our Guns

It surprised me when Jerry and I had a major disagreement over a story one day. I thought I would earn his praise for my report; instead, I was left with mouth agape at the end of the workday.

I worked especially hard on the story because Jerry's schoolteacher wife had told us about a workshop to be held by an after-school community-service group. Its purpose: Teach prepubescent girls essential information about their anatomy.

Sounded great.

An association selected mostly black girls from neighborhoods where teenaged pregnancy was common. The program aimed to reduce teen-pregnancy rates by informing the developing teenagers about the reproductive function of their bodies.

As a one-woman band on the story, I did the interviews and shot video. I used the tripod to capture the young people as they listened to the speakers; the latter were doctors who spoke in matter-of-fact medical terms. One speaker projected a drawing of the female anatomical parts on a large screen and discussed the purpose of each body part. He used words we all know: uterus, cervix, vagina, fallopian tubes.

In shooting video for a report, it is basic to show a wide shot of the room; this establishes the setting. That is followed by an MCU—a medium close-up shot—to single out a person involved in the event. This personalizes the event or the topic. Then, skilled shooters show the TV-viewing audience what the people in the news story are themselves observing. For instance, if the folks in the camera shot are gazing upward, it's natural for the reporter to show the TV audience the thing at which they are gazing—a tall statue, for instance. This last shot completes the basic editing sequence. Therefore, I utilized such a shot.

I thought it a benign thing to show the black-and-white line illustration of the female reproductive tract. How was I to know that doing so would cross a line?

Seemingly seconds after my package aired on Channel 41, Jerry's wife called the newsroom to complain. She had found disturbing the image in my story. I didn't understand. How could it be that what the fifteen girls were learning from health-care professionals *was not supposed to be shown* to girls not present at the event?

I felt that the story, the real story, was not that the association was teaching girls. For me, the *information* the association members were teaching formed the real story. I reasoned that girls in our viewing area, the ones who had not been present, could still learn what every adolescent needed to know about her body. After all, wasn't the issue useful for all girls and not just for the fifteen in the room?

I believe Jerry's answer to that question was something like, "Well, yes, but do not put a diagram of female body parts on television."

I thought about the target audience of the story—girls who needed to understand the biological functions of their bodies. For some of them, our news report would provide a rare opportunity to see sensitive anatomy information discussed in a serious manner. "Journalists must use their platform to take an event to the people who cannot attend the event—no matter what the event," I argued.

I failed to persuade Jerry, and Jerry refused to see the video as anything but offensive and inappropriate. He insisted I replace it for the replay of my story on the late newscast. Briefly, I wondered if a minority manager, or even a female manager, would have supported my scope of the story.[19]

Of course I deferred to Jerry and did not rerun the original footage, but the feeling of powerlessness frustrated me. I lacked influence in the newsroom, so I could not affect what viewers would see in the replay.

A Bare-Bones Existence

My frustration over feeling powerless added to another frustration I faced in Macon: the drop in pay I had wholeheartedly accepted when I resigned from my position in retail advertising. My WMGT-TV job paid in the range of ten thousand dollars a year. I don't recall whether that new paltry sum was my take-home or my gross pay, but in group crying sessions we held after work, my Macon colleagues and I lamented the low wages. One day, we vowed, we would all break out of Macon, Georgia, and earn some real money.

I lived in the economizing mode for the fifteen or so months while getting my feet wet in TV journalism. I budgeted by taking my lunch or dinner to work, instead of buying something on the road. Because of the feeling of community with my on-air colleagues, the studio cameramen, and the production team, I would sometimes splurge and order a hot meal from the family-style restaurant near our station. I would occasionally find the $3.80 to enjoy with the

---

19. "Women are not equal partners in telling the story, nor are they equal partners in sourcing and interpreting what and who is important in the story," according to the report *The Status of Women in U.S. Media 2017*, released by The Women's Media Center. Women news directors in television reached 30 percent of the total for the first time in 2013. It was 33 percent in 2017. Accessed June 30, 2018, womensmediacenter.com.

crew a meat portion, two vegetables, cornbread or dinner rolls, and dessert. The fried chicken wings proved to be the most popular. Most days I would forgo the sweet tea, which cost extra.

Anissa Wilkins, the weather woman and former Miss Warner Robbins beauty-pageant winner, would write down the orders and call them in. She was lovely and personable. A male colleague would make the run to the restaurant to perform the pick-up duties because the heavy lifting was too much for our popular Anissa.

We would eat together—something short of ten people—in our drab dining hall. News director John Gimlin and redheaded and polished anchorwoman Julie Gilreath would join us. Early-shift reporters Kym Clark and Dave Kurpius would sometimes stay behind after their workday ended. We would talk and laugh and find some camaraderie while enduring our financial frustrations.

In my severe economizing mode, I would order a man-sized dinner with its meat dish and accompaniments but eat only half the meal. I would leave the rest, in its Styrofoam packaging, in the station's employee refrigerator. A petite person, I could satisfy my hunger and justify the price. Two meals for $1.90 each seemed reasonable to pay in 1986.

One day, I left a beautifully presented meal to be finished off on another day. The day I planned to sit down and eat it, it was gone! I nearly collapsed at the sight of the empty refrigerator shelf where my leftovers had been. I had been bitten, my colleagues told me, by the same burglar who had helped himself to other free meals. I would have to work the rest of that night without food.

I made the theft known throughout the station. I spread word from the basement where the journalists worked to the executives' top floor. I reached an unprecedented level of low spirits that day at WMGT. I told everyone I saw why I felt that way.

As usual, I did not sulk long. I bounced back with an action plan. To feel safe about using the employee fridge, I decided I would always choose a chicken meal. That meant the end of meatloaf with tomato sauce, ham with cheese potatoes, even spaghetti—all of which were delicious. To protect day two of my man-sized carry-out dinners, I would eat half the chicken dinner and leave inside the container the bones from the chicken parts eaten on day one. No one other than the person who cleaned the first round of chicken bones would have the courage to move them aside to finish off the meal.

Problem solved! Offensive-looking leftovers proved to be the best defense. No one ever stole another of my meals.

Happy days were back for me in middle Georgia.

CHAPTER 7

Why Did Rosa Parks Hug Me?

In my next job, at WTVM-TV in Columbus, Georgia, I landed a position that came with a prestigious title: bureau chief/assignment editor in a one-person news department. That gave me the freedom to decide the stories I wanted to report and to conduct myself in any way that I chose while in the field. To do my job, I traveled my territory along the Alabama-Georgia border in a four-wheel-drive car that I was free to take home with me. I shared a tiny office with a good-natured and respectful white colleague named Gerry Potter. As the station's sales rep, Gerry sold airtime to clients in the east Alabama region. He treated me as an equal in every one of our exchanges during our fifteen months as colleagues in the Opelika, Alabama, office.

In this role as a one-woman band, the assignment of my life fell into my hands. The newsmaker at the center of the assignment left not only a lasting change upon my spirit but a lingering question in my mind, even decades later.

Why did Rosa Parks hug me longer than I hugged her?

I met world-history icon Rosa Parks on February 4, 1988, at her seventy-fifth birthday celebration given by the city of her birth, Tuskegee, Alabama, and its mayor, Johnny Ford. On that memorable day, I had been a TV news reporter less than two years and was enjoying my new status as WTVM Channel 9's bureau chief.

Though a cub reporter, I took pride in being professional, polished, prepared. I had covered Alabama state politics in the capitol building in Montgomery, and everyday politics on the streets of Opelika and Auburn and in five nearby counties. Despite being young, I thought I presented the air of a veteran.

Before the event began, I spied Mrs. Parks, who was standing alone. I wondered how that could be! How could the woman to whom the event was dedicated be waiting in silence when, all around her, men and women in business clothes and teenagers in school uniforms buzzed with activity?

I walked toward her.

As I did, I recalled the pictures of Rosa Parks I had seen in school books. Crisp black-and-white images of a prim, light-skinned African American woman with dark, silky hair pulled back from her face. Her tranquil yet determined expression preserved in her Montgomery, Alabama, police mugshot—with the inmate number *7053*. On December 1, 1955, she had refused to obey a bus driver's direct order that she give up her seat, triggering her arrest by Montgomery police. The city's black population responded with an overt, business-crippling bus boycott.

At the same time, in a significant but largely unheralded chapter in history, four other black women filed a lawsuit against the bus company.[20] During the year that commuters stayed off the bus, the four plaintiffs scored a landmark Supreme Court victory that changed public transportation nationwide. The court's decision in favor of Aurelia Browder and the others ended the legal segregation that white operators had lorded over riders of the buses. The brain trust of the boycott called off the economic protest on December 20, 1956. From that date forward, as Dr. King expresses in comments made at Holt Street Baptist Church, fifty thousand black people in Montgomery and sixteen million black people in the U.S. were free to sit wherever they chose on public transportation.

---

20. Petitioners Aurelia Browder, Susie McDonald, Claudette Colvin, and Mary Louise Smith, with attorneys provided by the NAACP, sued the privately run Montgomery City Lines. Like Rosa Parks, the women had routinely faced degrading conditions on the bus. The U.S. Supreme Court case, *Browder v. Gayle*, challenged the constitutionality of segregating local public transportation. (For more details about the court's ruling, see Endnotes.)

Mrs. Parks was not a part of that anti-discrimination lawsuit. However, she became the public face of the organized rebellion and the spark, most people believe, that ignited the blaze. And now, I was moving toward her.

I need her to remember me! my inner voice shouted.

I reached her and realized we stood at nearly identical heights. I was five-foot-three, so she must have been, too, at that stage of her life. Her signature dark hair was mostly gray and pulled into an updated French twist—still neatly pinned in place. Modified cat-eye glasses with light-pink frames had replaced the wire frames on historical record. Her lilac-colored rain slicker and baby-blue flapper's hat beautifully set off her honey-colored skin. Her clothing choices, and the overall vision of her, stirred a familiarity in me—as if my paternal grandmother were present.

Mrs. Parks was the focus of my report that day because she had helped upend the daily race-based indignations and the inequality of the world into which she, and both of my grandmothers, were born.

She was no ordinary woman! And here she was, beside me, within arm's length, full-color and in the flesh.

I'm standing here with Mrs. Parks! the voice inside of me shouted. My mind raced to find something enduring to say. How could I leave an impression on a woman who had done so much?

I formally extended my hand to shake hers. It was what I always did with the white males I interviewed in government and business. I stated my first and last names clearly. I wanted her to truly hear them. I was determined to maintain a professional decorum.

Then something changed.

Her eyes had settled on me as she listened to my name. I looked beyond the frames of her glasses, gently meeting her gaze. *These eyes, the eyes of Rosa Parks, have seen so many changes*, I thought. In that moment, I became aware of how petite and thin her body was; in her lifetime of activism, she had endured so much. Death threats, insomnia, ulcers, and extended financial stress had ravaged her life and the lives of her loved ones.

I suddenly knew, in that instant, that I needed to pay something back to her. There was no death-defying sacrifice I could make for her in that moment. Nothing I could give to repay her for what she had done for black people and for society beyond the American borders. Nothing—except myself. My physical self.

I shed my professional demeanor as if I were slipping out of clothing and said, "Excuse me, Mrs. Parks—I never do this—but is it OK for me to hug you?"

Without hesitation, she replied, "Sure, baby," and sounded just like my beloved maternal grandmother.

I leaned in to embrace her, shoulder-to-shoulder, the skin of our cheeks touching. For a petite elderly woman who appeared frail, she offered a surprisingly firm hold. I returned a powerful squeeze, contracting the muscles in my forearms to pull her close to me. I closed my eyes and lost myself in the force of her arms.

For me, the world became silent.

Our hearts rested in proximity in our quiet cocoon. We breathed in slow and unhurried breaths. I can't recount the number of seconds it lasted.

But then, too soon, the quiet ended.

With my eyes still closed, I again heard street sounds and nearby conversations. Stirred from my peaceful reverie, drawn out of a state of intoxication caused by another's maternal affection, I drifted back into awareness—and suddenly suffered a moment of embarrassment. What happened to my signature professionalism? Had I stepped over a boundary by initiating a hug with the Mother of the Civil Rights Movement? Had I intruded on her personal space?

Even as I thought these things, she still held me, and I still held her. We embraced so long that I felt I should signal the release. After all, I knew *her*, but she did not know me. I was hugging her in gratitude, thanking her for what she had done for my life, for what she represented to the world. But I had done nothing for *her*—had given her no reason to embrace me. I felt I was being unfair by keeping her locked in our embrace. *Do not impose on this precious woman, this treasure. I don't have the right*, I thought.

I let go first. Regretfully.

But for a second or two more, Rosa Parks continued to hold me. She hugged me longer than I hugged her, and I do not know her reason.

Nearly thirty years after that 1988 embrace, I still search for the answer. Did she see herself in me? If she had been born not in 1913, but in 1963, we might have been trendsetters together in television journalism. Was that her thought? Did she see, with all her wisdom and civil-disobedience training, that my career in television journalism added a stone of triumph in a road of opportunity she had helped to pave? Was she embracing *me* at all, or was she holding onto what she considered to be a victorious symbol in the cause for equality?

I will never know the answer, for Rosa Louise McCauley Parks died on October 24, 2005, at the age of ninety-two.

If I had been fortunate enough to meet her a second time, as a mature journalist and a socially aware African American woman, I could have questioned her about her intense desire for worldwide human rights. She was not an accidental participant in social movements.[21] And while she appeared acquiescent, my research reveals that she believed in self-defense. She even called Malcolm X her personal hero.[22] If I had met Mrs. Parks again, I could have mined her vast experiences as an internationalist, an opponent of the war in Viet Nam, and an objector to apartheid in South Africa. Her activism knew no boundaries; her present-day impact knows no borders.

Without the steadfast push for social and economic equality by legions of self-sacrificing activists, I would not have been a television bureau chief/reporter/one-woman band at WTVM-TV in Columbus, Georgia, and in position to embrace Rosa Parks.

To this day, I carry the fleeting seconds we spent in that puissant hug. Though I will never know the real reason Rosa Parks held onto me, I do know why I asked for the embrace: I was thanking her. She had courageously offered herself on the front line in a prolonged

---

21. Jeanne Theoharis, *The Rebellious Life of Mrs. Rosa Parks* (Boston: Beacon Press, 2013).
22. Id.

resistance movement against legal racism. I had benefited from the way she organized to improve American institutions during what would become seventy years of activism. But even as she and I held each other, I knew that what Rosa Parks wanted from me was not a *thank you* but *action*—a continuation of her fight against injustice.

Somewhere deep inside, I felt the beginnings of resolve.

CHAPTER 8

A Serious Body of Evidence

But then I got hired in Huntington, West Virginia.

I worked in the city for nearly three years. I could easily describe it as a negative chapter in my life—because of my workplace interactions with Bill Cummings and Roger Lyons, the white male news director and assignment editor, respectively, at WSAZ-TV. However, I will choose a more affirming statement when I recall my West Virginia years. I will parrot words written by the irrepressible Coretta Scott King, a woman widowed at age forty-one with four school-age children to raise. I will "count it all joy."[23]

One major positive that came out of that challenging period was my improvement as a television journalist. This happened because I had the exemplary reporting of white female colleague Cathy Brown in front of me most workdays. As the top investigative reporter in the entire market, she covered the hard news, the breaking news, the high-profile court cases. No matter what the breaking story, if you tossed it up in the air, Cathy would catch it and turn it into a sizzler. She would enterprise (TV-industry term meaning "to create") stories to present with a delicate touch and always with a memorable use of the most appropriate words.

Cathy produced a brilliant story about a deaf teenager who played a team sport—soccer, I think it was. She and the editor put together

---

23. Coretta Scott King, as told to the Rev. Dr. Barbara Reynolds in *My Life, My Love, My Legacy* (New York: Henry Holt and Company, 2017), p. 317. In her comment, she borrows language recorded by the Christian apostle James in chapter one, verse two, of the Bible book that bears his name.

a package that took viewers inside the teenager's hearing-deprived world. When the young player's hearing teammates appeared on screen, TV viewers heard the same sounds the players heard. Laughs and shrieks, yells and whistles, hand claps and thuds against the leather ball. When spectators seated on the bleachers appeared on screen—again, vibrant audio. But when the featured athlete appeared—no sound. Mute. Dead silence. The story demonstrated how powerfully a story could be presented to the viewers when a reporter and photographer lived up to their expectations as professionals and worked together as a team.

Viewing her quality packages on a daily basis pressured me to perform better—to perform the Cathy Brown way. She is the first colleague who pushed me in my career.[24]

I first noted Cathy's influence on my work when my photographer colleague Jim Backus and I shot a story about teenagers who drowned in Kenova, a city to the east of Huntington. Each spring, swimmers, mostly young people, attempted to leave the bank of the Ohio River near the 6th Street bridge and make it to a cement platform some twenty-five yards away. As you would expect, drownings occurred. It would often take an agonizing number of days to recover the bodies of swimmers who lost the challenge to conquer the river. They would eventually float up to the surface of the water downriver.

Jim and I shot interviews one evening with some young people who had lost one of their group in that way. At the time of our story, the body had not been recovered.

Pained by what the young people were experiencing, Jim and I tried to chat our way out of feeling low as we drove back to the WSAZ headquarters. Jim said, "If Cathy were doing the story, she'd say, 'The popular teenager disappeared in a watery grave in the Ohio River.' "

At first Jim and I scoffed at the tone of the words; they sounded dramatic and insensitive. However, after a quick moment of reflection,

---

24. Cathy Brown became an attorney and started a West Virginia law firm in 2009.

Jim concluded, "That's what it is, isn't it?" He was right; the tragedy did, indeed, culminate in a watery grave. A Cathy Brown piece would have included the blunt description. Therefore, I used that line in my package, and thus began my push to write with more force and courage.

In another case, I watched Cathy cover the high-profile murder trial of affluent local accountant Lyle McGinnis. While Cathy's work was stellar, I strongly disagreed with my news manager about the way WSAZ reported the initial crime.

McGinnis, a white male member of the business class, was bound with rope or other restraints inside his office building. Once rescued, he told police that two black men tied him up and set a fire. McGinnis said that he saw from his office window that the men drove off in a blue car. Our script on the late newscast included an alarming full-screen graphics page with a description of the suspects that the Huntington police were seeking. "Two black men in a blue car," we reported on WSAZ, treating McGinnis' account of events as unimpeachable information.

I went directly to Bill's office the next day. I asked if he saw our newscast and the description of the suspects in the alleged break-in and fire. He told me that he had.

I asked him what was the validity and usefulness (to the police and to the public) in saying "two black men in a blue car." How could that vagueness aid in the search? How could it do anything but indict all black men in blue cars? I pointed out the lack of approximate ages, skin tones, face shapes, facial hair. One or both wearing afros? Shaved heads?

I failed to persuade Bill. He staunchly supported the producer and the scriptwriter's decision to air the vague alert. His imperviousness planted a grain of discontent in me about his management style. It reminded me of the female-anatomy dispute I'd had with assignment manager Jerry Gunn in Macon. Again, a manager had failed to meet what I learned to be the standard for news judgment: *How does the information serve the public interest? Does the information meet the public-service or community-service obligation?*

As it turned out, the police found the body of Kathy McGinnis, wife of the accountant, in nearby St. Albans, West Virginia. In 1990, the jury convicted McGinnis of murder. To cover his own crimes, McGinnis had created the phony tale that accused two black men. While the jury saw its way to find guilt, was our WSAZ newsroom also guilty of something? First, would a culturally sensitive news manager have aired and then defended the initial story that roped in nondescript black suspects? Secondly, our news team provided false information to its audience. The team implicitly trusted and aired unconfirmed statements, possibly stirring public fear of black neighbors and friends—when the facts later proved that no black people were involved in the murder.

In addition to admiring Cathy's work, I liked her immediately. I not only benefited professionally from closely observing her journalistic methods, social advantages fell in my lap because I worked across from her desk. She invited me to her home for my first Christmas in Huntington. I really got lucky with the invitation because I started my job on December 1, 1988. I did not know, at first, what I would do on Christmas as a newcomer to the community and far away from my Augusta family base.

Cathy's invitation included a home-cooked meal and an outing to see *Twins*, the ridiculous movie with Arnold Schwarzenegger, the six-foot-two former international bodybuilding champion, and four-foot-ten actor Danny DeVito, not a bodybuilder. They played twins separated at birth. However, the premise of the story is not the wackiest part of Christmas 1988.

Cathy had invited two male guests, both black males and her friends. *Great timing!* I thought. *I am arriving in Huntington and I'll kick-start my social life in the first month.*

An attorney nicknamed Butch arrived first. His physique provided irrefutable evidence to the jury (me!) that, yes, he had entered the weightlifting room and had, indeed, lifted weights. I also saw evidence that he had wholly invested in the sexy, clingy menswear approach of the day, the style made popular by the handsome characters Sonny Crockett and Ricardo Tubbs on *Miami Vice*, a hit detective show. The day we met, Butch's light-colored sweater hugged his athletic frame, revealing bulked-up shoulders and a rock-solid midsection. He would later tell me that, in the full flavor of the 1988 music videos, I would find parachute pants and belt-skimming, Michael Jackson *Thriller*-type jackets in his closet.

Before the Christmas date ended, Butch asked me out. A week later, we went dancing at Robby's nightclub, a trendy venue in Huntington. Butch reserved a table, an impressive and expensive move. The nightclub package included seating in a prime position and a New Year's Eve champagne toast at midnight.

On our first date, I had learned that Butch was a kind-hearted, family-oriented man. When not in the gym, he lifted a saxophone to his lips; he became so accomplished that he sat in on jazz improv sessions at after-hours bars. I did not get to learn much more about him on our second date, however, because people kept interrupting us. Because we were seated, we were stationary targets, allowing Butch's former clients to repeatedly stop by our table. Each one praised Butch's legal work and the winning outcome he had delivered on a case. The clients' inhibitions were lowered because of the drinks that were flowing; many of them stayed a bit too long in our space.

And then, not even one hour into our evening—as if things weren't awkward enough for Butch—our waiter tipped over Butch's drink. The liquid spread quickly on the table and dribbled off the side to soak into the crotch of Butch's pants. With the waist-cut jacket Butch wore (the style MJ made famous), there was no fabric to hide anything lower than Butch's belt. The large wet spot screamed that he had urinated in his pants.

While I guess that's not *too* odd an occurrence on New Year's Eve, it spelled disaster for a man trying to woo a woman. Butch rushed off to the restroom to assess his pants. After several long minutes, he returned with a mix of anger and embarrassment on his face. He suggested we sit out the dances. I was disappointed, but I agreed and understood. As a well-known attorney, he could not risk being seen in the largest nightclub in the state with a wet stain on the front of his slacks.

We watched while the other revelers danced to the year's hottest songs, including Terence Trent D'Arby's "Wishing Well" and the Pebbles' hit "Mercedes Boy." It was not a love match between Butch and me, but we were comfortable with each other because of what we had in common: being two black professionals in a state with a small percentage of blacks. Probably fueled by this need to racially connect, we dated a few more times. He eventually moved to another part of West Virginia. I would read later in the newspaper that he had married and settled down.

That was just as well. My divorce would not be final until mid-summer 1989, the following year.

CHAPTER 9

End of the Love Affair

As a child, I knew that my brown skin gave me something in common with the dark-skinned people I saw on our family's black-and-white TV. Sammy Davis Jr., Dr. Martin Luther King Jr., Diahann Carroll, a few others. And yes, I knew that beautiful Jayne Kennedy's brown skin, which I later saw on our color TV, mirrored my own. I knew I was *Negro*, as my birth certificate proclaims, or *black*, as my hometown icon James Brown proudly sings. I knew my race was black—but I did not know that meant I was also politically black.

In other words, I never realized that being a baby born in the year of a monumental civil rights act meant that I would face societal limitations—that constructs would be erected to restrict the possibilities of my dreams and desires. That is why I was taken aback by the resistance I received in my career path.

It is probably also why my mind and heart were open to entering a kind of marriage that American society had long said a black woman should not consider.

Blair Robertson and I were college sweethearts who married after four years of dating. We studied together in the Augusta College communications program, completed many top-quality projects in our television classes, and received our degrees in the same graduation ceremony in May 1986. A white Canadian with a mass of dark curly hair, dimples, and a Cary Grant cleft chin, Blair and I relied on each other through the rigorous video-production and journalism classes. Blair said "a-boot" when pronouncing the word "about," as did my favorite newsman Peter Jennings.

However, teenaged boyfriends and girlfriends, even though they marry, often grow in different directions. As adults, Blair and I discovered we were not well suited. I filed for divorce in the fall of 1988, less than two years after the wedding. Moving to Huntington to work, I closed that chapter of my personal life.

It was not, however, the end of my interaction with white men—personally or, of course, professionally.

I do not paint all my white male colleagues at Huntington's WSAZ with the same brush that I use for Bill Cummings and Roger Lyons, my immediate managers who attempted to stymie my progress.

Anchorman Bob Brunner, for example, presented to me a vast new world to be conquered in the business of news. He backed my work and gave me access to his professional contacts across the United States. Bob presented his segment of the newscast from our Charleston, West Virginia, studio in the state's capital city. He performed his duties fifty-three miles away from the Huntington newsroom—but he was even further away in figurative miles from the thinking that sought to limit me. The well-connected newsman set my career on a path that I, as a newcomer from the South, had not known existed before I met him.

Bob recommended me for the Radio and Television News Directors Foundation's Michele Clark Fellowship.[25] In doing so, the veteran broadcaster aligned his name and reputation with me, a nascent entity in TV journalism. The prestigious RTNDF annually designates a minority cub reporter as someone to watch in the industry.

Michele Clark had been that person, an up-and-coming black female television reporter in the burgeoning business in the early '70s. Her hiring on the national level added the diversity the industry

---

25. The organization added "digital" to its name in October 2009 and became the Radio Television Digital News Foundation, with the Radio Television Digital News Association as its parent organization.

sought. However, Ms. Clark died in a plane crash on her way to an assignment for CBS News in 1972.

In 1989, thanks to Bob's heavyweight endorsement, I won the one-thousand-dollar fellowship, to be used for an educational purpose. The award also included an all-expenses-paid trip to attend the RTNDF's Excellence in Journalism conference in Kansas City, Missouri. The conference culminated with an awards banquet attended by CNN creator Ted Turner and the network's lead anchorman, Bernard Shaw. NBC's Washington-based reporter Andrea Mitchell delivered an address and posed for pictures with us, the night's award winners.

Starting off the slow-paced meal, diners sipped a champagne apéritif and followed it with a white wine, to be enjoyed with a fancy salad with walnuts. (I particularly remember the walnuts because Grandmama, who was still alive at the time, regularly prepared Waldorf salad with a healthy portion of walnuts. I smiled each time she set the dish in front of me.)

To harmonize with the flavors of the *plat de résistance*—a choice between chicken and lamb—a diner could continue with white wine or nod to the server to pour red wine into the large-bowled glass in front of the diner. In the dandified setting, I went with the safe choice of chicken because I had never tasted lamb. How inelegant it would be of me to choke on something because I did not like the taste!

When I first sat at the round white-linen table with seven others, I recognized immediately my bread plate on the left and my water glass on the right. My memory had clicked back to high school home-economics classes, with utensils and plates carefully arranged in a high-toned table setting. However, not until the meal's progression did I begin to understand why we had so many wine glasses. As a member of a family that rarely went to restaurants, the wine-and-food pairing was a ritzy first for me.

The bestowal of the Michele Clark Fellowship capped the night. One of NBC's New York-based journalists, Claude Matthews, described the significance of the fellowship and then read my name as the recipient. Until that moment, I did not realize it was the top honor of the evening. I walked to the podium feeling poised, thanks to my years of modeling on the J.B. White fashion board back in Augusta. Actually, I believe I floated. The bright lights flooding the stage prevented me from seeing the faces of the people seated in the dining room, but I knew it was packed with the industry's stars of the day. I remember absorbing the rapturous applause.

In front of the stellar crowd, I thanked the foundation members in a succinct and sincere message. "I'm deeply touched by this award," I concluded.

Claude Matthews returned to the podium to wrap up the ceremony. "She *is* truly touched by the award," he quipped, "because she left her check!" Everyone laughed again.

An evening of splendor! I was surrounded by journalists who had set lofty goals and reached them. I knew I was in the right place.

I returned from the Radio and Television News Directors Association convention and the RTNDF award night feeling aligned with my destiny. Buoyed by this belief, I found the courage to confide in my boss, Bill Cummings, about my most sincere goal in television: becoming a sports reporter.

I knew I could do the job in a special way. I had always viewed sports reporting as a study in the planned collisions in the lives of would-be champions. Only a select few wear the uniforms and perform at the appointed time and place, giving spectators something bigger than their own lives to embrace. And the attitude of the players was clear: No excuses. Be there. Bring your best despite the harrowing path you may have traveled.

For years I had trained to tell these stories with honesty. I sought to put at the forefront the beauty of the athletic realm's human drama—to awaken the latent interest most people have in another person's story of conquest. After all, most people awaken from sleep with the desire to succeed at something. We get out of bed every day to win, don't we? Sports reporting grabs onto that private battle, that great shared human need, and gives it a public stage on TV.

Along with my interest in competition's drama, I had a head for facts, including statistics, about an array of sports. Beginning in childhood, I followed professional baseball and boxing and auto racing, along with basketball, football, golf, and tennis. I could recognize the international field of dominant players and pronounce the difficult names of tennis stars of the 1970s. Guillermo Vilas, Vitas Gerulaitis, Ilie Nastase, and Vijay Amritraj. Also: McEnroe, Connors, Borg, and Ashe; I knew them all.

At age fourteen, I met Arthur Ashe during his promotional visit to Augusta.

John McEnroe? While still a teenager, I interviewed him during the Tennis Over America events that brought him to my hometown.

I may have been twenty years old when I met and interviewed 1979 Masters golf champion Fuzzy Zoeller for my college newspaper.

Just bring it on—I could talk about it.

I began developing a knowledge base in NASCAR when I was a second-grader. My days of sitting on the couch in my family's home on Hazel Street in Augusta started—approximately, in 1972—with Richard Petty, A.J. Foyt, and Bobby Allison (not yet Davey Allison) on the ovals. Dale Earnhardt Sr., who would later capture the media spotlight in the American-born racing circuit, had not even debuted in the top tier. When I was tuning in, he was still five years away from gaining his full-time ride.

Baseball? I could discuss catcher Biff Pocoroba and most of the Atlanta Braves lineup. My dad preferred the Los Angeles Dodgers, so I followed them and their right-handed pitcher Don Sutton.

In 1981, for my high school paper, *The Westside Story*, I wrote an opinion piece on money's overreach in baseball. "Don Sutton to Houston?" I ask rhetorically in the article. I complain about the fact that the hurler could be uprooted from sunny California and his fan base in the free-agent spending spree. (The free-agent period is the time during which baseball teams throw money at star players who are up for grabs because of their contract situations.)

In 1992, I would meet Sutton in the media center at the Atlanta-Fulton County Stadium. Sutton, the Braves games broadcaster at the time, stepped out of his booth. Though eleven years had passed since the insult had occurred, I told him how I still felt burned about his free-agent contract with Houston. "Mr. Consistency" seemed more than a bit flattered that a twenty-eight-year-old woman had followed his career so closely.

What Sutton could not know is that I had begun building my baseball knowledge as early as age six. I adored the sport and devoured newspaper feature stories. I would read recaps of games in the paper, memorize the stats of players, and note the trends—up or down. In the pre-internet days, I could access the pertinent facts in my mental files as if flipping through a Rolodex on my desk. Later in life, one of my colleagues would remark, "Nita can write the heck out of a baseball story!" What more could a sports department need?

"You memorized the batting averages of your favorite players as a child. I wondered what you were going to do with that stuff," my dad has said many times over the years.

I had waited for the right time to suggest to Bill Cummings how I might align my background in sports with WSAZ's interests. Sure, I had landed the job of general-assignment reporter for the station, but by performing well, I felt I had qualified to take on an expanded role. Such progression is what I had experienced in my previous jobs and in my academic studies.

So, that day, soaring with unbridled anticipation (for I just knew I would receive a *yes*), I told Bill about my desire. I not only had the endorsement of a national journalism organization, I also was laden with knowledge and passion—with a foundation I believe should have earned for me his endorsement.

I did not get it.

"You don't know anything about sports," Bill said. "Besides, Joe Public will not accept a woman in sports."

After asserting that the Appalachian television audience would not respond to me in a sports role because I was a woman, Bill hesitated.

He did not say, *And because you're black,* but the implication hung in the air between us.

At the time, I was the only full-time African American journalist on air in that TV market. (This reflected the general state of things in West Virginia. The Marshall University basketball team, for instance, did not hire a black head basketball coach for the men's team until Dwight Freeman got the job for the 1990-1991 season.)

True, African Americans were less than 5 percent of the viewing area's population. For that reason, one could argue that catering to black interests would not be a wise business move. But allowing a reporter to draw viewers to the sports show with a unique type of reporting—one that focused more on the person than on athletic feats—is neither a race nor a gender matter. Besides, someone at WSAZ had thought enough of my abilities to let me in the door as news reporter. Why not expand upon the risk? Wouldn't there be a greater payoff in viewer loyalty?

Apparently, none of this mattered to Bill, which frustrated me. His decision also frustrated me because it ran counter to the ideals of the most important body in TV, the Radio and Television News Directors Foundation. That organization had branded me someone to watch in the industry, but what did that mean if my boss shut down my attempts to add a new skill?

In a letter dated September 10, 1989, the founder and treasurer of the RTNDF wrote:

> Congratulations, Nita Wiggins!
>
> We are delighted that you are the winner of our Michele Clark Fellowship! [...] It is almost always our most emotional experience for our conventions, as the audiences [...] wonder where Michele—had she lived—would be today. And they will look at you, and wonder whether the challenge of being her surrogate in a career sense weighs in for you.
>
> ...

With best wishes always,

Col. Barney Oldfield, USAF (Ret.), Founder &
Treasurer

RADIO AND TELEVISION NEWS DIRECTORS
FOUNDATION, INC

The words of the letter make it clear: The Clark award had a
tender meaning to those who bestowed it. They carefully selected
as its recipient only someone they truly believed would expand her
wings in the field of journalism.

However, the matter of my branching into sportscasting was a
closed issue for Bill Cummings. A nonstarter. What burned me the
most was that he didn't even ask me what I knew.

Sometimes, being a black woman in the workplace can be much
like ordering in a restaurant. Faced with a choice of two entrees—
gender or skin color—a server politely informs me that each of
those dishes comes with a side of discrimination. "And ma'am, are
you OK with that?"

CHAPTER 10

My Big Mouth

WSAZ-TV 3 held a coveted place in the Huntington-area broadcast market. As the station with the most viewers, and by a wide margin, our personnel received the respect of the local Marshall University. When the school hosted a discussion on the topic "How to Cover Minorities in the '90s," the organizer invited my news director, Bill Cummings—naturally. Bill was, after all, manager of the top-rated news station. Who better to talk about decision-making in news coverage?

The rub came when I also got the call. As the only full-time black journalist on TV in the market, how could the school's panel credibly address the topic without hearing from the journalist who held that dubious distinction?

For the event, the university opened the doors to the public, but the greater part of the audience comprised students and university personnel. There was not a large black presence at the event because the city itself did not have a large black presence.

On stage, a few seats separated Bill and me at a table that included six people. Place cards let audience members see the name and job title of each invitee. Each person made opening comments. I promised to give frank responses and to cite names, dates, locations, and other specifics to back up whatever I might say.

Once we moved to the question-and-answer portion of the event, a teenaged or twentysomething white student in the audience said that she wanted to hear an answer from Bill and from me.

"Why do I get the feeling, as a viewer, that whenever there is a story about the NAACP or black issues, Nita is reporting it?" the student asked.

I allowed Bill to have the first shot at a response.

"It's only natural," he began. "Nita's black and she has more comfort covering those stories."

I heard exactly the response I expected from him. My calm demeanor camouflaged two things. The first was a hot flash of displeasure caused by insult. How dare Bill imply that my race, rather than my professional training in journalism, made me the right reporter for a job. Second, I was reasoning my way through a quick internal battle. I could defer to my manager's position and remain quiet, or I could correct his deeply erroneous explanation. To clear up misunderstandings about minorities and the media—isn't that what I was there to do? Doing anything less with the journalism students, their professors, and other people in the audience would cheat them in the discussion.

So, I spoke.

"I am a reporter," I said. "That means it's my job to cover the story. If the people are black or if the people are white, a reporter is supposed to have the skills to develop a comfort level with the people involved."

I looked at the audience as I spoke, tempering my voice as if I were recording an audio track for a TV show. I wanted my words to be crisp and clearly understood.

"If we follow what Bill is saying, does that mean that I do not have the skills to cover a story that does not have black people in it? Does it mean that the only comfort level I can establish is with people from my race?"

Though I kept my focus on the audience, I detected with my peripheral vision that my manager was fidgeting at the table. Despite this, I continued speaking that which I believed to be truth.

"If I am not working on the day that the NAACP has a meeting, does that mean the story is not covered or does it mean I must come in to work because no one else can cover it?"

My rhetorical questions hovered in the air. I was grateful for the young audience member who had triggered my responses. Her question offered more intelligence and insight into the responsibility of the media than did Bill's answer.

Now, with the door to sensitive discussion fully opened, another audience member presented a pointed question.

"Why is Nita the only black person on WSAZ?"

Again, I allowed Bill to give first answer. He explained that with a black population of roughly 3 percent, it would be difficult to attract black people to work in the Huntington-Charleston market.

After Bill's response, the audience members seemed to turn in unison toward me, as if watching the ball in a tennis match.

"I disagree," I volleyed on cue. "This is a number 48 market. It is attractive to anyone who wants to move up."

That had been the case with me in 1988. I had read with much excitement the ad about a job opening at WSAZ. At the time, I worked as a one-woman band/bureau chief in the Columbus, Georgia, market, which ranked above 100—which means it was a market with a viewing audience smaller than Huntington's.

I told the university audience that when investigating the WSAZ ad, I had not checked the minority breakdown of the population in Huntington. Instead, I was focused on upward mobility. Huntington, an industrial center, would be the largest city in which I would have lived at that point in my life. More importantly, because I expected to work one day in the top-10 Dallas market, I focused on the market number of my new opportunity. At No. 48, Huntington outranked my then-current job in Columbus by more than 50 points. Moving that far up the Nielsen scale would mean doubling my viewing audience on the way to Dallas.

Therefore, after learning about the challenging new possibility, I had looked for magazine articles and encyclopedia entries about the three-state market of West Virginia-Ohio-Kentucky. I researched the industries, the traditions, and the leisure activities of the cities. This included, of course, finding out which pro sports teams the Huntington-Charleston viewers supported.

The racial breakdown of the Appalachian region was not a factor in my analysis because I was looking forward to immersing myself in new American experiences—and that includes all races. I saw the move as a step forward in expanding my cultural knowledge of my country. Who were the people I would meet and interview in Appalachia? How did they live and work—and play? Could I tell their stories? Surely, their experiences would differ in regional tone from those I reported in Georgia and Alabama. I felt the lure of discovery.

So, I disagreed with Bill. With my answers, I had publicly embarrassed him. That had not been my intention, but I could not backtrack.

I am sure Bill was relieved when the discussion softened in tone. I shared a brief account that demonstrated my ability to feel comfortable—and to provide comfort—regardless of a story's circumstances. The example also showed that the race of the person I was interviewing mattered not at all. I recounted a flood story I covered with my cameraman and good friend Jim.

Jim drove us to a neighborhood in eastern Kentucky, a place where he told me he had shot the devastation of flooding several times before. People in the area had the habit of throwing their old washing machines, water heaters, and other unwanted appliances into a nearby creek, Jim told me. The debris added to what was already a natural problem: The spring storms and melting ice from the mountains caused the water in the creek to rise.

When we arrived on the scene, we found a heartbreaking sight. Water had crept onto the property of a homestead and covered the lower level of a split-level home. The sloping backyard had essentially been turned into a pond. Jim parked the car. He jumped out and began shooting video before any distraught homeowner could tell us to leave.

To do a complete story, though, we would need an interview. I summoned the courage, in the midst of the watery damage, to walk up to the front door. I would have entirely understood if the family facing such misfortune simply refused to talk to me.

The homeowner, a tall white man who appeared to be in his eighties, opened the door wearing wet light-colored boxer shorts and a wet white T-shirt.

I tried to mask amazement that he had answered the door while not fully dressed. "You have serious flooding here," I said gently, stating the obvious with genuine concern.

The man looked at me but seemed distracted and did not speak. Maybe he was getting his first view of the flooding from his front door. Finally, he focused on me. If he were, indeed, in his eighties, then I was looking at someone who was born into a world in which the average black woman worked as a domestic or some other menial laborer. She certainly would not have stood before him with the authority to use a microphone to invade his privacy.

Empathy colored my voice and eyes. The man must have discerned this, for his stressed face softened a bit as he looked at me.

"I'm Nita Wiggins from WSAZ. Would it be OK for us to show our viewers how bad the flooding is?" I asked.

The elderly man said that the truly dismaying images were inside his home. He opened the door wider and motioned us into the living room and then into the kitchen. Murky ankle-deep floodwater covered the floor. To avoid stumbling over anything that might flow underfoot, we carefully dragged our feet as we walked. The man pointed out the water marks on the walls, refrigerator, and console television—proof that the level had been much higher. Jim captured incredible video. The homeowner willingly gave me an interview.

My account of the news story seemed to impress the audience at Marshall University. Some people nodded as though they remembered seeing our flood coverage. Later, some of my friends expressed surprise that the homeowner had so easily let down his guard and shared his concerns with me. Based on Bill's opinion about which journalist is capable of developing a comfort level and rapport with whom, such a trusting interaction and sensitive story should never have happened.

Upon arriving for work the next day, I walked into Bill's office. He was seated, so I caught him flat-footed. I resumed our discussion from the night before. I told him that I thought it had been my duty to say what I had said at the university, even though it meant disagreeing with him.

Bill had three sons, one of whom was an infant in 1990. I said, "One day, your sons might work for a black boss. They will need to be comfortable with people who are not white." As a TV station, I continued, we do not serve anyone when we use race to categorize people instead of using our reports to enlighten them.

What a headache! he must have thought. *Mouthy at Marshall University and mouthy the morning after!*

CHAPTER 11

Whose Lane Is It, Anyway?

I knew I was on borrowed time in my reporter position at WSAZ, for my relationship with Bill, the news director and my direct supervisor, developed into a long-running clash. Specifically, our point of contention was this: I did not accept someone's attempt to set limits for me. I had not allowed my family to steer me even on minor things. "Why change now? Whose lane is it, anyway?" I mused.

Here's a telling example. When I was about eighteen months old, I caused an uproar while my family visited my grandparents at their Poppy Avenue home in Macon. As we stood together on the walkway leading to their front porch, my grandfather put a scarf around my neck. Others tell me that I showed my displeasure and yanked it off. I must have had my own reasons for not wanting that scarf around my neck—I don't remember—but my grandfather and I were stalemated. Each time he wrapped the scarf around me, I removed it, becoming more emphatic with every removal. Finally, I firmly took hold of the scarf and, frowning, threw it on the walkway. I stomped on it, making my wishes unmistakably clear. I had not yet started watching major league baseball games, but according to the description my father gave, I must have looked like a team's manager determined to *one-up* an official in a heated on-field dispute. And I was not yet two years old!

"Good God!" my grandfather exclaimed, exasperated.

I'm not sure what moved me that day. However, in the showdown between Grandfather and Toddler Nita, the result stands: Game over. Point communicated.

A variation of this stubbornness reared its head in Huntington during a conversation I had with a photographer colleague, Charlie Hill. Charlie was fiftyish, with closely cut reddish hair, freckles and, on occasion, a bushy beard. He held the same position as did my buddy Jim, but I worked infrequently with Charlie. Our interactions were a definite change of pace from the ceaseless conversations Jim and I would have in the news car. For one thing, sounds from the radio filled the air whenever Charlie and I were in the car. I first heard Conservative broadcaster Rush Limbaugh while listening to Charlie's radio. Like a hound dog chasing a scent, Charlie would hunt down Rush's signal no matter where we found ourselves driving in rural West Virginia, Ohio, or Kentucky. Limbaugh did not disappoint, with his piping-hot servings of opinions.

Charlie offered an uninvited opinion of his own one day: his career strategy for me. He knew of my sports-reporting desire because *everyone* knew. I had been telling my friends in the newsroom, in the entertainment division, in editing, and in production about it ever since the RTNDF banquet. I was also in the sports office with Bob Bowen and Kenny Bass as often as I was at my own desk in news.

Thus, during a long trip into Ohio, Charlie advised me that I would be better off abandoning my aspirations of covering sports. The news director, Charlie reminded me, rules the roost in the TV business. My current boss or the next one, Charlie said, held the cards when it came to opportunities and assignments. It was unlikely my chance would ever come, Charlie told me. In short, he was telling me to stay in my lane.

I was not sure whether to regard Charlie's advice as kindly paternalistic or blindly chauvinistic. Either way, I was not accepting any of it.

"I'll cover sports in Dallas, or I'll die trying," I announced gravely.

The words slipped out of my mouth before I realized it. I would *die* trying to get there? Did I mean that? The words had sounded like an icy threat, but to whom? Was I saying I would take drastic action against someone who impeded me for too long? I had never linked blind ambition with my goal. Had never realized the goal might have been driving me toward delirium and desperation.

However obscure this underlying sentiment had been, Charlie liberated it for me that day, and there was no taking it back. Like the incident with my grandfather, game over. Point communicated.

After the awkward admission in the news car, I knew that the fire of my stubbornness would not die out. I often told myself, "If my getting a role as a sports reporter is a waiting game, I will outlast anyone foolish enough to work against me."

What other viable recourse did I have? Even with the existence of civil rights laws against job discrimination, I hesitated to file a claim. Suing a station would effectively lead to my being labeled a troublemaker, which could short-circuit opportunities for me at other stations. Mulling over the predicament, a solution appeared on my television screen.

At that time (the late 1980s), Oprah Winfrey was unfurling her wings. Unrivaled in attracting audiences and crashing ratings records, she stomped on the limiting thoughts and excuses offered by managers everywhere, just as I had stomped on the scarf in the incident with my grandfather.

I chose to latch on to Oprah's mantra, which was: *Learn something every day and learn from mistakes.* Mistakes, she says, are going to happen; just don't make the same mistake twice. Additionally, I heard Oprah say (in a televised interview in 1989, I think it was) that education is the great equalizer. Her words, along with her skyrocketing success, galvanized me and spurred me on.

I charted a plan of action. I needed to know more. I needed to groom my journalism skills and pump up my résumé with more credentials. I had to show on paper what I knew because I felt my black female face gave newsroom bosses a chance to reflexively reject my appeals for career advancement.[26]

So, I looked for additional sports-related education, training, and certifications. I achieved an unusual duo of credentials in late 1989 and 1990: registered basketball referee and licensed Junior Olympic boxing judge. I vowed that my future news directors would not be justified in limply saying that I did not have the background to be a sports reporter. My résumé would reflect my verifiable qualifications.

---

26. The following sheds light on the author's experience. Nilanjana Dasgupta, researcher at the University of Massachusetts-Amherst Department of Psychological and Brain Sciences, writes: "[R]esearch suggests that intergroup preferences and prejudices are influenced by two different psychological forces—people's tendency to prefer groups associated with themselves as a confirmation of their high self-esteem versus their tendency to prefer groups valued by the mainstream culture as a confirmation of the sociopolitical order in society. Second, these implicit prejudices and stereotypes often influence people's judgments, decisions, and behaviors in subtle but pernicious ways." See Nilanjana Dasgupta, "Implicit Ingroup Favoritism, Outgroup Favoritism, and Their Behavioral Manifestations," *Social Justice Research* 17(2), June 2004. Accessed March 2019 at researchgate.net/publication/226439218_Implicit_Ingroup_Favoritism_Outgroup_Favoritism_and_Their_Behavioral_Manifestations.

PART II

Hazards Ahead:
Seen and Unseen

CHAPTER 12

Putting on the Gloves

I had followed boxing ever since I was a preschooler, but how does one write that on a résumé? To augment my homegrown knowledge with legitimate credentials, I decided to join a local boxing club, an LBC, on the suggestion of Huntington police officer Austin Hairston.

I had met Austin, an unpaid volunteer boxing coach in his free time, while I was working a crime story. My photographer and friend Jim knew Austin well and had told me about the man's position as the only black officer on a police force of about one hundred men and women.

At his PAL gym, a Police Athletic League boxing gym, Austin trained Junior Olympic boxers. The run-down facility in the center of one of Huntington's government-supported housing projects put the community-minded officer in the ideal place to make successful outreach to his target population of preteens and teenagers.

Austin explained to me the gym's motto, which incorporated the D's of *discipline, direction,* and *determination.* He told me that the school-aged boxers could only train if they had attended school that day and only if they had obeyed all the school rules that day. Teachers had Austin's home and gym phone numbers, and he encouraged them to call if any of his young charges stepped out of line.

I loved the discipline of the gym. I loved also that the girlfriends of the boxers could exercise there if they adhered to the same guidelines. When Austin told me that he needed female supervision at the gym, I offered to work with the youngest boxers and to lead boxers of all ages on training runs through the city. As a runner at the time (two to three miles several times a week), I took up the new responsibility with excitement. Immediately after working hours at WSAZ, I would drive to the gym, change into ratty, un-chic layers of workout clothes, put on my Everlast hand wraps, and prepare to run with the athletes—the boys and the girls.

In boxing circles, wearing ratty, un-chic workout clothes is like wearing a badge of honor. Rocky Balboa, the fictitious icon of the Sylvester Stallone *Rocky* cinema saga, dressed in an unspectacular gray sweatpants-and-sweatshirt combination on the way to dismantling his underdog standing. He wore his shirtsleeves cut off above the elbows and a towel tucked into the neck to hold in the heat and keep out the Philadelphia cold. In this drab outfit, Rocky became an enduring image of punching through the odds.

My young boxing companions dressed similarly for our Huntington runs. Though I had too often felt the chill of loneliness in my adopted city and state, it melted away in the warmth of the boxing-gym community. I felt enveloped within the comfortable, multi-generational, multi-ethnic family unit.

Time with my gym family felt so fulfilling that I was not concerned about the dingy surroundings some might have found depressing. Our gym smelled musty, like sweat-soaked and dried boxing gloves and hand wraps; like old sneakers worthy of being retired; like the protective headgear that had covered its share of drenched afros, asymmetrical fades, cornrows, mop tops, and tangled mullets. However, the good far outweighed the grubby for me. We had each other, in our gym, and we used the equipment at our disposal to try to bring out the best in every member.

But one day, Austin asked me a question that would turn the tide of my career. He asked if I would study to obtain a license as an amateur boxing judge. At first, I deflected the question. The easy routine of engaging in TV work, fitness, and relaxation pleased me enough to not want to alter it. On top of that, I had not yet made the connection between having a judge's certification and building sports credibility.

I continued to hesitate a few weeks more, so Austin told me why he was being persistent. The boxers trained and anticipated reaping the rewards of their sweat, he said. Often, they would go to boxing meets, only to find that there were not enough judges for all the matches to take place. The kids from the gym faced too many closed doors, he said.

That stirred me; I knew something about closed doors. I also knew that having more judges meant that more kids could box. More kids could get to know police officers at the PAL gyms and not on the streets on the wrong end of a confrontation.

I agreed to become a judge.

The process included studying the manual of rules, passing a written exam, interviewing with a currently licensed judge, and finding three character references. It was a good move and, for me, a painless one mostly because it benefited the youngsters around Austin Hairston. But it also helped me. As a certified judge, I suddenly held a passport into new places.

I soon encountered a commanding and interesting person in the boxing universe, promoter Bill Picozzi. While covering a story with Jim, my trusty friend made it a point to tell Picozzi that I held an ABF (Amateur Boxing Federation)[27] judge's license. It was the perfect icebreaker. Bill told me about his upcoming boxing promotion with living legend Muhammad Ali. Bill put me on the backstage guest list.

In Search of a Champion

I needed fortifying.

I had to take on the task of slaying the dragon that stood in my way, namely, my news director's admitted prejudices against women sports journalists. I additionally felt that he wanted me, as a black journalist, to stay in my lane and progress at a pace that did not exceed his expectations. Oprah's televised words had inspired me to become armed, but now I needed the strength to fight, and I needed someone to champion my cause.

---

27. Later renamed USA Boxing.

I received both things I needed in the forms of then-heavyweight boxing champion James "Buster" Douglas and Ali, perhaps the greatest boxer of all time. For a promotion called *The Latest and The Greatest*, Bill Picozzi brought in the two champions to observe the Golden Gloves matches at the Huntington Civic Center in March 1990.

As I dressed on the morning of the matches and the heavyweight promotion, I fretted over what to wear. One wants to make an impression when meeting Muhammad Ali, one of the world's most charming athletes and a dapper dresser. But how to do that? Pretty? Feminine? Not too polished and coiffed—it's a boxing event, not an opera.

I finally settled on a tailored skirt suit from The Limited, a popular clothing store at the time. The suit was burgundy and deep blue, of woven fabric. It had cost a pretty penny when I bought it three years earlier. A three-button jacket detailed with four pockets, it was fitted but not too sexy to wear around teenaged boys, a boxing entourage, and the champs. Besides, it was my go-to suit. I had worn it when interviewing Rosa Parks in Tuskegee, Alabama, in 1988, some two years earlier. Actually, as I now reflect on the choice of the special outfit, I realize it was probably the only good suit I'd had in my closet!

❦

At the Golden Gloves event, Jim shot video of some of the matches, video of the spectators, and video of Ali's signing autographs. I asked a few people how it felt to see The Greatest in person and to receive his valuable signature.

As I orchestrated conversations about Ali, I kept my distance from the champ. He was seated near the boxing ring. A long line of people waited to meet him. The fans at the Huntington Civic Center deserved their time with him. I sensed that he wanted to give it to them. So, I waited.

But that wasn't the only reason I waited. I had known since childhood about the boxing world. Knew its luminaries. Ali was one.

He exhibited, as a young fighter, fleet-footed and quick-punching grace in a physical body that was sculpted and beautiful. In addition, the People's Champ had become a leading anti-war voice and a righteous symbol in the fight for the civil rights of black Americans in the turbulent 1960s and '70s. The cocky and boastful and bombastic showman was also lyrical and good-natured and funny. People loved him. There's no way to summarize his impact around the world, nor to list the places he visited and the people he influenced.

I found promoter Bill Picozzi and asked about interviewing Ali. To make it happen, Bill brought over Ali's road manager, an African American named Mahdi. Bill told Mahdi about our friendship, that I worked for the dominant television station in the city, and that I held a boxing judge's license. Apparently impressed, perhaps by my smart suit, my job, and my certification, Mahdi asked if I would be available to make appearances with the champ during the four days of the Golden Gloves. The entourage needed a female touch, he explained, and he said that my television station would benefit from the association with Ali.

I agreed without hesitation.

Mahdi said he would take us to the champ when the right moment came. When Ali took a break from the autographs and stepped out of the public view, Mahdi walked Jim and me over to him. Ali was seated. As I approached, my eyes widened with each step, as did Ali's.

I drank in the features of his smooth, healthily glowing toffee face. First, his eyes. Ali had said so much with his mouth over the years. Now, his eyes spoke. The expressive, dark, chestnut-colored spheres focused on me. Without speaking, each of us gazed with approval at the one returning the look.

Six years earlier, in 1984, Ali had announced that the incurable, progressive neurological condition, Parkinson's, was stealing his ability to speak. The once gregarious and humorously poetic man had delighted fans when he boasted that he could "float like a butterfly and sting like a bee." But the handsome and nimble athlete had become a forty-eight-year-old with neurologically slowed speech and movements. But this did not mean he wasn't still a striking and strong-looking man in 1990.

Ali stood up from his chair. He was six-foot-three and solidly built. He stared back at me with his well-preserved, manly good looks. Mahdi told the Champ that he had invited me into the entourage for the Huntington events. Ali nodded slowly with approval.

Lunch with a King

Because he was relying on his eyes and head nods to take the place of his words, Ali spoke very little during the days I spent with his crew. He smiled shyly at me many times during a private family dinner party, at a celebrity party at the Radisson Hotel, and during a lunch at the famous Jim's Steak and Spaghetti House. The lunch occurred one afternoon after a slate of amateur boxing bouts. Ali and company, which included me, were ready for lunch. We pondered the simplest way to move the ten of us from the civic center to the restaurant. Mahdi considered calling taxis, but we finally decided it would be simpler to walk.

We strolled from the civic center on Third Avenue to the restaurant, which was on Fifth Avenue. Nothing remarkable happened as we walked the first two blocks on a side street. After turning left onto Fifth, we still had some five blocks to go, walking in a direction that faced Fifth Avenue's oncoming one-way traffic flow. This wasn't at all dangerous because of the in-city speed limit and the wide sidewalks. People who obeyed the speed limit got a thrill because they could recognize Muhammad Ali and react before completely passing by the group.

Honking horns and cheers of "Champ! Champ!" sounded the entire five blocks that we walked on Fifth. What an adventure! Surely, none of those drivers had expected to see the Champ with a motley crew in the central district of their city. I got the feeling, though, that the unusual experience was nothing new for The Greatest. During that phase of his life, squeals of excitement and cheers of adoration must have followed him daily.

CHAPTER 13

Destiny's Child and Emotional Rescue

Having Muhammad Ali and James "Buster" Douglas on the same card for a boxing promotion in Huntington, West Virginia, showed the genius of Bill Picozzi. Putting the opposites together amplified what made each athlete special.

Ali proclaimed his greatness unabashedly. On the world stage, he won an Olympic gold medal (Rome, 1960) and the heavyweight title three times as a professional. He stoked the anti-war consciousness of the U.S. and became a revered symbol of resistance. Whatever he did, Ali did it out loud.

On the other hand, soft-spoken James—he told me to call him James—made his point with his fists. This was evident when he toppled the most feared boxer of the late 20th century, Mike Tyson. Yet, James did not boast.

I spent the late hours of Friday night and the wee hours of Saturday morning with James and learned more about him. I considered him to be a child of destiny, one chosen by fate to become an unlikely conqueror in the boxing ring, in front of the entire world. The writers on ESPN's *Page 2* column list Douglas' win as the No. 4 all-time upset in sports history and added: "[W]e were stunned to see a mammoth underdog take out an unbeatable favorite."[28]

---

28. The column lists as number one what it calls *The Miracle on Ice*, the United States' hockey victory over the Soviet Union, 4-3, in the medal round of the 1980 Winter Olympics. Accessed Nov. 1, 2017, at https://espn.go.com/page2/s/list/010523upset.html.

I needed to know how the man who accomplished that feat stayed on task because I was anticipating a make-or-break moment in my own journey. When that moment arrived, I could then knock down the ogres of sexism and racism that stood in my way. For me, the prize meant receiving a fair shot at living *my* destiny as a sports broadcaster.

This is how the evening unfolded.

Muhammad Ali returned to the Radisson Hotel around nine thirty p.m. on Friday night. As the youngsters in the group and full of late-evening energy, James and I rendezvoused in the hotel lobby around midnight. His hired limousine took the two of us and his bodyguard to the popular Robby's night club, where the doorman noticed our limo. As one would expect, he made it his focus to usher us into the club.

The bouncer recognized James, maybe from photos and videos taken after the Tyson fight. Or maybe he saw James in the coverage on the local television stations. News reports from the previous day announced that the man who had unseated Mike Tyson was in town. Surely, the twenty-nine-year-old newly crowned champion would have on his itinerary the city's hottest night spot.

So, Robby's was expecting us even though no one had called ahead to grease the wheels. Handling us with kid gloves, the bouncer guided us over to the club's host, who set up a table right beside the dance floor. Seating us there was a strategic move on the part of management. Everyone going to or leaving the dance floor would see Buster Douglas and his date and would chatter about it for years to come. The marketing possibilities justified our free admission.

I don't remember whether we danced. I won't rule it out, though, because I love to dance. And we drank sensibly. I believe James had fruit juice. I probably enjoyed one Sloe Gin Fizz or a Fuzzy Navel, something fruity. James' bodyguard stood watch behind us, with his broad back to us, to keep at a distance the partygoers who were uninhibited by their potent beverages. He stood *behind* us because obviously the toughest man on the planet and the holder of the three heavyweight boxing titles could dispense with any incoming trouble from the front. Besides, James had such an agreeable manner that he could diffuse with words the belligerence of clubbers.

Two Peas in a Luxury Pod

Though Mike Tyson had knocked unheralded Douglas to the canvas in the eighth round of their fight in Tokyo, Douglas stunned the fight world by getting up. Steadying himself over the next two rounds, he finished off the previously undefeated champion with a knockout. Boxing observers everywhere, Americans among them, awoke on February 11, 1990, to meet the new holder of the unified heavyweight crown.

Less than one month later, at Robby's in Huntington, men and women came over to our table to shake the hand of this champ. He expressed thanks for the admiration. I watched people walk away beaming, as if enriched by the few words Buster Douglas had said to them.

Coming from Ohio, a state that borders West Virginia, made Douglas a close cultural kinsman to the people he met at Robby's that night. This fact, coupled with his endearing modesty, must have fueled his Mid-Atlantic fans' pride in his achievement. Their underestimated Midwest cousin had become the champion for all the world!

What a rush, being out with James. There's an undeniable amount of sizzling allure to the world of boxing: the bling-bling of the characters, the physical danger of the bouts. The attraction to a competition that ends literally with the last man standing. Anyone who is the world's heavyweight champion effuses an aura different from that of everyone else. Star power and raw animal magnetism are the twin offspring of athletic supremacy. With boxing, there is also the essential internal component, the mental fortitude needed to outlast whatever comes.

James was a denizen of the boxing world, so my being with him made me a temporary inhabitant of that world, too. During our night of partying, I felt what others might experience as a high. My skin tingled. I felt rapturous and floaty amidst the chatter and the maneuvering of others to get up close to James. I was awash with deep satisfaction.

For James, however, the night's activities became too much. He suggested we leave.

When we slid into the limousine, James and I were finally alone. We did not immediately order the chauffeur to drive us away. Instead, we sat outside of Robby's in the quiet and stillness of the plush automobile.

We had escaped the crush of well-wishers so that James could decompress. In the whirlwind month since defeating Tyson, James had been constantly in front of television cameras. Adding to the need to catch his breath, he also needed to mourn. He was just a few months removed from burying his mother, his number-one supporter.

Lula Pearl Douglas died in January 1990, three weeks before the boxing main event in her son's life. In that fight, emboldened by having lost her, Douglas summoned all his might to show up physically, to throw one punch, and then another, to keep his appointment with destiny. However, in the training camp he attended before the fight, he said he had felt at the end of his rope.

Imagine being depleted to what you think is a point of no return, he said. You've pushed your body to its physical brink. You need food and you need fluids. Would it ever be possible to eat and drink enough to satisfy the biting hunger and the intense thirst? And your spirit—you've lost your bearings about who you are. You're searching for your inner force. In every possible way, you're a tank running on empty. Inspiration gone.

James said that he was in such a condition when he collapsed into a chair at the end of a grueling pre-Tyson workout one evening. At that point of utter loss, a spirit entered his being, he said. That spirit infused him, bit by bit, with everything that was missing; his body and his soul absorbed the force, he said. It replenished everything he had expended. Physical and mental fortitude returned. A cool, reassuring presence rained down over his sweat-drenched body and occupied his being. The presence sought out and eased away the aches in his throbbing muscles. It reconstituted all that was broken.

James said his Christian beliefs reawakened in that moment, bringing with them a remarkable steadfastness. Not invincibility, not indestructibility, but rejuvenation and sure-footedness—enough to outlast the physical challenge in the ring and the pitfalls that awaited the man who would hoist the champion's belts.

This is the conversation James "Buster" Douglas and I had in a private limousine parked outside a nightclub in the wee hours of the morning. Two twentysomethings, we were both prepared to rise to the challenge of our futures, to answer when Destiny called on us.

But hunger called first.

After maybe two hours of the soul-cleansing conversation, James and I were so hungry that we left the sanctuary of the limo and prepared again to face his probing public.

Oh, the joy of eating pancakes and bacon at five in the morning!

A Heavyweight Champ on Each Arm

Back home by eight a.m., I hurriedly prepared an outfit to wear for the Saturday events with Ali. I would have to leave home around ten a.m. to meet up with the entourage.

At some point during the day, while I was with the entourage of the former heavyweight boxing champion, the reigning heavyweight boxing champion called and left a message on my recorder. The message began simply enough. "This is James," he said, as if the sound of his voice alone weren't enough for me to identify him.

He asked to see me again.

Unfortunately, I would not know this until after midnight, for my fun and satisfying day with Ali stretched longer than I had anticipated. Ali's road manager, eager to get a break from the routine of eating restaurant meals, had gladly accepted an invitation to attend a dinner at a private home. "Anywhere that Ali and I can get a home-cooked meal, we'll accept," Mahdi said.

Would I go as Ali's dinner date, Mahdi wanted to know.

Why, *sure!*

I telephoned my friends, Jim Backus and Tina Trigg, to tell them about the dizzying slate of events. I had the phone message from James to play back to them—to provide evidence of what sounded like a tall tale. If my friends doubted me, however, their doubts would soon be erased; I asked Mahdi to make a detour on the way to dinner.

Let's go to the television station with Ali, I told him.

CHAPTER 14

"My Wife is Married,"
Muhammad Ali Told Me

By the end of Saturday night's Golden Gloves matches in March 1990, I had figured out how to move within Muhammad Ali's inner circle—how to maneuver within an entourage as television crews and people from the public try to get up close to the champ. Ali and I had met two days earlier. His road manager was right. I was getting a kick out of seeing the life of Ali from an insider's vantage point. He was also right in knowing that the entire endeavor would look more polished if the group included a professional woman.

As a television journalist, I knew how to flash a smile on cue for photos with the fans and how to chat comfortably with people who were waiting to take pictures with the champ. All the better for the followers to pass the time in line more enjoyably. I picked up this series of tasks without anyone's asking.

I witnessed Ali, champ-like and tireless, shaking hands and posing for pictures. He seriously approached his statesman and sportsman duties, making children smile, women giggle, and sponsors feel on top of the world.

Wonderfully, Ali also found time to focus on me during a few scattered moments. The tenderness with which he looked at me let me know that he thought of me as a special part of his West Virginia stopover team—not a hanger-on in any way. He didn't say it, but he began to rely on me as a steadying force when road manager Mahdi had to put his energy into other matters.

When Ali did talk, it was sparingly, but in the sparseness of words, he managed more than once to call me pretty.

As Saturday evening wound down, I finally asked the question that had been on my mind from the day we met.

"Are you married?"

"My wife is married," he wittily replied.

Yolanda Williams and Ali had married nearly four years before his visit to Huntington. He conducted himself as a married man around me. A *flirty* married man, yes, but he never crossed the line with me, nor with anyone else that I observed. I saw only the behavior of an upstanding forty-eight-year-old gentleman.

At age twenty-two, Ali joined the Nation of Islam,[29] drawing derision from some people. He evolved into the role of social leader for millions of others. During the conflicted years in the 1960s and 1970s, America's civil-disobedience soldiers applauded Ali for his staunch disapproval of the gap in the quality of life between black and white families. Peace advocates embraced him as the ultimate celebrity spokesman against the Viet Nam war. Thus, Ali established himself as an agitator and one who creates opportunities for the black race.

By the time I met Ali, he had long held enough leverage to open doors for blacks. By agreeing to visit my place of work, he was about to do so for me; he was about to become a champion for my personal cause. He may not have been aware of what he was to do, but manager Mahdi knew. I had told Mahdi that my manager tried to marginalize me and stifle my contributions. Mahdi knew that when the People's Champ escorted me to my workplace, his presence alone would become a figurative battering ram against the obstacles in my way.

29. Born Cassius Marcellus Clay Jr. in Louisville, Kentucky, on January 14, 1942, he changed his name to Muhammad Ali in 1964 after joining the Nation of Islam. Citing his religious beliefs as justification, Ali refused military induction in April 1967. He was stripped of his heavyweight championships and banned from boxing for three years during the prime of his career. See muhammadali.com.

Ali and Mahdi and I settled comfortably into the limousine after watching that night's amateur bouts at the civic center. In a few short blocks, we arrived at the side-door entrance of WSAZ. The weekend writers, producers, and technicians were working as usual. The security guard, a slightly-built, eagle-eyed man named Manny, spotted the stretch limo as it slowed and stopped at the curb.

I exited the limo first, signaling to the observant watchman that we needed neither further investigation nor police backup. Mahdi followed me out of the limo. As limousine protocol seemed to dictate, the star attraction let the drama outside build up before he presented himself to onlookers. It wasn't choreographed, but we each moved through the steps just right.

When the limo first arrived, the faces of my newsroom colleagues began appearing in the row of windows of the station's building. Tina, one of the production crew members, told me later that someone said, "It's a limo. We know Nita's in there." Not one of them dreamed, however, that Ali would step out onto the curb. Even better, no one dreamed that on my Saturday night off, I would bring him to the station to meet them.

Security guard Manny opened the employee door. The champ shook the hands of overwhelmed employees, many of whom had run to the side entrance to ensure they would not miss him. Manager Mahdi drank in the appreciation that blanketed his client. He also liked hearing my colleagues thank me for the treasured moment.

Ali and Mahdi and I walked through the corridors to find and speak to employees who may not have seen the limousine drive up. I took Ali inside the studio control room, which is, by design, buried in the bowels of a TV station. I wanted to ensure that the hard-working technical people got the chance to greet the champ. After we left the techs, I asked Ali if he wanted to see my desk. We went to the newsroom. There, I offered Ali my chair. He sat.

Word of Ali's presence had spread throughout the two floors of the building, so people flooded the newsroom. Mahdi talked with a few of them while Ali busied himself with something interesting on my desk: shortbread Girl Scout cookies. I had bought them from my friend Jim's daughter Chelsea. With half of the canister remaining, the legendary Ali peeled back the paper and started eating. (The impromptu drop-in was delaying his dinner.) He finished off the cookies, leaving Jim to say, about his daughter, "Now *that* is something we can tell her about in the future."

My champ and his manager wrapped up the visit after we felt that everyone had spoken to Ali or had taken pictures with him. (In the days before smartphones, luckily some colleagues had cameras with them.)

As much as I anticipated my evening out with Ali and company, an important question rocketed into my brain and momentarily distracted me in a good way: What would be the impact on Monday morning when the news director heard of my personal connections with the sports world's greatest living legend?

CHAPTER 15

The Underdogs Go to Las Vegas

On Monday, WSAZ general manager Don Ray—curly-haired, white, energetic, and youthfully fortyish—cruised into the newsroom.

"So, Muhammad Ali was here this weekend?" he asked.

"Yes," I heard someone reply. I maintained my focus on some task at my desk.

Don asked how it happened that Ali had been in our building.

"Our *news* reporter Nita brought him in," a different voice volleyed from somewhere in the room.

Don lingered and seemed to want more details as he stood on the very carpet on which Muhammad Ali had walked less than forty-eight hours earlier. Despite Don's winsome personality, no one offered more than the brief responses—and I think I know why.

The colleagues who responded may have been some who excitedly met Ali or were friends with those who did. But the brevity of their responses, and the overall coolness in the room toward Don in that moment, might have signaled something else: my colleagues' disagreement with the station's intractability in its dealings with me. Many of them told me they believed I deserved a shot in sports and, for them, my contact with an international icon as high up as Muhammad Ali cemented it.

I witnessed it all, laughing inside and feigning work. *A journalist with contacts like that could not possibly be an asset in the sports department,* I thought with sarcastic amusement. Even as Don asked his questions, I was devising. In the wake of Buster Douglas' win, the general manager and many of our viewers had a renewed interest in boxing. How could I channel this interest into an assignment in sports?

Don had a reputation for making the right call when business was on the line. I believe that is why he had achieved the responsibility of general manager at a relatively young age. I took advantage of this sterling trait of Don's. I used Ali's unannounced visit to give Don the chance to do the right thing in connection with my sports future.

Two Underdogs

Buster Douglas had signed on to follow up his blindsiding win over Mike Tyson with a bout against Evander Holyfield. The match would take place in October 1990, a few months after Douglas became champ. My contacts within the fight crowd promised to get me up close to the insiders of the main event. That meant I would have to be there—in Las Vegas!

I floated the idea with WSAZ sports director Bob Bowen, who anchored the Monday-through-Friday sportscasts. "Go for it," Bob said, giving me the nod to do a report on the match for his segment.

Bob and weekend sports anchor Kenny Bass were welcoming whenever I entered their workspace. They talked with me regularly about the goings-on in the games and in sports, in general. Both men knew that WSAZ could present something better than the competitors' coverage of the next Buster Douglas match if I were on the scene.

I valued my alliance with Bob, and not just because he was the decision-maker for his department. A white man, sixtyish in age, Bob was working in journalism during the time when men openly expressed the belief that female reporters belonged only on society pages. In fact, Bob had worked so long in the business that he remembered when he could smoke in his office while writing scripts. He even looked like the previous generation of sports journalists. He wore the plaid jackets and wide striped ties, the uniform sports anchormen typically chose to distinguish themselves from the sleekly dressed news anchors.

Yet, despite his old-school appearance, Bob was ahead of his time. He never behaved as if he were threatened by my interest in his field of expertise. He was wise enough to know that one day in the broadcasting industry, one's getting hired in sports would not be dictated by the politics of anatomy. Bob even joked that he preferred having women, rather than men, sitting next to him in the office. In his opinion, a physically attractive and competent female sports reporter offered a *double* good deal.

That the leader of our sports department felt this way was a plus for me, but it did not mean I was in the door. Bob did not have the authority to make me a permanent sports reporter. Over him, there was news director Bill Cummings, who made it clear he did not want me in that role.

Still, I was confident I could convince Bill to let me have the Vegas assignment. My inside angle with James Douglas would benefit the entire WSAZ operation. Douglas was the sports world's emerging media darling. West Virginians and Ohioans were especially proud of him, for he was one of their own who had succeeded. Additionally, his rags-to-riches rise created a significant audience of Americans from all regions who wanted to see him capitalize on his stunning win.

On the top-rated *The Tonight Show with Johnny Carson*, the champion scored with a comedy punchline. The comedian Carson suggested Douglas might choose the Trump Plaza in Atlantic City to stage the next fight. "If you go to Trump Plaza, you could get Donald and Ivana on the undercard," he quipped.

The live audience laughed.

James seized the moment. "In that case, I might be upstaged," he said, generating an even bigger laugh. At the time, the media had widely reported that Trump and his first wife's marriage was in a phase of stormy separation.

Carson shook with laughter at the clever comeback, flashed a wide grin, and tugged at his collar while the audience added applause to its roaring laughter.

With Douglas as the nation's hot media property and with sports director Bowen's endorsement, I decided to propose to Bill that I cover the boxing story. I had my argument points ready. Destination, Las Vegas: an exciting venue that our viewers would enjoy seeing. A likeable subject: James held incredible appeal among fans. I had seen that for myself during our late-night date. Furthermore, my license as an amateur boxing judge qualified me professionally for the assignment. Because I coached boxing, I could dissect the combinations of punches thrown in Vegas. I could evaluate Douglas' ring generalship and his strategy of attacking the body to chop off the head—a boxing basic—from a perspective matched by few local sports broadcasters.

Later that day, I put in my request to Bill Cummings.

"No," Bill said without missing a beat.

I wheeled around and, without a glance at anyone in the newsroom, marched up to GM Don Ray's second-floor office. I don't remember seeing the secretary or any other gatekeeper. I found Don alone, sitting at his desk and more than a little startled by my entry, even though he had an open-door policy. I strode in, confident that my recent coup with Muhammad Ali had given me *carte blanche* to fight for the assignment.

I began by explaining that coast-to-coast and across the sports universe, people wanted more coverage of Buster Douglas.

Don agreed.

I explained my unique interaction with Douglas, citing my overall boxing connections and the Ali visit. Also, I told Don that WSAZ could have a story no other station in the market would have.

He said the idea sounded great.

I told him Bill was against it.

I continued without pause, saying that I was going to Vegas, anyway, and that I had agreed to share my boxing expertise in an article I was selling to a newspaper based in Charleston, West Virginia. I told Don that I was going to further cement my connection to the Douglas camp by attending Farm Aid IV. James was scheduled to participate in the fund-raising concert.[30]

---

30. The author decided to go to Farm Aid IV to watch James "Buster" Douglas introduce

An expression that looked like puzzlement crossed Don's face. His brow furrowed and he stood. He stepped from behind his desk and blew by me, walking at such a swift pace that his necktie caught the wind. Trailing him, I had to shift into another gear to catch up. He bypassed the elevator. I followed him down a flight of stairs to the newsroom. There, he walked into Bill's office and closed the door.

Minutes later, the door opened and Don exited briskly, though not as briskly as he had entered. From the doorway, Bill called me in. I clearly read his discontent. For more than a year, it had been the recurring expression I saw on his face when he looked at me. He said that, yes, I could report from Vegas—but that my report would be a phone report only. (In 1990, television stations spent money on satellite video reports primarily for disasters and national politics, not for sports.) Still, the result of going over Bill's head pleased me. I was going on a *sports assignment* for a TV station in a market that ranked 48 in the Nielsen rating system! I wasn't even rankled by the fact that I would have to fund the trip myself.

A huge step forward for womankind.

I spent three, maybe even four days in Las Vegas, wearing my press credentials and navigating the lavish and palatial complex of The Mirage hotel. Amongst the boxing press, rappers, and celebrities, I met Spike Lee, Heavy D, ESPN's Dick Schaap and Tony Kornheiser, CNN's Fred Hickman and Nick Charles, and future president of CNN worldwide, Jim Walton. I also enjoyed time with my West Virginia boxing connections, chief among them, Bill Picozzi.

I learned that covering a big-time sports event meant going from one press conference to another. Taking notes from conversations with the newsmakers in the interview room and reading press clips provided by the media liaisons. What an afternoon's work! When there was not an official interview session going on, I used my time

---

singer John Cougar Mellencamp. The boxer supported the fundraiser because his underdog status before the Tyson fight linked him to the long-running struggle of the American farmers who would benefit from the event. "One underdog to another," he told the author.

to engage in earnest conversation with the significant members of a boxer's team—the managers, trainers, cornermen, and former boxers who had become sparring partners. With the trust of these people, I could learn how well a fighter's training had gone.

Real Deal, Real Punch

On October 25, 1990, Evander "The Real Deal" Holyfield out-worked Douglas. Three rounds into *The Moment of Truth* bout, Holyfield, the more active boxer, put Douglas on the canvas with a straight right. The punch landed squarely on Douglas' chin.

I stared in disbelief.

There was James, flat on his back. He attempted to roll over to place his gloves on the Caribbean-blue canvas to push himself up. But then ... he didn't. Unlike Tokyo. Eight months after breathing life into the hopes of underdogs of all types, his ride ended. *Our* ride ended—shipwrecked and spent on the bright-blue canvas.

I listened to the victor and the vanquished in the post-fight interviews. In both the defeated warrior and in the newly crowned champ, I found a mantra to adopt for the battle that waited for me back in West Virginia.

Holyfield told Showtime interviewer Al Bernstein, "A lot of people thought I could not do it because I was a small man," said the twenty-eight-year-old, who gave away two inches in height and more than six inches in reach. Those two factors matter in boxing because a shorter man with shorter arms has to punch *up* instead of punching downward. Plus, he has to go in closer than the opponent in order to land punches. "This displays to the kids that if you work hard, you train hard, and you work at anything, you can be successful," concluded Holyfield.

James admitted his miscalculation. He went for a haymaker, the right uppercut that would have certainly rocked Holyfield. However, James weighed fifteen pounds more than he had weighed against Tyson, and this slowed James down. By being off-balance after the miss, Douglas gave Holyfield a clear shot at his unprotected chin.

James was counted out at the 1:10 mark of the third round. In the post-fight interview, he said he would regroup and consider what to do next.

After I returned to Huntington, I would be in the situation of both fighters. Like James, I was toggling between being off-balance and being on track and deciding how to regroup. And like Evander, I would need to stand before my news director with the assurance that my physical traits did not disqualify me from being able to claim my goal. So, I went home determined to land just the right punch.

Leaving Las Vegas

But first, I had to test my opponent. I had to land exploratory punches, the kind that jar or sting but don't fell the other fighter. The kind that weaken.

I delivered such a punch when I returned home from Vegas. I covered the promotional visit that the Cincinnati Bengals NFL team made to Huntington during their off-season. The football players took part in a charity basketball game to boost fan interest and to ultimately sell expensive jerseys and tickets for the coming year. For me, the visit offered up a story combining sports with social justice: equal access to job opportunities and a look at workplace attitudes in America.

The season before, Cincinnati coach Sam Wyche had bumbled into a controversy that dragged in female sports reporters. Following a loss in early October 1990, the team instructed a security guard to prevent *USA TODAY*'s female writer from entering the locker room to conduct interviews. This violated the National Football League's rule that guaranteed that reporters, regardless of gender, could have professional access to locker rooms.

NFL Commissioner Paul Tagliabue fined Coach Wyche thirty thousand dollars, the highest in the league's history.[31] Coach Wyche

---

31. Associated Press, "Bengal Coach Fined Nearly $30,000," in *Los Angeles Times*, Oct. 6, 1990.

said the high penalty would not cause him to change his mind. A woman, he believed, should never be present in a locker room with naked men. Wyche's case came on the heels of a highly publicized incident in which players from the New England Patriots harassed a female reporter from *The Boston Herald*.

Men and women across the country were talking about sports locker rooms. So, I proposed focusing on the players' views about having women in their midst as they moved through various stages of showering and dressing. The WSAZ sports anchor accepted my angle.

So, there I was, in the locker room of an NFL team!

Fourth-year player David Fulcher, the star safety and a team leader, said that he had no problem with female reporters in the locker room. Mature athletes recognize that women could interview and report as professionally as could men, he said.

My first NFL locker-room story was in the bag. And with Fulcher's supportive comment, a second sports figure, along with Muhammad Ali, had hit against a door of opportunity that was still not fully opened for me.

CHAPTER 16

Ohio Road-Tripping

I worked primarily with photographer Jim Backus in doing stories for the WSAZ late shift from December 1988 until mid-1992. Our identical work schedules, Monday to Friday, two thirty p.m. to eleven thirty p.m., threw us together every day. He became my best friend at the office and away from the job. He had a wife and preschool-aged daughter, and we lived in the same neighborhood. With our other WSAZ friends, we would organize house parties and group dinners.

I adored Jim, a native West Virginian, a man quite blond and just shy of thirty years old. He and I had many outward differences, but just as many unseen similarities. The similarities began with our Taurus birth sign and spilled over into our interest in playing two-on-two basketball.

On the basketball court at the YMCA, Jim and I became the NBA's hotshot teammates, Stockton and Malone,[32] with my creativity in dishing the ball to Jim, the sharpshooter. Jim disguised his basketball prowess in a compact, stocky, rugby-man's body. He would score from nearly anywhere on court. As his Stockton, I would bounce-pass the ball to him, occasionally no-look the pass, or lob the ball over an opposing team that half-heartedly tried to get back on defense. Jim

---

32. Point guard John Stockton played 19 seasons with the Utah Jazz, 18 of them with prolific scoring power forward Karl Malone, known as The Mailman (he always delivered the goods). Stockton, born in 1962 and retired in 2003, set numerous NBA assists records. Malone, born in 1963 and retired in 2004, scored 36,928 points, second only to Kareem Abdul-Jabbar (38,387)—and ahead of Kobe Bryant (33,643) and Michael Jordan (32,292). See nba.com and basketball-reference.com.

would bank in the shot. He was not a nothing-but-net scorer, but he was a scorer, nonetheless. "The bank is open!" he would boast, capping off his marksmanship with trash-talking. Our opponents would cringe. We won many more co-ed showdowns than we lost.

Jim appreciated my idiosyncrasies in the workplace, and I, his. Fortunately. As the evening reporting team, we would drive to Ironton, Ohio; Athens, Ohio; and Gallipolis, still in Ohio. He would tirelessly take the wheel of the WSAZ station wagon and safely drive us two hours into the Buckeye State, paying close attention on the two-lane highways. That did not prevent him from cutting up sometimes, though. He clued me in to the stereotypical cracks white people in the Appalachian region made about themselves. Of course, I had never heard the putdowns before, and I found them hilarious. We'd laugh together each time he crisply delivered a punchline.

Jim often remarked about having the same name as Hollywood actor Jim Backus of *Mister Magoo* and *Gilligan's Island* fame, but he did not imitate the white actor's comical characterizations. Instead, on occasion, Jim would imitate the signature line of a well-known African American comedian and actor, Redd Foxx, by declaring, "I'm comin', Elizabeth!" Mimicking Mr. Foxx's shtick as junk dealer Fred Sanford, Jim would clutch his chest as if a cardiac crisis were about to end his life and send him to join his beloved wife beyond the Pearly Gates. "What dead-on comic timing and imitating ability," I thought the first time I saw Jim's performance.

Jim would conjure up Mr. Foxx for the emergencies that happened at work. Meeting President Jimmy Carter in May 1989 at Ohio University in Athens spawned one such important emergency.

Time with Jim, Jimmy, and James

We set out early on the drive to the university to avoid the pressure of the clock. Jim promised I would see picturesque, pastoral scenery for most of the eighty miles. Grassy fields of springtime, freshly painted barns, rolling hills, lazy horses grazing, he predicted. I left for the road trip with excitement not only because of the rustic scenes that would flow past my window, but also because I would be interviewing a president of the United States for the first time.

Before leaving the station, we stopped by the office of meteorologist Tony Cavalier. Jim wanted to pump Tony up about the video Jim would shoot for future weather segments. Weathermen customarily use flattering pictures of surrounding areas as background video over which to superimpose temperatures. Jim planned to capture such video on our trip to Ohio.

"Super!" acknowledged Tony. As a transplant from Pennsylvania, which borders Ohio on the east, Tony was familiar with the Ohio countryside and knew that Jim's video would be a treat for viewers. "I need at least four minutes," he reminded Jim. Tony required uninterrupted, four-minute-long clips of weather scenes. Airing a two-minute video on a loop left open the possibility that viewers could see a jump cut (a sudden cut from one video scene to another) at some point during the report. As a skilled photographer of weather scenery, Jim was on the same page with Tony. We promised to stop and shoot the weather videos on the return trip from Ohio, for we wanted nothing to delay our arrival at President Carter's event.

In a conference room on the Ohio University campus, Jim and I set up our gear along with the other assembled reporters. We waited for the entrance of the former president, sixty-four years old at the time. Mr. Carter took his place not at the head of the oval table but in a seat or two away from the oval's point.

Mr. Carter spoke about Manuel Noriega's "shameless" theft of the Panama election. General Noriega was that country's former dictator who had dealt with the U.S. government as far back as the 1970s.[33] The Panamanian power broker was not on the ballot himself in 1989, but Mr. Carter decried Mr. Noriega's attempt to usurp power by stealing ballot boxes. Jim filled two twenty-minute tapes with Mr. Carter's patient question-and-answer session.

---

33. For a discussion about the Panama affair, see Mark Tran, "Manuel Noriega—from US Friend to Foe," *The Guardian*, April 27, 2010.

In the end, I focused my story on Mr. Carter's work with Habitat for Humanity, but not because the issues surrounding Panama were over my head. The reason for my focus is found in the television-news proverb about making chicken soup out of chicken *s%#**. In other words, no matter how badly the story falls apart, you had better put something, anything, on the air, to fill the block of time allotted by the producer. More about that in a minute.

On the drive back to WSAZ, Jim and I remarked on covering a big-time event. We were excited to have been in a conference room full of journalists, hearing important information straight from a former leader of the Free World. Feeling like champions, we stopped several times to capture the Ohio sunset and the orange glow it cast over horses we saw in the fields—bay and buckskin breeds. We also recorded some of the painted barns, capturing a minimum of four minutes per scene.

Jim filled one twenty-minute tape and grabbed another to over-de-liver for Tony, whom we regarded not just as a colleague but as a friend. Jim shot six or seven scenes that Tony could use for future weathercasts.

More than satisfied with our international-politics story and the weather shots, we packed up the tapes, camera, tripod, and microphone. Back in the car, we soberly discussed the Carter story and agreed on some memorable sound bites. When I asked whether he had been rolling tape on a particular comment, Jim reassured me that he had captured the entire give-and-take. He also told me that he had shot several reversal shots of me, called reporter cutaways. Based on this information, I wrote a script and began practicing the lines so that I could record an audio track immediately upon entering the station.

After the unstressed drive home, we cruised into the street-side parking spot right beside the TV station's back door. "All systems on go!" I thought.

We jumped out and met at the back of the station wagon, where Jim opened the hatch. He pulled the camera out of its case and pressed "eject" to get the last weather tape out. Jim passed it to me. He then began riffling through the utility bag for the two twenty-minute

Carter tapes. One, he handed off to me right away. He continued to dig. Then, puzzled, he looked toward the other gear neatly arranged in the rear of the wagon.

He gasped, blinked, and shook his head.

Back to the utility bag.

It must be there, his expression seemed to say. Frantically, he paddled through all the gear, swimming as if to save his life. He dislodged every piece of equipment from its usual place. At this point, with face flushed red and sweaty, he wiped his blond hair back from his forehead. He grabbed at his heart and rocked back on his heels in Fred Sanford style. His best Sanford impersonation ever! He didn't cry out for Elizabeth, though. He lamented, "I shot weather video over the president!"

There was nothing for me to say because the clock was ticking toward the eleven p.m. show. Because of Mr. Carter's high profile, the producer had placed our story high in the show's rundown.

After exchanging glances of support, Jim and I kicked into our Stockton and Malone high-performance, get-it-done mode. We would use what remained of President Carter's interview on the one surviving tape. Fine.

But suddenly the material from which to edit was not forty minutes in length, as I had imagined when writing the script. Tape two contained only twelve minutes of footage! Comments about Panama had been on the first twenty-minute tape. Furthermore, we would have to create a story and choose meaningful sound bites on the spot. The script I had leisurely written with attention to every word was now out the window. Too bad the president had not talked about the beauty of Ohio landscapes!

With our basketball-court teamwork, Jim and I got our story done. It aired on time and received compliments from colleagues. Neither chicken soup nor chicken s%#*. Many years passed before I told anyone what happened on the day that President Jimmy Carter finished behind a few Ohio bay horses.

When Jim and I interviewed Godfather of Soul James Brown, I momentarily drew the iconic singer into our circle. In the moments that Jim needed to connect camera cables and the microphone and such, I explained to Mr. Brown that the three of us were born under the Taurus sign. I informed him that he and Jim shared the May 3 birthday. Once the tape was rolling, I asked Mr. Brown to offer a birthday message to Jim. James Brown looked at the camera, not hesitating a bit, and said something like, "Happy Birthday to Jim, my fellow Taurean, on May third."

The gesture surprised and pleased Jim, which pleased me. I wanted to leave him something special in the video vault, a fitting memento to honor our years of working together while having a ridiculously entertaining time.

Not in 1990s America

Living nearly three years in Huntington, I dated a number of men, black and white. One of my suitors was a black engineer who lived in Ohio. Each time he came to my home in West Virginia, Theo[34] drove on Ohio's Highway 52 in Lawrence County. Though the stretch was less than twenty miles long, Theo said that, without fail, some law-enforcement officer stopped him every time. He insisted that he was not drawing attention by speeding. He was convinced that his being a dark-skinned black man in a dark blue souped-up sports car put him on law enforcement's radar.

I could not relate to Theo's story. True, I believed that gender and maybe racial discrimination were happening within the corridors of WSAZ—a subtle discrimination involving polite professionals in business clothes. I viewed those as psychological confrontations, mental battles, microaggressions. But Theo's? He was describing regular unwarranted physical proximity with gun-toting law officers. Something that could lead to deadly consequences for a black driver. After all, officers held the tools of domination: weapons,

---

34. The name has been changed.

the cover of night, and the confidence that any legal investigation would go their way.

I did not want to open my mind to that reality. *Of course, our institutions protect everyone equally. It's the social contract,* I reassured myself. Thus, I did not buy Theo's assertion that he was being targeted. By all measures, Theo had played the game the right way. He had acquired advanced education and lucrative employment. He steadfastly obeyed traffic laws.

So, when he repeatedly confided in me about his disappointment in the system—maybe even also his hurt and fear—I pressed him to find out what *he* had done to get stopped every time. By doing this, I negated his firsthand experiences. I invalidated his concerns about his personal safety. My dismissive reaction probably left him feeling more belittled about the injustices than his encounters with the police had done. This short-circuited the deeper connection we might have reached as a couple.

Was I so strung out over my own battles that I fell blind to racial intimidation that was not directed at me?

Yes. Simply, yes.

Not surprisingly, Theo eventually stopped taking the roadway risk to visit me. We faded from each other's lives. A handsome and educated man, a cherished member of a close-knit family, his mama's baby boy—why habitually undertake a dangerous road trip to see a woman who does not *see* you? Why repeatedly endanger your life for a woman who fundamentally fails to connect with you?

CHAPTER 17

A Time to Legislate

Protection of citizens against unreasonable searches and seizures was written in the 4th Amendment to the U.S. Constitution in 1791, centuries before my Ohio friend Theo and I came along. In reality, however, the modern-day application of that section of the Bill of Rights left Theo unprotected.[35]

Occurring much later than 1791, my birth practically coincided with the signing of the Civil Rights Act of 1964. Less than two months after I was born, President Lyndon B. Johnson wrangled enough support from U.S. senators and congressmen to pass the slate of anti-discrimination measures. In doing so, the president stressed the belief that all Americans should have the right to self-actualize, or to fulfill their highest needs. President Johnson called the signing "a turning point in history."[36]

A specific portion, Title VII, calls for equal opportunity in the nation's workplaces by prohibiting employment discrimination on the basis of race, color, religion, national origin, or sex. The modern-day application of that section of the law left me unprotected, in reality, on the job at WSAZ.

---

35. An officer may conduct a traffic stop if he has reasonable suspicion that a traffic violation has occurred or that criminal activity is afoot. Accessed Sept. 8, 2017, at uscourts.gov.
36. Library of Congress (*loc.gov*).

West Virginia's Honorable Weapon

In 1961, the state of West Virginia put in place its West Virginia Human Rights Act,[37] predating the national legislation by three years. An abbreviated version of the WVHRA describes its merits in this way:

> *§5-11-2. Declaration of policy.*
>
> *It is the public policy of the state of West Virginia to provide all of its citizens equal opportunity for employment [...] Equal opportunity in the areas of employment and public accommodations is hereby declared to be a human right or civil right of all persons without regard to race, religion, color, national origin, ancestry, sex, age, blindness or disability.*

The denial of these rights to properly qualified persons by reason of race, religion, color, national origin, ancestry, sex, age, blindness, disability or familial status is contrary to the principles of freedom and equality of opportunity and is destructive to a free and democratic society.

In contrast to the law, in my West Virginia newsroom, news director Bill Cummings had made it clear that he was denying me in-house progress because he did not think his Mid-Atlantic and Appalachian viewers were ready to see a woman in the role of sports reporter.

Because of Bill's stance, I took my case outside the confines of the TV station. I had become friends with one of the daughters of a

37. West Virginia's Human Rights Act created the nine-member West Virginia Human Rights Commission (WVHRC) to "encourage and endeavor to bring about mutual understanding and respect among all racial, religious and ethnic groups within the state and [to] strive to eliminate all discrimination in employment and places of public accommodation." 1961 W. Va. Acts 135, § 1 (Reg. Sess.)

heavy-duty West Virginia civil rights attorney, Herbert H. Henderson,[38] a firebrand for achieving equality for all Americans.

When I met him, Henderson had never lost a civil rights case. This, of course, placed his services in high demand. Despite that, he spent thirty minutes of his billable time during one workday to address the obstacles I was facing on the job.

The day before, Bill had demanded I sign a document that he hastily created on his own typewriter in our pre-computer days. He said that I could not work at WSAZ until I had returned the paper, signed. The document stipulated that I would not work for the farm team of the Chicago Cubs baseball franchise. The team had set up minor-league operations in our city for the 1990 season and looked to develop its executive office from local talent. Team president Edward Poppiti, after a brief interview with me, had offered me the position of community-relations director. I could perform the part-time commitment when I was not on duty for WSAZ.

My job would entail behind-the-scenes organizing of public appearances for the baseball players and driving them around in my Ford Mustang. Working in this role meant I could continue my long-running love affair with baseball and earn extra cash.

The team also offered to hire my sports-loving WSAZ colleague Randy Yohe, someone with whom I had a good professional relationship. With loads of personality and energy, Randy would become the ballpark announcer for the minor-league Cubs games. We were both happy to land the side gigs and live out our sports fantasies on the team in Huntington.

But in stepped Bill with his document. He said it would be a conflict of interest with my reporting job if I worked for the team.

I showed the document to Henderson the morning after I received it. I told Herb that Randy, despite also being a reporter, had not been given a document to sign.

---

38. Born in 1929 in West Virginia, Herb Henderson bridged generations of prominent African American legal minds, from Supreme Court Justice Thurgood Marshall (1908-1993) to attorney Johnnie Cochran (1937-2005).

The veteran of employment-equality battles knew immediately what to do. His instructions were simple:

"Go to work today. Tell Bill that you talked with me. Tell him that I need to see what Randy has signed. The only thing your boss can do to you is change your schedule. He can give you the dog schedule, and believe me," he added knowingly, "he will."

Herb gave me his legal letterhead with nothing written on it. "Give this to Bill," he advised. "He can call if he wants to talk with me."

I left Henderson's office, grateful but skeptical. Can this simple sheet of letterhead obliterate the biggest obstacle in the way of my career goals?

When I leisurely reported to work after visiting Herb's office, I went to see Bill.

"I'd like to see what Randy signed," I said politely.

"What?" Bill asked. "Randy didn't sign anything. I asked *you* to sign the paper."

I waited without saying a word.

When a poker player believes his cards will crush his challenger's, he may have trouble maintaining a poker face. He can't wait to present his hand to seal the win. Unable to suppress this excitement, he may let out nervous laughter. That was Bill Cummings that day. He stumbled into my trap of feigned patience. His laughter slipped out to fill the uncomfortable silence.

"Do you have it?" he pressed, unable to stop a grin from broadening his face.

He even jutted out his chin as if he thought he were gaining an advantage over me. The gesture made me think of how Muhammad Ali and others showboated in the ring by dropping their arms to leave their chins unprotected or to pretend to be weary—only to recover and dominate the bout.

But Bill Cummings was no Muhammad Ali. Once he fully exposed his chin, I finished him off. I lowered the boom on him.

I said, "I talked to Herb Henderson. He said he needs to see whatever Randy signed."

Sometimes, a boxer's been hit so hard he bounces on his hind-quarters. He can't get his hands down before landing on his butt. That happens when a powerful punch comes from out of nowhere. That was Bill Cummings that day. When he heard Henderson's name, Bill gulped. Fell silent. The embarrassed red face that I saw at the Marshall University panel discussion returned.

The year-and-a-half of his controlling my aspirations had ended with one swift blow. My haymaker.

Finally, he recovered his voice. "Why did you make this so serious?" he asked.

"When you asked me to sign that paper, *you* made it serious," I returned. "I thought about signing it yesterday when you gave it to me. I know that being coerced into signing something negates it."

No response from Bill; after being knocked to the canvas, he was standing again but was suddenly the fighter absorbing unanswered punches.

"I wanted to have the day off yesterday," I explained. "I knew I wouldn't sign it, but I wanted you to think about it all day."

I imagined my words landed like a battery of body shots. It took Bill a moment to regain his bearings. Afterwards, he told me that we would need to talk with the human-resources manager, a woman named Wanda Bailey.

Wanda was white, about age sixty, and an aunt, she said, of the popular Cincinnati Bengals receiver Chris Collinsworth. She was coiffed to perfection and pleasant every day at the office. Whenever she appeared in the newsroom, she would either deliver yogurt-covered almonds from upper management to the birthday girl or boy of the day, or she would announce that the company Christmas bonus checks were ready to be picked up. In her office that day with Bill, I saw a different side of her. She repeated Bill's question.

"Why did you make this so serious?"

I answered her with the same words and tone I had used with Bill.

"When he asked me to sign that paper, *he* made it serious."

Sitting before Wanda, I suddenly realized two things. She worked for a system that had hired no managers of color. That was the case during my entire time at WSAZ, from December 1988 to the summer of 1992. The second thing I realized was that *human resources*, in that instance, meant keeping a lid on the violations of the West Virginia Human Rights Act and the national Civil Rights Act.

In WSAZ's case, such violations stifled economic opportunities for individuals. The highest-rated TV station in the No. 48 market in the country paid a handsome salary to managers. Had no person of color ever applied? (Remember that Bill had told the audience at Marshall University that minorities did not seek employment in Huntington.) If those applicants existed but were unfairly dismissed because decision-makers had thoughts like Bill and Wanda's, what recompense could the applicants receive for the violations?

In that crucial moment in Wanda's office, Bill sat in silence, waiting for her to act as fixer, to neutralize the storm he had created. He needed *her* to concede the victory to me. He could not do it. He could not bear to admit that he had been bested by me. Could not bear to admit that I had called upon the spoils of victory that Rosa Parks and others had secured for me, that I had employed my legal rights and could work for the baseball team, and that he was not the boss of my destiny.

In the end, Wanda affirmed my argument. I had brought to life the words of the legal documents that promised opportunity to all. Over Bill, I had won.

But there is a dark side to such battles, an emotional strain and a kick to one's self-esteem that come even with a victory. You may have won a battle for inclusion or freedom, but it nags at you that you had to prove yourself worthy enough, human enough, to be included or unrestricted in the first place. In an interview with *The Law Works* program, which aired on West Virginia Public Broadcasting, Attorney Henderson describes the effect this way: "To force a beautiful little chocolate girl to go into a restaurant, or something like that, and she knows that she must go there because of the color of her skin, it warps her for her entire life to be a part of it."[39]

Because of all the beautiful little chocolate girls who had endured such a humiliation, I had won a victory at work. Because I listened to Henderson's advice and handed to Bill Cummings the letterhead of a respected warrior,[40] I got to enjoy my work with the Cubs baseball team. And who knows? If Herb had not become my shield against discrimination, I might not have made a trip with the Cubs to Chicago, where the most influential woman in television shared her Midas effect with me.

I had intentionally retraced Oprah Winfrey's path into the potentially dangerous "hotbed of racism" in Forsyth County, Georgia, in 1987. Three years after that, and thanks to my civil rights victory that allowed me to work for the Cubs baseball team, I accidentally encountered her in person. The chance meeting happened in Chicago in the calm and luxurious restaurant Oprah owned.

The Chicago Cubs' home office had invited the front-office staff of the Huntington Cubs to attend a game at Wrigley Field and spend the weekend in the Windy City. Each staffer could bring along a guest. I asked my best friend Terri. Her mother and grandparents lived in Chicago and, upon their suggestion, we all went for dinner at Oprah's self-named restaurant. As we waited for our meal in the tony establishment, Ms. Winfrey and a male companion walked by our table. Terri's dear grandparents said, "Go talk to her! Go talk to her!"

I resisted their urgings for as long as I could, but eventually I relented because everyone at our table loved Oprah and wanted me to find out what was on her mind that evening. I would proceed,

---

39. Transcribed by the author from *The Law Works: A Conversation with Herb Henderson* (2007).

40. Attorney Herbert H. Henderson fought passionately for decades to stamp out inequality. He passed away in October 2007 at the age of 78, but in the life of the author, and in the lives of many others, his work marches on.

however, only if Terri would do it with me. (That was our way. We were twenty-six years old at the time and together had pulled off many crazy capers since the age of fourteen.)

Together, Terri and I walked over to the dimly lit and secluded section, where, instead of being met with cold annoyance, we received a warm reception from Oprah. Her meal had not yet arrived. She did not seem in a hurry to send us away. She asked both of us what we did in life. Relaxing in the presence of greatness, I refrained from answering and drank in the beautiful scene that included my friend and Oprah. I listened as Terri said she worked as an engineer.

Then, Oprah, ever the inquiring journalist, turned to me. "And what do you do?" she probed, looking gently and patiently at me.

"I'm a news reporter at a television station," I answered. "But I want to be a sports reporter," I added.

The television mogul lay her right hand upon my left shoulder. The pressure was steady, reassuring. I believe that, through it, she connected me to the vein of her remarkable success.

With the hand resting upon me, Oprah leveled a perceptive stare at my eyes and, in that rich timbre that is uniquely hers, assured, "It'll happen."

It'll happen, Oprah had said. *It...will...happen.*

The prophetic and potent words, her beautiful assurance, entered the deepest part of my spirit and stayed with me for twenty years beyond our 1990 meeting. Like an audio file I could access on demand, Oprah's affirmation soothed and motivated me until the last interview I conducted in my last television job.

With Victory Comes Painful Retaliation

Attorney Herb Henderson had seen decades of on-the-job intimidation, so he correctly predicted I would experience some form of workplace retaliation from Bill Cummings. When handed down, Bill's spiteful reassignment caused me not only mental abuse, but physical pain.

Bill changed my job from the prestige of weekday reporting, with the quality video of WSAZ's photographers, to weekend one-woman-band duty. I would work alone (or with an intern) and shoot video for my stories—the same as I did in my first television job. Though I had received the top award at the TV industry's 1989 RTNDA convention, I found myself demoted in 1990 in Bill Cummings' newsroom. I had not thought about contacting the RTNDF selection committee to announce the *opposite* of job progression, but it seems like an interesting idea now.

The physically grueling work included loading the Betacam, in its protective shipping case, into the WSAZ station wagon. I would do all the tasks while dressed in business clothes and heels. I was the only woman shooting video at WSAZ. I suffered two back injuries while doing so.

With the first injury, I fell while shooting backstage at a play. I slipped and landed hard on my butt with the television camera on my right shoulder. To protect the expensive camera, I held onto it with both hands, which meant I did not brace myself during the fall. Thus, the weight of the camera slammed down on my shoulder. A tremor of hot pain shot through my spine. I recovered, dusted off, and completed the night's shoot.

The injury that still physically pains me thirty-one years later occurred on election day in November 1990. Bill and assignment manager Roger gave me a slate of one-woman-band shoots spanning the entire workday. From morning until after the six p.m. news, I shot interviews of candidates, mainly in the counties WSAZ covered in Ohio.

My back screamed "Uncle!" during one such interview. It gave up trying to support the weight of the camera after more than nine hours of loading, unloading, and capturing the election day's nonstop activity. At the twelve-minute timecode mark of shooting a candidate's interview, the camera dips and the candidate falls out of the frame temporarily. A lightning bolt of hot pain had zapped me in the back and caused a collapse of muscle control. I shook off the discomfort, hiding the crisis from the man in front of my camera. Once I steadied myself, I reframed the candidate and finished the interview. I even finished the work that night and deposited the tapes at the station, as scheduled.

The next morning around nine a.m., I called the newsroom and asked for Bill. "I can't get out of bed," I informed him.

"Why not?"

"My back. I do not know how I can work today."

He did not question me any further. Within the hour, the newsroom assistant called and told me that I should fill out a workman's injury form and contact a doctor. My Occupational Safety and Health Administration (OSHA) claim entitled me to seventeen weeks of chiropractic care, at which time I began seeing Dr. Rob Ballard, whose office was a short distance from the station. The OSHA claim specified no shooting until I determined my back had recovered. I moved on to another station before my back recovered well enough to resume shooting at WSAZ.

Over the years, I have tried to forget the job retaliation—but I can't. Nearly every night I lie in bed and wriggle and contort my neck and upper back until I feel a release of the tightness that accumulates during the day. Sometimes, a pain stabs me before I pour my morning coffee.

Admittedly, my pain is small compared to the violence inflicted upon the backs of many Africans who were enslaved in America, and on the backs of black American citizens in the wake of the Civil War. But the aches I feel in my body in these modern times link me to my ancestors and the stings of mistreatment they endured. It is an unbroken chain from them to me. And though the oppression suffered at one point in history may exceed the pains endured in another time, each form of oppression burns in the heart and in the soul in its own burdensome way.

CHAPTER 18

And Now: Heeeere's...Failure!

Bill Cummings finally conceded and assigned me once to fill in as sports anchor. However, before he did that, two white male reporters had already sat in the seat. One of them, my baseball-team colleague Randy Yohe, eagerly wanted to do it again, but he did not perform well enough to get a repeat performance. On the rare occasion when the regular sports anchors were absent, news director Cummings preferred Tom Zizka in the chair. Tom, however, saw himself as a Peter Jennings type of presenter, for news only.

Tom, in his twenties, as I was, with side-parted dark hair molded into place, gracefully read the information and connected with viewers through the camera lens, but his presentation was a bit too sleepy for the sports fan. On top of that, Tom took the sports assignment lightly, which became glaringly evident on the day he fumbled the name of well-known golfer Chi Chi Rodriguez. He knew the name, as did every sports fan in the 1990s. But I heard Tom's joking around before his segment by saying the name with a long *i* sound, making it rhyme with *eye*, instead of correctly using the long *e*.

In the heat of the broadcast, Tom had to turn to the correct camera on cue, reference the golf video being shown, brave the studio lights, and read from the teleprompter. Having so much to manage, he reverted to his mocking pronunciation of Rodriguez's name. Tom realized his error immediately. Before his on-air co-anchors could react, he nervously laughed and explained, "Oh, I know it's *chee chee*. We were playing around with his name before the show..." That didn't remedy the situation at all. The stunned co-anchors knew of Tom's lack of interest in presenting sports, but they had not expected to be on set with him when the viewers saw it, too.

Tom anchored WSAZ's sports for the last time that night.

With Tom out of the mix, my colleagues intensified their backing of me in the fill-in role. Bill Cummings recognized that the rising tide of support in his newsroom had turned toward me, a black female. His own troops wanted Bill to break down the barrier against diversity that he had fought to keep in place.

He finally buckled. But it was an incident that had me remembering the old saying *Be careful what you ask for.*

Bill assigned me to anchor the sportscast on what was, for me, the worst possible day of the entire sports calendar, NFL Draft day. It happened unwittingly, I am sure. There was no way he could have known about my aversion to America's college football system (which is the springboard to the drafting of players into pro football).

I unapologetically spent many years avoiding the wholesale exploitation of nineteen- and twenty-year-old college athletes. The vehicle of this exploitation, known as the National Collegiate Athletic Association, or NCAA, to this day profits from the sweat, blood, broken bones, and broken dreams of athletes.[41] As of 2021 (the year of this book's second edition), there is movement toward economic empowerment for the athletes through unionizing. A study entitled *How the NCAA's Empire Robs Predominantly Black Athletes* states on its opening page that "the NCAA has built its enterprise on racial inequality and injustice for decades. The industry that the NCAA has shaped and regulates is infused with systemic racism that emanates from its insistence on adhering to a principle of amateurism..."[42] [43]

---

41. Mark Schalch, "NCAA: Where Does the Money Go?" *espn.com*, July 12, 2011. Accessed in 2017 at http://www.espn.com/college-sports/story/_/id/6756472/following-ncaa-money.

42. The report continues: "Increasingly acknowledged as a mechanism that serves to direct wealth away from the players and toward college sport industry leaders and institutions, the NCAA's principle of amateurism and its attendant regulatory system routinely suppresses player value while trapping players in a nationwide economic cartel that strips them of basic rights available to U.S. citizens." (From "How the NCAA Empire Robs Predominantly Black Athletes of Billions in Generational Wealth," Huma, R., Staurowsky, E.J., & Montgomery, L., Riverside, CA: National College Players Association [2020]. Accessed March 14, 2021.)

43. NCAA Chief Legal Officer Donald Remy posted, in part, the following on *ncaa.org*: "This union-backed attempt to turn student-athletes into employees undermines

While the NCAA's rules block athletes from getting paid, member universities, broadcasters, and construction companies that build their stadiums earn billions of dollars because of the athletes' performances.[44] (See Endnotes.)

Undoing some of the economic lynching of the NCAA's business model may be tied to the widespread outrage over the actions of white police officer Derek Chauvin in Minneapolis, Minnesota. He restrained a black father until the man, George Floyd, expired on the street. In all, four police officers were videotaped on the scene. In broad daylight, three were shown pinning Mr. Floyd to the pavement while a fourth officer positioned himself between the actions of his colleagues and the people who gathered. The deadly incident took place in May 2020.[45] The next month, I conceived Good Cops Only At Game, a program designed to reduce the harm of police violence and avoidable deaths, such as Mr. Floyd's.[46]

---

the purpose of college: an education. Student-athletes are not employees, and their participation in college sports is voluntary. We stand for all student-athletes, not just those the unions want to professionalize." He also says: "Many student athletes are provided scholarships and many other benefits for their participation. There is no employment relationship between the NCAA, its affiliated institutions or student-athletes." Accessed March 14, 2021 at http://www.ncaa.org/about/resources/media-center/press-releases/ncaa-responds-union-proposal.

44. In "Where's Our Money: The Fight for Black Economic Justice," decorated broadcast journalist Roland Martin points out that the wealth-building "game is rigged" in the sports industry, as in other fields. The segment's discussions focus on the expertise that black-owned businesses have to land prime contracts in construction, legal, financial, advertising, and audiovisual services, as well as game-day merchandising and catering. Martin, the National Association of Black Journalists Journalist of the Year in 2013, is host and managing editor of the daily online digital show #Roland Martin Unfiltered.

45. On April 20, 2021, a Hennepin County jury in Minnesota returned guilty verdicts against fired police officer Mr. Chauvin "on Count I, unintentional second-degree murder while committing a felony, Count II, third-degree murder, perpetrating an eminently dangerous act evincing a depraved mind, and Count III, second-degree manslaughter, culpable negligence creating an unreasonable risk," according to Source: Judge Peter A. Cahill's Memorandum for the Sentencing of Derek Chauvin, Court File No. 27-CR-20-12646, dated June 25, 2021, accessed July 31, 2021. https://int.nyt.com/data/documenttools/Chauvin-Sentencing/c14b8665cad28229/full.pdf. Judge Cahill sentences Mr. Chauvin to 270 months under the custody of the Commissioner of Corrections.

46. Good Cops Only At Game calls on sports fans to contact the athletes and teams they follow and insist that only law-enforcement officers free of brutality or related charges can work security at games. Lydia Toukal, a Toulouse, France-based political science student concerned about safety, joined GCOaG as co-developer, content creator, and community manager in January 2021. (See page 314.)

My stance against athletic racism was and is a noble one, but it severely hampered me on that fateful weekend when opportunity finally intersected the path of my goals. Because of my long-standing quiet protest against the NCAA, I did not have the full knowledge I needed to report about the NFL draft.

What is an unprepared journalist to do? The same thing an underrated athlete does: Suit up and give it a shot. The desire for this goal had burned within me for so long, there was no way I would do anything but muster the grit needed to meet the challenge.

The result?

I would like to say I scored, but the truth is far from it.

I floundered the first time I sat as sports anchor. No one was using the internet in 1992 to track the draft, so an untold number of our West Virginia, Ohio, and Kentucky viewers tuned in to hear where the top college players were headed. The fans of pro football teams wanted to see the projected lineups for their favorite teams for the next season.

What those viewers saw was laughingly bad, amusingly bad. A train wreck.

Viewers saw an ill-equipped sports anchor, one who knew neither the backgrounds nor recent information about the players. I stumbled through names as if I had never seen them before—an ultimate display of incompetence for a broadcaster.

Writers Karen Gutmann and Betty Sosnin summed up the incident in an article they published in *Gravity* magazine in 2014. Under the headline "Nita Wiggins: Game Changer," they wrote:

> Nearly three years after she arrived, under repeated pressure from Wiggins and a campaign of support by her peers, the news director caved and assigned her to anchor the sports report on the evening news. It was draft weekend for the NFL.
>
> And?
>
> "I stunk," she said, still cringing at the memory.

"I cannot emphasize how terrible I was. I mis-identified Heisman contender David Klingler in a video. I mispronounced player names. My earrings were too large and overpowering. Plus, I had a Donna Summer hairstyle. Problem was it was 1992 and not 1979, so I was not even a pleasing picture on the screen."

But what do champions do when they fall? They learn something, pick themselves up, and try again. So she did.[47]

Yes, I did recover and try again. And to be fair, I have to say that Bill Cummings did not gloat after my colossal fail. Still, in the immediate wake of my first sail, I wanted to hide under a rock.

I admit, without reservation, that I flubbed. The failure belonged to me alone because I did not know the subject—a subject I had chosen not to know. Despite this, I maintained my strong disagreement with news director Bill over his contemptuous women-shouldn't-be-sports-reporters stance. I continued to put front and center, as often as possible, my discontent over being limited to a news-reporting position. I knew I would have to somehow maneuver myself into sports-related reports and prove I was the person for the job.

47. Karen Gutmann and Betty Sosnin, "Nita Wiggins: Game Changer," *Gravity* magazine, Spring 2014.

CHAPTER 19

Making the Climb

M̲y eighteen-thousand-dollar-a-year salary in Huntington eventually exceeded twenty thousand, allowing me to travel on a whim and live comfortably. But I remained restless and, frankly, agitated. Tired of the confrontations with my restrictive West Virginia boss, I walked away from the television business—and returned to Augusta in the fall of 1992.

Despite being out of television, I did not feel as though I were entering an uncertain phase in my professional life. I believed what Ralph Ellison writes in *Invisible Man*, that "the beauty of discipline is when it works."

The discipline that propelled me to early successes as a student I took to another level, by studying the comings and goings in the boxing world and keeping my focus on the Dallas Cowboys games. I knew I would be back in journalism and that I would stick. I knew this because, at age twenty-eight, I could conceive of nothing else I wanted to do professionally until retirement. I simply needed a breather, to step away from a field that allowed a manager to follow his whims and discount the efforts of an industrious, award-winning worker.

I had a financial cushion I had built on my own, so no worries on that front. My family expected me to pull through and to do it independently—except for housing, the offer of which I did freely accept. I moved back into my pre-college bedroom in the Montclair family home. I picked up intermittent paychecks as a substitute teacher.

I also volunteered at the Augusta Boxing Club as an assistant coach under director Tom Moraetes. This let me tie into the sports pulse and interact with young people who wanted to move their lives in positive directions. However, I needed to get back to what I was born to do: the media. Brainstorming, I quickly found the avenue.

I called on the relationship I had established a decade earlier with the city's daily newspapers, *The Augusta Chronicle* and the *Augusta Herald*. As Westside High School's sports editor, I reported to the newspapers, with unfailing regularity, our school's football scores. So, in 1992, in restarting my association, I cold-called sports editor Ward Clayton, a white male manager who proved to be fair-minded. Ward gave me many opportunities to write tennis, racing, and college-basketball stories for the sports section. My byline appeared often in the daily newspaper.

One afternoon while in the *Chronicle*'s newsroom, I answered a phone call that the switchboard operator sent to my desk.

"Hello, I'm Sherry Lorenz, the news director at Channel 12," the female voice said. "Is it OK for me to call you there?"

"Yes," I answered, curious. My heartbeat quickened.

"I've seen your byline on the sports page, but I know you have a television background. I'd like to talk with you about a position here, if you would be interested."

The station had a part-time sports anchor-reporter-shooter job all rolled into one and available right away, she explained. I said that of course I could meet with her to talk about it.

Sherry specified on the phone that it would be a twenty-hour-a-week job. Because it was not full-time, there was no healthcare insurance. The job entailed working two ten-hour days. In other words, the person hired would shoot sports video on Saturday and Sunday. On both days, it would be the person's responsibility to change into anchoring clothes, do her own hair and makeup, write scripts, edit videos, and then read the sportscast on TV.

Oh, and there were two shows, at six p.m. and eleven p.m.

I knew that the job, as written, did not meet my standards. I accepted the interview appointment, anyway, to practice my interviewing and negotiating skills. I visited Sherry at the WRDW headquarters in North Augusta, South Carolina, just across the Savannah River. My aging 1982 Ford Mustang had what was, for it, an incredibly steep climb to reach 1301 Georgia Avenue at the top of a hill. The car's engine struggled and gurgled. I was in no financial position to replace the car, further letting me know that I would have to think long and hard about accepting a part-time job.

Sherry was a rarity in the television business in the early 1990s: a female news director, maybe in her mid-thirties, white. She posed fair questions. We talked comfortably and I enjoyed being courted for the position. I recognized the immense possibilities of working at a CBS station. After all, the Dallas Cowboys games aired on CBS back in those days, before the move to Fox. So did the Daytona 500.

After Sherry laid out all she expected from the person hired, and after she insisted that the job's multifaceted responsibilities could aid a journalist in developing multiple skills, I responded honestly.

"I appreciate the chance to talk with you. Thank you for your time. However, I'm not interested in a part-time position and I would not like a job that includes shooting video."

Sherry listened. A petite blonde with dimples, her pleasant facial expression stayed intact.

I continued.

"I feel that for me to do the best job possible, I need to work in a newsroom where I am not shooting video and anchoring the show on the same day. I'd want to do a good job, but I don't feel this situation would allow me to do as well as I'd like."

She left me more time to continue, so I did.

"And because I want to have insurance, I am looking only at jobs that are full-time."

Her reply surprised me not because she offered what I had called for but because of how quickly her reply came.

"Then how about a full-time, forty-hour-a-week job and no shooting?"

She sweetened the offer even further with a clothing allowance. I would anchor the weekend sportscasts and fill in on Monday through

Friday in the absence of the main sports anchor, so new clothes, to help me look the part, would be necessary.

That sealed it.

Because I was only a per-story contributor for the Augusta newspapers, I was free to start immediately with the TV station. I do not remember the television salary, but it eclipsed the per-article rate I was getting. The money for clothes? The figure of four hundred dollars twice a year sticks in my mind, though I am not certain that is accurate. Whatever it was, it was more than zero—which, to me, was all that mattered.

A new wardrobe was not the only perk in my new position. I remember the first day the legendary *Sports Illustrated* magazine arrived at 1301 Georgia Avenue with my name and *WRDW TV Sports Department* on its mailing label. I was elated! My professional life was back on target.

That is, until a few months later, when director Sherry Lorenz left WRDW to work in public relations.

During my first scheduled meeting with her replacement, I detected that he was not pleased to see me in the position I had negotiated to my liking.

Here we go again.

I worked at seven television stations in full-time positions for twenty-one years. The first three were news-reporting jobs, including general-assignment reporter and bureau chief/one-woman band. In my fourth job, I worked at my hometown station, CBS affiliate WRDW, from 1992 to summer 1993. It was there that I met news director Brian Trauring, a slightly-built white male, probably five-foot-six, early forties, with close-cut graying hair.

Brian scheduled each member of the WRDW-TV news team to have a closed-door conversation with him during his first few weeks. A positive leadership move, actually. However, his strained expression and snarky tone in his private meeting with me told me clearly what he did not bother to say with words: He did not want me in the sports department's reporter and weekend-anchor position.

"The new boss is going to take me off the sports desk," I told my father right away.

How could he have arrived at that level of professional contempt for me so soon?

Could there have been professional jealousy?

In the TV game, market ranking means everything. Brian had come from the combined but still tiny broadcast market that consisted of Wheeling, West Virginia, and Steubenville, Ohio. By contrast, I had worked in the top-50 market of Huntington-Charleston. It was also in West Virginia but perhaps one hundred markets larger than Brian's previous experience. If one had called "scoreboard," the transplanted news manager would have lost. Was that part of the reason I was the object of his apparent dislike? Perhaps. But there was definitely another reason: I was in the way.

Brian had come South bringing with him one of his former on-air sports people, a wavy-haired athletic white man named Steve.[48] I was friendly with Steve and with other staffers who, for the most part, had gone to journalism school together in Illinois. They followed Brian to Augusta. Steve initially worked as a photographer at WRDW, but only because I was in the job he had been promised. I learned that the news director had lured Steve to Augusta to work in *front* of the camera, not behind it. To Steve's credit (and mine), my handsome rival and I had no problems on the days that he shot video for my stories.

Still, the manager, Brian, needed to remove me from sports to complete the deal he had offered Steve.

It proved difficult, however. While most of the on-air staff came from other regions of the country, I had graduated from a respected high school and college in the city. The communities of my alma maters, Westside High School and Augusta College, took pride in having a graduate in one of the few TV sports positions in the city. Furthermore, members of the news staff complimented my work and, as journalists, they liked being part of a team that offered something out of the ordinary in 1992—a female sportscaster. They did not like

---

48. The name has been changed.

what they suspected Brian wanted to do. A manager from Ohio and journalists educated in Illinois should not push out the homegrown journalist who was doing the job well.

One day, out of the blue, Brian's disapproval of me manifested itself in a peculiar attack.

"Bangs—not for TV," he criticized. "You'll never get anywhere with bangs."

What an idiotic statement! But I knew what it was: Brian's attempt to badger, discourage, and destabilize me. At that very moment in TV history, CNN's Bobbie Battista's beautifully styled blonde hairdo marked the norm on daytime national television. Ms. Battista held her audience and her CNN job from 1988 to 2001. She did it, somehow, with full bangs.

Master of My Career Path

In three of my four sports posts, three female news directors (plus one female general manager) hired me. If more women had been in position to hire TV reporters and anchors, a higher number of qualified female journalists might have been in sportscasting. In Augusta, Memphis, and Seattle, I worked within multi-ethnic and multi-racial news staffs, but I was the only woman in the sports departments in those three cities.

In Dallas, things were different. In the KDFW sports office, which had ten full-time positions, I happily worked beside a woman for five of my nine-and-a-half years—but with only one woman at a time. We even worked at adjacent desks. One of the women was ten years younger than I was, came from a broadcast-journalism university in the Midwest, and had a cultural background different from my own. She specialized in hockey and did her work off camera, producing shows. I worked with a different woman in the department during my final year.

I find it objectionable to think that employers that hire one woman in a sports office could be deciding *one and done*. That is, the hiring of one woman means that under no circumstances will another qualified female applicant have a sliver of a chance at getting hired. The equal-employment-opportunity laws prescribe precisely a protection against gender bias like that, but how closely do employers abide by the law—inside and outside the world of broadcasting? And when they do abide by the laws by conducting fair interviews, how does the course proceed for the women who break through? I know other women who experienced some of the same opposition I did.

In Augusta, Brian Trauring finally succeeded in unseating me, reassigning me from sports as quickly as he could maneuver it. After the 1992 Masters golf tournament, which I covered, he circulated a memo. It emphasized the need to find "someone who could provide credible golf coverage" with sports director Chick Hernandez for the next Masters. Despite the memo, I would also cover the 1993 tournament for Channel 12, with credibility in interviews and writing.

Brian's insult did not wound as deeply as it might have because golf never interested me as an assignment. I welcomed a release from golf-course duty. My desire to discard the Masters assignment was reinforced by a brief but hateful incident. During one of the rounds that I covered during tournament week at the Augusta National golf course, a spectator said, as I walked past him, "We even got the bunnies in here." While carrying a heavy tripod and sweating through the humidity of the April afternoon, I knew that he was calling me a "jungle bunny." The slur referred to the African jungles of some of my ancestors.

Brian's declaring that I had no place in the station's future golf coverage left me ecstatic. Similarly, Brian's shady, engineered transfer of me out of the sports department was not a discouragement. Instead, it energized me in my quest to find a new and better sports job—sooner, rather than later. I knew I would profit, in the end, from what Brian had done. I knew it because I was going to become a sports reporter in Dallas, Texas—or die on the road to getting there.

CHAPTER 20

Too Pleasants

The beloved, telegenic, and popular midday anchor Cindy Pleasants gave me an unexpected and private endorsement while at WRDW-TV. "You go, girl!" she said to me in the ladies' dressing room one day.

A North Carolinian by birth, Cindy, with sandy-blonde, shoulder-length hair, and a beautifully bright smile, told me that she had aspired to be a sports reporter. However, in her home state, Cindy's breaking into the sports-broadcasting game had proven to be too tough, she said. Outdated notions about women's roles on TV had blocked her progress. But external obstacles had not been Cindy's only enemy. She confided to me that her fight to meet her professional goals had given way to a fight to stave off cancer.

That day in the ladies' room, we talked like two little girls playing with dolls. When girls have dolls in hand, guardedness melts away, make-believe rules the moment, and every dream seems attainable. The girls as make-believe mothers feed their dolls invisible milk; the girls as dreamers freely admit their hearts' desires, no matter the impossibility of realizing those desires. In that precious space when two little girls are caring for plastic and cloth figures as if they are flesh, what is real? What isn't? In an unbridled moment of swirling visions and emotions, it is all real.

Cindy and I shared an ease and familiarity we would never have experienced in the bustling co-ed newsroom. In the comfort of our gender sanctuary, we learned about the pleasant truth that bonded us. As children, we shared the same vision of fulfillment in sports journalism. As little girls, we both had untethered our dreams so that we could chase them to lofty places. As we matured, we each kept grasping onto a promissory note in the form of our country's laws—the laws that obliged American institutions to protect us and our precious dreams from gender-based and other biases on the job. In the quiet of the dressing room, Cindy and I still wanted Section VII of the Civil Rights Act, the equal-employment clause, to become a reality for us, and for everyone who needed the provision.

Cindy told me that she knew she would never again take up her pursuit of sports reporting—but not for lack of desire. Doctors had found more worrisome cancerous cells in her lymph nodes. She told me this with neither sorrow nor pain in her voice; she could well have been reading a script about someone else's medical condition. She seemed to have accepted the cards she held, though she said she had undergone aggressive measures in previous rounds of medical treatment.

Most people in the tiny circle of Augusta television journalists and in Cindy's loyal television audience knew about her health. She would disappear from the air when the treatments left her too haggard. She would return for spells when she felt comfortable enough to have the cameras and lights focused on her. Each time, it reignited her followers into believing she would recover completely.

Hearing the news about the cancer, and drinking in the details of her courageous face, moved me to hug her unabashedly. She returned the gesture. We almost sobbed together.

Then, as TV broadcasters do daily, we became aware of the clock that was ticking toward show time. We released each other. She turned on a radiant smile and repeated her supportive statement: "You go, girl!"

Cindy Pleasants died of melanoma later that year, 1992, at the age of thirty.

Pleasantville, the TV Station

While holding the reassigned *news*-reporter position at WRDW in Augusta, I read in the trade magazines about a job opening in Memphis, Tennessee. At WREG-TV Channel 3 in Memphis, sports reporter Glenn Carver ran the sports department. It is he who orchestrated the interview process, which, it turns out, was the most strenuous of my entire television career.

Unlike every other interview, Glenn required me to send video clips of everything I put on air during a given weekend.

Then, after my work made that cut, he asked me to send everything I put on air the following weekend. Glenn's thoroughness in the preliminary screening signaled to me what lay ahead in the high-stakes career of a sports reporter.

My skills measured up to his strict standards in phase one, earning for me an interview and visit to the western-Tennessee city.

During the two days I spent in the Memphis newsroom, I noticed an impressive amount of cohesion. It moved me to ask Ethel Sengstacke, the assignment manager:

"Is everyone on happy pills?"

Ethel, a forty-one-year-old tall and fit black woman, ran the assignment desk. She wore a close-cut curly hairstyle and a flattering rich shade of black currant lipstick—or something similarly striking. She answered my question with only a purse of the lips; no words necessary. Maybe she wondered about the working conditions at the job I hoped to leave.

Ethel led the newsroom in such a confident and organized way that photographers, even white chief photographer Steve Hutchinson, fell in line under her command. (Imagine Academy Award-winning actress Viola Davis in charge.) During my two days there, I heard little grumbling among the photogs and reporters about jockeying for assignments, scheduling, and the other minutiae of newsroom politics.

"Now this is a place where I can work!" I thought to myself.

After about two months, Glenn recommended me for hire as a sports reporter and weekend anchor.

I concluded sixteen months of service and left Augusta's WRDW in mid-June 1993. The move to Memphis more than doubled my salary to thirty thousand dollars a year. When I accepted the new job, I called my own closed-door meeting with Brian to resign from my news position.

"Where are you going?" he asked in the privacy of his office.

"It'll be in the newspaper at the right time," I replied. I placed no importance on his knowing my plans, even though I would work out the customary two-week transition period.

"I don't think you have a job," he said skeptically, his manner condescending. "If you had a job, you'd tell me."

A totally unprofessional line of questioning. Something about it reminded me of the conversation I'd had with Bill Cummings about signing a conflict-of-interest statement in West Virginia.

"That's fine" was my response to Brian's doubt. I told him I had something pressing to do in the newsroom. I left his office. In effect, I brushed him off. My insubordination was nothing new; months earlier, I had begun turning a deaf ear to most of what Brian had to say.

While Memphis' WREG courted me, the WRDW job in Augusta was in my mental rearview mirror. Because my deepest friendships were with people outside the newsroom, I was not tempted to reveal my plans to any of my colleagues, even the ones whose interactions with me had always been appropriate. Cindy Pleasants had died a year earlier. Without her, there was no one with whom I wanted to share the news of my exciting new career move.

When I arrived in Memphis for my new reporting opportunity, I interviewed Ed "Too Tall" Jones, my first interview with a Dallas Cowboys player. We held the interview on the rooftop of the historic fourteen-story Peabody Hotel. Because of Jones' six-foot-nine height, I chose an interview location positioned high above the ground. I wrote a script centered on the theme of reaching personal heights. The story served as a foreshadowing. I knew that one day, I would interview members of my deified Cowboys on a regular basis.

As I had learned to pepper my writing with forceful words because of watching Cathy Brown in Huntington, I witnessed the rewards of unyielding work ethic while working in the Memphis sports department with Glenn Carver. I observed his constancy, his thirst to know more than the other reporters and anchors. With that approach, he gained the credibility that is crucial in earning the respect of athletes, especially celebrity athletes. In the seventeen years that I was a full-time sports reporter/anchor, I never worked with anyone who chased success as did Glenn.

CHAPTER 21

Michael Jordan, John Daly, and The Preacher

While working in Memphis with sports reporter Glenn Carver and weekday anchor Mike Heller, I interviewed PGA sensation John Daly at his home at the TPC Southwind golf course.[49]

To land the Daly exclusive, I asked a contact of mine outside of journalism to give me John's home phone number. I had known this personal contact since 1989 but had never asked for his help. It was imperative that I ask now, in 1993. I wanted a direct line to Daly, who, as a twenty-five-year-old, electrified the golfing world with his win in the 1991 PGA Championship. Golf spectators responded to John's game in a way that the sport had never seen before.

"John Daly turns a golf tournament into a football game," Glenn cleverly wrote for a video package. I wished I had come up with that line.

But I did do something in November 1993 that no one across the country could do.

At that time, John was a Memphis sports personality who always commanded interest beyond the golf community. From the uniqueness of his bristly platinum-blond hairstyle to a lifestyle rife with bouts of public drinking, Daly caused tongues to wag. TV cameras loved to catch him.

---

49. TPC Southwind, a championship golf course on the PGA Tour, hosted the FedEx St. Jude Classic in Memphis, Tennessee.

So, there was Daly, a sports figure whose appeal stretched beyond the fairways and beyond his monstrously long drives off the tee, trying to display his skills at the Kapalua International in Hawaii in November 1993. Double-bogeys marred his play. People playing ahead of him had complained that he was hitting his golf ball into their group.

Irate, John picked up his ball mid-round of the mid-week Pro-Am. He walked off the Kapalua course and disappeared from public view. Reporters everywhere speculated about where he might be.

I had Daly's number.

I called his home phone, which he answered. What's more, he said yes to my coming over with a photographer to shoot an exclusive interview.

It was monumental.

My Preacher, My Teacher

I drew a winning card in the station's selection of a photog for the assignment: Greg Tate, a cocoa-colored black man of medium build and height, and a few years older than I. Though an experienced shooter, he was focusing on the next phase of his life and would, therefore, study the Bible during downtime on the job. He accepted good-naturedly that my colleagues and I nicknamed him The Preacher. Greg created a warm and supportive cocoon whenever we worked together. His support came not only from his close walk with God, but also from living up to the expectations of a professional.

He did not move very quickly, however, but moved with thoughtful deliberation and few wasted steps. When we would shoot high school football games on Friday nights, I would fret (on the inside) because nothing ever happened with Greg as fast as I thought it should. Greg, on the other hand, never sweated anything. If we left late for a long road trip and all circumstances indicated we would miss the event or return too late to edit with quality, I would feel torn up inside. Not Greg. He would say something like, "In God's time."

He was right. Truly, in two years at WREG, we never failed to meet a deadline or to meet our own standards of quality. After several instances in which we delivered against the odds, I stopped fretting. *Let go, let God,* I learned to think. It was an expression I had heard others use to let go of worry.

So, at John Daly's home with Greg, the three of us decided on a certain camera shot we wanted. John was showing us around the second home he was building in the luxurious and pricey TPC Southwind development. We needed wide shots of the lot and the building materials. To establish me as the reporter on the scene, we needed the standard reporter-walking-with-newsmaker shot. Greg positioned himself around a corner of the structure. He told John and me to wait behind the wall and, on cue, walk around the corner and pass by the camera.

OK, no problem.

Take one: Greg did not like the shot. Maybe our heads were cut off. Maybe our feet. Maybe we were too close to the camera as we passed it.

Take two: Greg did not like the shot. He did not explain; he just asked for a do-over.

John led me back to our starting mark out of view of the camera behind the same corner of the house. On cue, we turned the corner.

Take three: Greg did not like the shot.

John showed no indication of being annoyed with the movie-making. For the fourth take, as he and I waited for the cue to walk, John said, "Let's try something."

We heard the cue from Greg and started walking.

"Dum...dum...da-dum-da-da dum-dum da-da dum-dum-dum," sang John, performing Mendelssohn's *Wedding March.* He took my arm and escorted me around the corner. He continued the tune in full view of Greg and the rolling camera.

"Oh, no!" exclaimed Greg, slightly irritated, slightly laughing. "I had the shot!"

Greg and I spent four hours at Daly's home. John played electric guitar for us in his man cave, a room filled with gadgets and games for John's amusement and located on the ground floor of his current home. He talked about his frustration on the golf course one week earlier. He discussed his image, his critics, and his sanctioning by PGA Commissioner Deane Beman for John's exiting the tournament in Hawaii. We hit all the high points of the Daly chronology at that point in 1993.

The interview was a symbolic hole-in-one for me. It made me remember Brian Trauring's memo that he sent out to the WRDW staff in Augusta—the memo in which he let everyone know he believed I was not equipped to cover a golf story.

Well, here I was in Memphis, having just gotten inside John Daly's house—and inside his head.

Golf credibility?

Check.

John had many memorable and trying public episodes over the next roller-coaster decade of his life. Despite that, he remembered me when we ran into each other backstage at the Lennox Lewis vs. Mike Tyson match at the Pyramid Arena in Memphis in 2002.[50]

"Come here, you," he said warmly.

He laid a heavy arm around my shoulder. Happily, we posed for a picture.

A Michael Jordan Home Run

Over the course of two years at WREG, I learned how a reporter and photographer can work as teammates for the good of the station. Listening to Greg "The Preacher" Tate, whether he was sharing wisdom from a scripture or a strategy to work smarter than the competition, paid off for me in many ways. Greg showed his journalism instincts during a video shoot in August 1994, a shoot as important as the one I'd had with John Daly at the golfer's home.

---

50. The author traveled to Memphis to cover the fight while working for Dallas' KDFW. Her report focused on the future bankability of Mike Tyson as his boxing ability was declining. No one believed the 36-year-old would ever match the invincibility of his past and command the purses. His record fell to 49-4-2, with 43 knockouts, after that night's loss to Lewis. The national Fox network aired the author's piece.

I had to fight to keep my exasperation about Greg's slow pace from bubbling up when we were packing to leave for a baseball story. It was nothing less than basketball legend Michael Jordan's first pro *baseball* game in Memphis. Instead of letting anxiety creep in, I consciously flipped the script in my head. I reflected on how much I valued Greg's genuinely respectful treatment of me. I let the soothing God-acknowledging mantra flow through my mind—albeit a bit altered:

Let go, let Greg.

I decided I would work at Greg's pace without mouthing off about timing and scheduling. Besides, in some magical way, he always got the job done.

In contrast to the fervor of my colleagues in the sports office—"Get a Jordan interview no matter what!"—Greg expressed early on game day that we would not run ourselves ragged. He had a strategy for covering Jordan, who had dropped basketball to take up the baseball bat and glove. At the time, Jordan was the world's undisputed best basketball player.[51]

We arrived before the crush of journalists at Tim McCarver Stadium, where the Memphis Chicks would play Jordan's Birmingham Barons. We parked and Greg outlined his plan. He said we should position ourselves along the right-field fence line. "He'll enter from over there," said Greg, pointing to a door in the outfield wall. Other TV crews would likely wait in a media holding area, he reasoned. If we actively watched the outfield door from a different location in the ballpark, he said, we could approach Jordan without the others following us.

Just as Greg had diagrammed the flow of events, Jordan, in the No. 45 pinstriped jersey, emerged from the outfield door.

---

51. Michael Jordan stepped away from the Chicago Bulls for the 1993-94 season but returned the following season. He played from 1984 to 1998 with Chicago, with a one-year break. During that period, the greatest of his generation won six NBA titles, six NBA Finals MVP trophies, and five NBA MVP trophies. Though he retired in January 1999, he later, at age 38, resumed his career with a new team, playing for the Washington Wizards from 2001 to 2003. In 1,072 NBA games, Jordan scored 32,292 points, ending with 15 in his last game on April 16, 2003.

Greg and I left our seats near first base and walked over to the field-access gate. We stepped onto the grass undetected by the competing journalists. With Greg's leading the way down the foul-ball line, I matched his brisk pace, though wearing heels and a flowery linen-and-silk-blend dress. I had thought it was wise to wear a dress—not a provocative one, but one that could catch the eye of Michael Jordan as he looked out over the sea of reporter faces and mass of bodies.

The dress paid off. As Greg and I closed in on Jordan, he spied us and stopped in his tracks. We reached him—alone. Carefully, I talked with him.

At the time, he was a thirty-one-year-old veteran of thousands of interviews given during his reign as a world champion with the NBA's Chicago Bulls. I knew Jordan could easily tire of a boring questioner (even a thirty-year-old black woman in a pretty dress). To give him a moment to develop some comfort with me in the one-on-one encounter, I first engaged him with a softball question—a lightweight question. I eased him into a discussion about the proving ground that baseball represented to him. I also made sure he talked about his reaction to our city. Viewers would be delighted to hear the superstar say the name *Memphis* and share his feelings about our community, including our renowned barbecue and hospitality.

By the time he had answered three questions, I sensed that other reporters were coming toward us. Jordan was not succinct but elaborated on each of his answers. That began to make me nervous. If he continued in that manner, everyone else would be in place to hop in on the conversation—which would kill my exclusive.

I asked one final question. Jordan was winding up the response a bit too slowly, so I interrupted with a quick, "Thank you."

Only then did Michael realize what I wanted. After all, he understood the importance of blocking out the competition. He gave me a knowing smile—a playful, conspiratorial, brother-to-sister smile, which I returned. "Thanks," he replied, then he pivoted and stepped away just as the others reached us.

A chorus of displeased voices assailed me, asking, "Why didn't you keep him longer?"

"I got everything I needed," I answered simply.

Greg wrapped up the microphone cable. His expression showed his pleasure that our strategy had earned us our prize. We returned to the news car feeling like champions.

With Greg's friendship, leadership, patience, and tutorials, I did, indeed, get everything I needed, time and again, in Memphis.

I left the city in the summer of 1995 when I landed the weekend sports-anchor position in Seattle.

CHAPTER 22

Breathless in Seattle

Through the window of the KIRO-TV sports office in Seattle, Washington, a mom-and-pop coffee establishment tantalized me constantly. I would slip out for a java in the middle of the workday. It provided an occasional boost from the fight for my fair share of high-profile stories—the type of stories, my agent argued, I was bound by contract to receive.

Unlike the mocha latte, which became my favorite coffee drink, the taste of Seattle resistance was not sweet. I received a serving of this bitterness in my first month—possibly my first week. A sports producer was editing Mariners baseball highlights for the show I was about to anchor. Usually, producer-editors insert a three- or four-second shot that is not part of the action of the game. They do this to give a clever anchor a chance to say something, well, *clever*. The producer sometimes offers his own idea about what the anchor could say—a play on words, a pun.

In this case, my colleague dropped in a clip of a bird in flight over the field of play. However, instead of freely offering a witty comment I could make about the clip, the white male producer-editor curtly said:

"You make all that money. You figure out what to say."

His terse statement surprised me. I was a new sports-team member and expected a professionally affable first interaction with him. For reasons I never knew, he did not give me that. I shook off his nastiness and, unfazed, forged on. I was happy in my new assignment; I was expanding my range of American experiences.

With the move to Washington State, I was now living as far away from my Southeastern roots as possible, without leaving the continental U.S. In rounding out my value as a sports journalist, I had thought that an assignment in the Northwest would be a good move. I could learn Nordic sports and hockey, I thought.

Also, I was in love.

You see, in my first sports love affair, I fell for diamonds. Baseball diamonds. Therefore, I arrived at KIRO-TV in Seattle with a lifetime of baseball behind me and one of my all-time favorites, Lou Piniella, as manager of the Mariners major league team. I followed his playing career closely when I was growing up in Augusta in the 1970s and when he managed the Cincinnati Reds to the wire-to-wire World Series title in 1990. In my new Seattle assignment, having Piniella as a regular interview capped my mirth.

It was also a joy for me to earn a nice salary, sixty thousand dollars a year, to go to the Kingdome Stadium to cover "Sweet Lou" and the transformation of his latest team. I watched the way the players formed a solid bond and grew in confidence. I recognized what was happening. I had seen a version of this when the kid baseball players coalesced around my dad, their coach. His teams became formidable units.

Lou's players were thirteen games down in the push for the postseason when I arrived in June 1995.

The disparaging views, including the *Seattle Post-Intelligencer*'s article calling them a team of "nobodies," did not matter to me. I religiously went to the Kingdome to get the players acquainted with me. I ignored the sentiments of the area's longtime sports reporters, even those at my station, who repeatedly labeled the team's situation as dire. "There's no need to focus on the team. It's a lost season," they said, as if they knew how I should best use my time as a newcomer to the Seattle sports scene.

I cast off the naysayers about the team just as I cast off naysayers about my own potential. My twenty-five years of stubborn blindness and strategic deafness got me to the precipice of my career. What did those other journalists know?

I became such a regular at batting practice that Lou, Edgar Martinez, Rich Amaral, Jay Buhner, Ken Griffey Jr., Luis Sojo, first-base coach Sam Mejias, and third-base coach Sam Perlozzo would pause to say a few words to me each day. More than a few words, if they were idle.

Other dividends would come.

On Base With A-Rod

One of those dividends, a reward for my loyalty, came from future superstar Alex Rodriguez, who came through for me on a personal level that magical season.

Alex (not yet known as "A-Rod" around the world) appreciated the fair and fun interview we had done in Tennessee when he was a teenager on the USA National baseball team. I asked him back then about the best negotiating advice he had ever received. At that time, he talked about toggling between accepting a major league contract and pursuing, as an amateur, an Olympic gold medal in baseball. He was playing the sides against each other, as one must sometimes do. In that negotiating game, he said that he valued his mother's words above all other advice: "Figure out your bottom line and keep sight of that," he explained in my exclusive story.[52]

It was an amusing response, a teenager's admitting that he took his mom's words to the negotiating table against a battery of male power brokers. But her advice apparently worked; the teen and his mother got the deal they wanted. Seattle made him the number-one overall pick in the 1993 draft. Alex played his first major league game the following season, on July 8, 1994, at age eighteen.

Probably because of our past interactions, Alex and I shared an easy familiarity when we became reacquainted in Seattle. He jokingly told teammates and journalists at the Kingdome that I had followed him from Memphis to Washington. When time permitted,

---

52. Selena Roberts retells these events in *A-ROD: The Many Lives of Alex Rodriguez* (New York: HarperCollins, 2009).

we would talk about his life away from baseball and mine away from journalism. In one conversation, he confided that he did not care for the grunge look of the Northwest. The fashion statement synonymous with Seattle brought together a lumberjack shirt, loose-fitting pants, a T-shirt, and possibly a fleece vest to manage the temperature fluctuations throughout the day. Birkenstock sandals worn with knobby woven socks finished the look. And nothing was ironed.

More of a dress-up guy, Alex knew he could confess his dislike of the look to a fellow outsider. He said it would be easier to go salsa dancing after a game, something he enjoyed doing, if he wore to the stadium an attractive button-down shirt, slacks, and dress shoes. Teammates thought him a little odd for dressing that way, he said. I told him that I had never connected to Seattle life, either. (We would both go on to Dallas for our next career jumps. *He* followed *me*, that time.)

One day during the 1995 season, nineteen-year-old Alex rescued me from being in hot water with my sports director. For some reason, the infielder/power-hitter had been avoiding interviews. He was missing in action during the usual media sessions for a string of days, so it became my job to get him on camera. I found him taking swings in the batting cage under the stadium seats. I walked up and asked him for a comment on camera. "I don't feel like interviewing today," he said. He seemed to regret saying no, but he had planned to stay out of the reach of the long arm of the media. That's why he was warming up in a semiprivate area, he explained.

"I wouldn't ask if my boss weren't on me about talking to you today," I persisted gingerly.

He relented. "Well, let's do the interview in here," he said. "I don't want to talk to everybody."

I accepted the arrangement. Camouflaging my excitement, I found my photographer outside on the Kingdome playing field. We nonchalantly ambled over to the opening in the curtains and slipped inside for the private interview. We had walked cautiously so that we would not alert the other crews that something interesting was behind Curtain Number One.[53]

Several reporters had faced pressure to get Alex on camera that day, as I had. One asked me, "Where was Alex today? How did you get the interview?"

"I asked him," I replied simply.

Rescued by the Griff

Just as A-Rod had done when he relented and gave me a much-needed interview, so did team leader Ken Griffey Jr. This happened when I traveled with KIRO-TV colleagues for four regular-season games played against the Texas Rangers in Arlington, Texas. KIRO was going to air some special programs from the city.

Thrilled to be sent with sports anchor Tony Ventrella and producer-reporter Bill Rockey (two white male decision-makers), I prepared a list of no less than eight story angles. Using the approach of baseball-beat reporters for newspapers, I was set to inform the viewers about some surprising subjects—not minutiae, but truly interesting stories involving our Mariners.

Nothing eventful happened in traveling to Texas, but at the game, my Seattle sports experience hit the rocks. Toward the end of the game, my boss Tony told me that there was no need for me to produce a story. He said that he and Bill had settled everything between themselves and that I could just chill.

I bit back disappointment and pressed him, trying to persuade him that one of the angles I proposed fit in nicely with the way the game unfolded. Furthermore, I pointed out that KIRO would not have financially invested in sending me on the trip if there were no expectation of my delivering a story.

He dug in his heels, saying that, really, I did not have a role in the show. His overall tone was, "Relax! It's all in the bag."

---

53. An American TV game show, *Let's Make a Deal*, is famous for making contestants choose valuable prizes or worthless gags that are hidden behind closed doors and curtains. The curtains are numbered, beginning, of course, with "curtain number one."

Erased from the coverage during the road trip! I was nonplussed, but I did not sulk. Instead, I wracked my brain to figure out why this latest obstacle was in my way. Had I not been a good soldier? Had I not worked the team to develop contacts? Had I not researched and studied?

Meanwhile, the Mariners won the game 6-2 on a Griffey grand slam in the eighth inning. The game over and already notched in the *win* column, Tony discussed the lineup of stories with news director Ilene Engel, who was on the telephone from the Seattle newsroom. When she asked what story I was doing, he told her I did not have one. I don't know whether Tony said that I did not *propose* one or that he did not listen to my eight ideas, but Ilene responded that I *must* have a story. (Good for her!)

After the phone call, either Tony or the producer Bill found me amongst the other reporters. Though the team's scheduled postgame interview period was ending, I suddenly had to jump into action. The planning I had done did not matter in that moment. I would have to grab a quick interview with someone on the team and turn it into a credible report reflecting the significant win.

Easily, I was in the position of failing—of disappointing either the viewers who loved the team or the news director, a woman who believed in me and had sent me on the road. How would I ever be able to explain away a failure?

Photographer Aaron Stadler and I met up. Aaron was a lumberjacket-shirt-wearing, long-haired, white male colleague who consistently shot great video with me. Together, we rushed into the Mariners locker room.

We found one player. On his face, under his eyes, were smudges of his trademark black grease paint. He was slumping forward, sitting on a bench with the number 24 written on tape on the locker behind him.

It was Griffey, the game's hero, alone.

I approached with Aaron. Griff's body language told us he was done for the night with his public life. He even said as much—that media time was done.

I gently urged Griff to change his mind. "Junior, I know that you're exhausted and I know we are the last ones in here interfering with the rest of your night. But I just found out that I need to have an interview. Our viewers want to hear from you more than anyone else because you won the game tonight," I said.

He was silent. I continued.

"You know I would not ask you if I didn't feel I had to."

It worked.

My interview with Griffey led the baseball program. My boss Tony told me I did a good job—but it was he who initially said that the show did not need my contribution.

Yes, personal favors from A-Rod and Griffey—granting me interviews when they were avoiding other reporters—amounted to sweet recompense for the time I put into covering the '95 Mariners. But there was more redemption to come.

Because I was present in the stadium's press box, I witnessed the two most important cracks of the bat in the franchise's first forty years. The first (in a do-or-die, one-game playoff) had to occur to make the second one possible in the team's first-ever postseason. If I had not stayed to watch the games after my afternoon interviews, I might not have witnessed these events. I certainly would not have found myself in the midst of a team's celebration, after arguably the most exciting major league baseball playoff series in history.[54]

---

54. Chris Donnelly, *Baseball's Greatest Series: Yankees, Mariners, and the 1995 Matchup that Changed History* (Piscataway, NJ: Rutgers University Press, 2010).

CHAPTER 23

Start Spreading the News:
I'm Not Going to New York!

On October 2, 1995, after Luis Sojo's broken bat rewrote the history of the Seattle Mariners, I was in the jubilant team's locker room. Luis, armed with a bottle of expensive champagne, sprayed everyone standing nearby. It is not proper for a reporter to inject herself into a team's celebration, so I stood at a safe distance from the hero of the game. Or so I thought.

Spying me, standing alone, Luis approached with a mischievous grin.

He poured the remaining cold, cold, cold bubbly over my head.

Gritting my teeth and shaking off the chill, I blinked multiple times to recover from the physical shock of just how cold the champagne was (8 degrees Celsius, or 47 degrees Fahrenheit). Luis watched me, laughing and enjoying the sensations of the champagne dripping down his own face. At the point of deciding whether to retaliate or not, I laughed.

On any other day, Luis knew it would have been out of order to douse me in my silk-blend pantsuit. But that day was different. On that day, the upstart Mariners changed history. They had hosted the California Angels in a one-game playoff to decide the American League West division champion in the 1995 baseball season. Sojo had unexpectedly made the biggest run-scoring play in the team's existence. (A team relies on a player such as Sojo in the shortstop position for fielding expertise. A light-hitting shortstop can keep his job with stellar defensive play because his value comes from playing on defense. If he produces runs, it's a welcomed bonus.) The result of Sojo's at-bat: The Mariners won.

Elated over the triumph, Luis had cast aside, momentarily, the rules of etiquette that separated the treatment one gives to a petite feminine reporter from that one gives to a burly, shirtless teammate. So, I accepted the drenching for its symbolic meaning. With the frolicsome act, Luis drew me into his historic moment, into the team's historic result, into a Northwest historic victory.

Seattle convincingly thumped California 9-1 to claim the American League West Division—and a berth in the next level of the playoffs, the American League Division Series against the New York Yankees.

But (cue the disappointment) the ultimate decision-makers at Seattle's KIRO-TV did not choose me to go to the two playoff games in New York. Despite the contacts I had built, the station sent Tony Ventrella and Bill Rockey.

Figures.

So, of course, I was ecstatic when the Mariners returned to the Seattle Kingdome for the third game in the best-of-five series against the Yankees. The M's had to win the three final games of the playoff series in order to advance. They had work to do. I did, too; I was back on duty in the home stadium.

Seattle pulled even in the series with a pair of wins (7-4 in Game 3 and 11-8 in Game 4). With that, the Mariners forced another palpitating do-or-die baseball game. Fans, sportswriters, and players began to call the season the "Refuse to Lose" season. It was a worthy label.

Perfectly Played Ending

Baseball is an accumulation of manufactured runs. Minor plays set up major plays. Emotions stay bottled up until the payoff pitch, the crack of the wooden Louisville bat on the tightly wound leather ball. Dynamic base-running might push one team further into the postseason while sending the other team home for five months of rebuilding.

On the fateful night of October 8, 1995, the game goes into extra innings with a packed stadium of fifty-seven thousand spectators. Seattle trails 5-4 in the eleventh inning, with no one out and two men on base, when the season's batting champion, Edgar Martinez, steps to the plate. He crushes a line drive to left field, allowing speedster Joey Cora to race home. By the time the ball rolls to the warning track in left field, Griffey, representing the potential game-winning run, is nearly at third base. With long, uninterrupted strides, he rounds the hot corner. The throw to the plate arrives too late and Junior scores standing up. Soon enough, though, he's on the bottom of the celebratory pile of Mariners players. With the two runs scored on the walk-off double, the M's win 6-5 in front of the ecstatic home crowd. The "Refuse to Lose" team secures the victory in eleven innings.

The play preserves the game in baseball lore. It culminates the work of the players, manager Lou Piniella and his coaches, the front-office decision-makers, and this reporter.

There is not supposed to be cheering in the press box, but most of the decorum flies out the window as the eyes of the long-suffering Mariners reporters lock in on the action on the Kingdome turf. Cora and all the others bounce around behind home plate in joyous celebration, like children. The men in the press box do the same.

Thunderous cheers rise from the crowd. The bleachers vibrate.

They did it! They did it! I am screaming on the inside. Naysayers had told them they lacked the talent, but the Mariners fought on. With the win, they qualified for the second round.

As I stand in the press box after the victory, the success of the underappreciated team touches me deeply. Their victory feels like mine. (So many times I had been told I could not.) Outwardly, however, I display nothing more than a smile and what I imagine are brightly gleaming eyes.

A perfectly played ending to wrap up the momentous American League Division Series.

After the astonishing comeback, Griffey tells an on-field interviewer that the Mariners can keep it up. They can take it to Cleveland in the next round, he avows. But it's not to be. The team left its offensive firepower on the field in the Yankees series. Cleveland ends the Mariners' season nine days later.

My season ended when Tony and Bill again got the assignment to travel with the team.

My Favorite Diamond

My heart beats at a quickened pace whenever the sensations of those baseball days stream back to me.

The shrill of Hall of Fame broadcaster Dave Niehaus' signature call: "Get out the rye bread and the mustard, Grandma. It is a grand salami!"

The tingle on my skin when Luis Sojo's broken-bat base hit earned the Mariners their first postseason berth.

The icy dribble of the champagne down my face.

The precious gifts of clutch interviews the players bestowed upon me.

I will always remember, too, the pride I felt when drinking in Sweet Lou's wonderful, knowing glances during our pregame conversations. From his warm brown eyes I interpreted a message of thanks for being around, thanks for believing that we were going to do something.

Singer Montell Jordan's thumping rhythm & blues song, *This Is How We Do It* (an American dance hit in 1995), provided our theme music. It blasted from the Kingdome speakers and in the clubhouse. The boastful and happy lyrics resonate in my spirit these twenty-six years later.

It all lives on like a summer love from the past, one that resides forever in the mind in illogical perfection. Though it ended, it is perfectly preserved. Such is, for me, the Mariners' 1995 baseball season.

CHAPTER 24

Unforgettable Jackie Joyner-Kersee

Despite the cool beginnings in the KIRO newsroom, I soldiered on to make my Seattle assignment worthwhile. I continued my practice of reporting on the person *inside* the athlete. I also progressed as an interviewer, thanks to a six-question research technique I developed in the early 1990s. I created this new way to prepare for interviews because I felt I had failed to uncover anything substantial when interviewing Rosa Parks in 1988.

I used my strategy when faced with the golden opportunity to interview another American legend: Jackie Joyner-Kersee.[55] *Sports Illustrated*'s "Greatest Female Athlete of the 20th Century" became my interview subject in the fall of 1996. She was preparing to play in a professional basketball game in Seattle, but it was not just any old game in any old league.

The new American Basketball League (ABL) revolutionized professional basketball for women because it was their first pro league on American soil. Before the ABL formed in 1996,[56] female basketball players from the States had to leave home and loved ones to earn a

---

55. Jackie Joyner, born in 1962 in East St. Louis, Illinois, played basketball for UCLA from 1980 to 1983, and then in the 1984-85 season. In 1984, while still a UCLA student, she focused on the Olympics and won her first medal, a bronze in the heptathlon. UCLA has recognized her as one of the 15 greatest players in UCLA women's basketball history. See jackiejoynerkersee.com.

56. The ABL lasted more than two seasons but folded midseason before Christmas Day, 1998. The Women's National Basketball Association, or WNBA, an offshoot of the powerful NBA, played its first game on June 21, 1997. The NBA required advertisers for the men's games to spend money on its women's product and, therefore, choked off the ABL's income and broadcast partnerships.

living playing the game they loved. They went to countries such as Turkey, Russia, Japan, and Italy—far from their American home. On top of that, the meager salaries insulted their talents.

By probing why this project had lured the thirty-four-year-old Joyner-Kersee to suit up, I discovered the inner woman.

An author as well as an athlete,[57] Joyner-Kersee constantly seeks new horizons to conquer. Thus, she said that she could not let this first for women take off without her aboard. The advent of the ABL toppled a long-standing barrier, and Jackie wanted to be a part of that. Why not finally have a pro league in front of American fans of women's basketball? Lending her prominence, JJK signed on for the inaugural season as a forward with the Richmond Rage team in Virginia. She and I met when Richmond came to town to compete against the Seattle Reign.

There are some things a trendsetter does for herself. JJK's singular goal of making the Olympics had driven her from the age of fourteen; she did that to satisfy herself. There are also things a trendsetter does to establish tracks for those next in line—once she attains a position influential enough to do so. With such selflessness, Jackie Joyner-Kersee joined the ABL.

A decorated basketball player at UCLA more than a decade earlier, Jackie was not a starter on the new ABL team but came off the bench for the game in Seattle. Not being a starter presented no problem for her. Her ego was buried somewhere beneath her three Olympic gold medals, two bronzes, and one silver in track-and-field. Young autograph seekers, primarily snaggle-toothed, smiling, and pigtailed black, white, and Asian girls, were Jackie's spoils that night in Seattle.

Unforgettable—that describes my first JJK encounter. It was also unforgettable for her, as she would inform me five years later.

---

57. Lindsey Johnson and Jackie Joyner-Kersee, *A Woman's Place Is Everywhere: Inspirational Profiles of Female Leaders Who Are Expanding the Roles of American Women* (New York: Master Media Publishing Corporation, 1994).

I Lose Again

In June 1996, I covered the NBA Finals with the Seattle SuperSonics playing against Michael Jordan's Chicago Bulls. However, even that did not surpass the emotional and professional attachment I had with the baseball team in 1995, '96, and '97.

I had gotten to know Mariners' manager Lou Piniella—well enough to know that his wife's name was Anita and that the family had a shih tzu like my precious Pepper. Lou wanted to know how I, as a thirty-two-year-old woman, could spend so many evenings at the games. *Don't you have a romantic relationship?* he inquired.

I did.

But during a two-year-long courtship, I found myself in the figurative seat that Theo, in Ohio, had occupied when he was with me. I had failed to empathize with him and the habitual nighttime police stops he experienced on the highway. Now, I was the one explaining how I felt targeted, not by the police, but with professional slights. I tried to convince my Seattle boyfriend of the truthfulness of the events in the KIRO-TV sports office, where my supervisor restricted me to a back seat for assignments and intentionally diminished my role.

For example, my contract specified that I would cover the NFL's Seattle Seahawks at home games in their stadium and that I would travel for road games. Only one road-trip assignment came through for me in two-and-a-half football seasons. That lone Seahawks' road assignment to Washington, D.C., came about after my agent reminded the news director of the job description in my contract.

In my private life, I failed to generate the understanding and support I needed to cope with such on-the-job mistreatment. Having a partner who could not empathize with me in my biggest battle left me feeling empty, as if I were a single woman.

In an attempt to win at something, I took an unexpected step to inject fulfillment and joy into my life. This step was the result of a pledge I had made to myself. Several years before, when I was a twentysomething novice journalist, I promised to re-evaluate my TV career after the first decade. If I were happily placed and winning praise and recognition for performing to the best of my ability, I would continue. If I were not living up to my own picture of success, I would punt, or—for non-sports people—quit.

Not every post had caused me intentional pain. WTVM in Columbus, Georgia, for example, with African American assignment manager Eric Ludgood, and WREG in Memphis, Tennessee, with white sports manager Glenn Carver, had offered me unobstructed chances to work and strive. I calculate, however, that of my first eleven years on the job after college graduation, six of those were spent laboring under oppressive managers in charge of my advancement.

So, the answer was simple.

I resigned from my television job in the No. 12 Nielsen market. In November 1997, I said "I do" to John Bennett. In marrying the light-skinned, hazel-eyed African American, the Harvard-educated son of two Harvard graduates, I hoped for the best. I told myself that I simply needed to be brave—that I was crossing the threshold into my happily ever after at the age of thirty-three. I was also pleased that my new married life would allow me to walk away from the headache my career had become.

John and I left the state of Washington and relocated twenty-eight hundred miles away near the East Coast, in Charlottesville, Virginia. He was four years older than I, and we had many points on which to build an untroubled, serene family life. For our later years, we both wanted a harmonious home and reconnection with the important people from our younger days. We valued healthy eating, and our hobbies, beginning with our love of dogs, meshed.

But...

I failed to understand him as much as he did not understand me. There were too many differences between us, not the least of which were our dissimilar socioeconomic upbringings. Neither of us found fulfillment in our marriage. Neither of us prioritized it, so its end was assured.

Besides that, I was compelled to continue to decry workplace mistreatment based on gender and race. I was determined to combat the system that routinely rejected me and other female journalists.

I was more determined to fight that battle than I was to save my marriage.

At the same time, I continued to believe in the solvency of American journalism. I kept telling myself that no matter how many times I got overlooked, benched, or knocked down, I was going to prove that meritocracy survives in the newsroom.

Thus, I focused on my career and pushed toward my Dallas destination. I did so to satisfy my personal desire and to validate the ideals espoused by the defenders of this Land of Opportunity. I wanted to prove them right.

Now, twenty-two years after my life with John, I finally see something he tried to tell me. Something I never before tried to understand.

During the run-up to the 2000 U.S. presidential election, John floated a political question that should have been eye-opening for me. We were still a couple at the time.

"Why is it that our choices for president are limited to two men the same age and from the same school?" he asked. Texas Governor George Bush, the Republican candidate, a graduate of Harvard Business School, turned fifty-five years old in 2000. His Democratic opponent, Vice President Al Gore, who earned an undergraduate degree at Harvard, turned fifty-two.[58] They represented the major-party options on the ballot. Not being a savvy political thinker back then, I placed little importance on John's question. I am sure I focused more on the prognosis of the Cowboys' next season than on the country's next election.

When the 2016 United States presidential campaign showdown between Hillary Clinton and Donald Trump took place, John's question seemed prescient. Again, voters had two candidates who shared too many similarities. I see this now because I shifted my analytical skills away from dissecting box scores into a full-on evaluation of

---

58. George W. Bush received his Harvard M.B.A. in 1975; Al Gore received his B.A. in 1969.

the game of politics. I am catching up with others who have long seen how the political elites are wresting away from voters, from the majority of the people, the power of real choice. The Republicans and Democrats conspired and colluded to keep proposals from outside parties away from the voters in 2016—yet another example of excluding the "other."

I am not OK with remaining silent about such exclusion. This suppression of ideas, a suppression directed at non-Republican and non-Democrat camps, threatens the entire election institution. It is this practice that produced the disturbingly similar pairs of candidates on the 2000 and 2016 final ballots.[59]

Leading to Election Day on November 3, 2020, national moods swing largely between outrage and fear on three fronts: deadly police violence captured on video, a raging and mysterious killer pandemic, and exploding job losses and homelessness because of the pandemic. Incumbent President Trump becomes a one-term president. He and Vice President Mike Pence lose to the Democratic ticket of former Vice President Joe Biden and U.S. Senator Kamala Harris of California.

The election of the Biden-Harris ticket temporarily eases the complaint of having too many similarities between the candidates on the final national ballot. The victorious Democrats arrive at their posts not representing Ivy League elite educational backgrounds, which history reveals had been the norm for the top two positions in the U.S. government. (See Endnotes.)

Ms. Harris, born in October 1964, is a *civil rights baby* as well as a *voting rights baby*, for she entered the world between the passage of the 1964 Civil Rights Act and the 1965 Voting Rights Act. In other words, she is the first U.S. vice president who was born at a

---

59. Hillary Rodham Clinton and Donald John Trump, ages 69 and 70, respectively, on Election Day, resided in the same city, New York City. They did not fully disclose to the public their political and financial connections to Wall Street bankers, which caused unease for American voters. Also, similarly, the two candidates operated family-run, multimillion-dollar foundations that engaged in arrangements with foreign entities. Neither candidate made full disclosure of the financial and other dealings with the wealthy foreign power brokers. Third-party candidates and noncorporate media called for transparency, but Clinton and Trump did not comply.

time when her right to vote was not guaranteed by law. Black women and women of color received voting rights, by law, when President Johnson signed the historic voting legislation in August 1965.

The great leap in voting participation that elects Biden-Harris in 2020 stirs a spate of voter-suppression proposals in January 2021. Insidious maneuvers to reduce access in more than 40 of the 50 states replaces the previous targets of suppression: third-party candidates and third-party policy input. Chief among Republican-led statehouses, Georgia passes an omnibus bill that severely restricts voting hours, ballot drop locations, and early-voting dates. Governor Brian Kemp signs it.

Across the aisle, national Democrats propose remedies to extend voting access, such as the For the People Act and the John Lewis Voting Rights Advancement Act.

Still, to have an honest election process, American voters need even more than this. To improve the future field of candidates, I target the access to the election-season televised debates that are hosted by the Commission on Presidential Debates. In television interviews I gave following the 2020 vote and the January 2021 inauguration, I strongly advocated that any candidate seeking the presidency or vice presidency should be required to provide, as a condition for taking the CPD's stage, no less than 15 years of filed tax documents. No tax documents, no podium on the debate stage.

This is vital because since 1988, the televised debate has been the make-or-break vehicle candidates use to introduce themselves to the public. Requiring candidates to furnish their tax documents for public scrutiny adds a layer of transparency needed when looking into the business and financial background of candidates.

The two dominant political parties influence all aspects of the Commission on Presidential Debates' televised presidential and vice presidential debates. At the time the CPD[60] was formed, co-founders

60. Its website states that the CPD was incorporated as a private, not-for-profit, nonpartisan corporation, but openly partisan figurehead and co-founder Fahrenkopf is a co-chair in 2021. Kenneth Wollack, a CPD co-chair in 2021, has ties to the highest levels of the U.S. political structure and has been involved in the U.S. Agency for International Development (USAID) and the American Israel Public Affairs Committee (AIPAC). The

Paul G. Kirk Jr. and Frank J. Fahrenkopf Jr. served as chairmen of the Democratic National Committee and the Republican National Committee, respectively.

I did not know any of this during my time with John, but I have such knowledge now, and I believe it gives me a balance I did not have in the past. In defense of my former self, however, I say only that from one newsroom battle to the next, I held on faithfully to my vision. On some distant date, I would tell myself, it would all be worth it. I believed it would be worth it. Because of the struggles, biases, trials, and triumphs, I had to believe it would be worth it.

CPD is a 501(c)(3) organization that receives its money from corporate, foundation, and private donors but not from governments, political-action committees, political parties, and candidates, according to *debates.org,* accessed April 14, 2021, and August 22, 2021. Additional information from https://www.ned.org/experts/kenneth-wollack/, accessed August 22, 2021.

PART III

Finally, Dallas!

CHAPTER 25

Kicking off the Dallas Decade

After two years and eight months in Seattle and an eighteen-month stopover as a wife in Virginia, I re-entered the TV business with my dream job—in Dallas! The new and fulfilling opportunity at KDFW-TV started in the summer of 1999 with a memorable conversation in the station's news car.

Dwayne Watkins, an attractive news photographer with broad shoulders, a deep brown complexion, a chiseled jawline, and the beginnings of graying hair along his temples, made me a promise the first time we were alone together on our way to a story.

"I will never do anything to shortchange you, as a black woman on the job. I will never do you wrong," he assured me.

His pledge caught me off guard, so I did not ask why he felt the need to offer me a professional harbor. I simply accepted the compact.

I was beginning my work in Dallas, Texas—finally!—at KDFW, Fox 4. On an unscheduled drop-in, I had visited the sports department five years earlier, in 1994. Since then, I had pictured myself in the work environment. Had envisioned details such as having my own workstation and phone extension and my coffee cup, which I would bring from home to reduce waste. In my vision, my brand-new work life felt rewarding and right to me.

And now, the vision had become reality.

My new station home, which served the huge Dallas-Fort Worth viewing area, broadcast the Dallas Cowboys games. That gave it immense prestige among sports fans and in the broadcasting industry.

175

This meant I also bore a badge of prestige. I was now a team member of an affiliate of the national Fox Network, the pearl of sports programming in the United States.

I entered my new setting never expecting to receive career resistance. Why should I? I had finally landed at the center of the pro-football-broadcasting universe. People there were as happy to be there as I was. That meant they would be qualified, conscientious, hard-working colleagues—not resentful and malicious. Right? Surely, in this broadcast heaven, no one had time to plant career-ending minefields such as the ones that had dogged me in the past.

Besides, it was Dallas! A city where, in 1995, a racial blend of voters had installed the city's first black mayor, Ron Kirk.[61] Diversity prevailed in the combined Dallas-Fort Worth market. Whites were the majority in the two cities, followed by Hispanics, then blacks, Asians, American Indians, and Alaska Native populations, according to the categories and statistics of the U.S. Census of 2000. Surely, with such a diverse audience, in such an opportunity-rich environment, a woman's finely tuned skill set would be enough to carry her through to success.

Another reason I felt optimistic is because my handsome salary, seventy thousand dollars a year, would enable me to afford any type of neighborhood or home that I chose. Anything I would consider was within my financial reach. Now I could buy my dream home—something comfortable and centrally located (but not a mansion like the Ewing family's homestead, Southfork, in the TV series *Dallas*).[62]

I was charged up about conquering the wide north Texas region. I strongly suspected that slackers need not seek work in the territory, which had evolved from processing cotton and cattle to firing on the pistons of railroads, aviation, banking, and oil exploration. No, it was clear to me that here on this north Texas plateau, the most competent people lasso and command the most important

61. Ron Kirk, born in 1954 in Austin, Texas, served as mayor of Dallas from 1995 to 2001 and as United States Trade Representative under President Barack Obama (2009-2013).
62. The popular CBS program aired from 1978 to 1991.

jobs. Perhaps that is why I felt uncharacteristically satisfied when a human-resources executive at Fox 4 congratulated me on beating a field of one hundred forty-one applicants for the sports job.

I had finally reached the land of milk and honey. But my new photographer colleague had said something that gave me a prick of concern. He had handed me a sort of brotherly shield of protection. Had just assured me that he had my back.

Why?

Would I need someone watching over me?

It was the color of desert sand, the sleeveless and tailored sheath dress I wore on my first day at the Dallas Cowboys training camp in 1999. I loved that dress; I thought it professional. Airy and cut from a lightweight fabric, I knew it would give me comfort on a workday that lasted from eight-thirty a.m. until eleven-thirty p.m.

Within my first few weeks of hire at KDFW-TV, I was on assignment at Cowboys camp at Midwestern State University in Wichita Falls, Texas. I took up a position at the entrance to the dorms that would house the football players for seven weeks. Television, radio, and print journalists jostled one another to catch first glimpse of the athletes' arrivals by car. Once they arrived, we would try to cut them off at the door to grab our interviews.

Like the longtime Dallas reporters working beside me that day, I recognized, on sight, the veterans and the rookie players. That served as no advantage, really, because every reporter in the crowd was clamoring for interviews. Each one of us would stick a microphone in the face of any athlete who stopped to talk. Standing shoulder to shoulder with the seasoned journalists and the interns, I was surprised to hear a male voice direct a question my way.

"Are you an intern?"

I turned. The inquirer was a videographer from competing channel WFAA-TV.

"What?" I replied with annoyance. I was there to work, not to discuss my biography.

"You're interning with KDFW?" the man, a slender African American holding a pro-grade video camera, continued politely.

"No," I replied curtly. I did not want to create an enemy, but I believed that the first day was better served getting into the scene instead of letting someone chat me up.

I later found out that the inquisitive man was Arnold Payne, a decorated photojournalist and Grambling University graduate. He would become a solid personal contact for me. On the day we met, I noted that he was good-looking, caramel-colored, tall, and around my age. Indeed, I could have found him a possibility for something more than work.

But determined, as always, to remain professional, I put first things first.

Arnold's questions were not the only source of mild irritation for me in those tense opening moments of the first day. Another African American journalist peeved me even more.

"You don't have to dress like that," said Jose Gant, a salt-and-pepper-bearded, muscular black man with a serious demeanor. *Great*, I thought. Now a second person from WFAA-TV is into my business, and this one's swiping at my dress! I noticed other women on the assignment—even those in their thirties, as I was—wearing shorts and T-shirts.

To Jose, I shot back, "And you are Elsa Klensch?"

Jose, unfazed by the tart retort, laughed good-naturedly. Most of the people who heard my remark laughed, as well. Certainly, all of them knew that Klensch hosted, at that time, a superb fashion program on CNN every Saturday morning.

And what luck for me: She had transmuted and was working outside the dorm at Midwestern State University.

Despite his verbal misstep with me, I realized within the next hour or so that Jose held a respected position among the gathered journalists. He was dean, of sorts, for the Cowboys media. That became clear when the team's media liaison on the scene, likeable, white and thirtyish Doug Hood, asked all of us to back away from the entrance to allow players to walk in, unobstructed. Doug repeated the request several times, louder and louder each time. Finally, Jose's voice rang out with an authority, a thunder, that Doug's did not have.

"The man said *BACK IT UP!*"

The mass of reporters cooperated.

He impressed me greatly.

"So, he's not Elsa Klensch," I thought. "He's General Colin Powell."

The "E" Exclusive

The job on that first training-camp day was not too big for me. I had done in-depth preparation to cover the current Dallas team. Add to that, I had nearly thirty years of following the Cowboys from afar. Thus armed, I quickly cultivated a positive relationship with Chan Gailey, Dallas' head coach at the time. We shared a Georgia upbringing, so I dialed up a languid Augusta accent when I spoke to Gailey, a Gainesville native and former Americus resident.

My boss saw how well I was doing at training camp, so he handed me a plum assignment.

"You're interviewing Emmitt Smith at lunch," said Kevin Morrell, an easy-going white Californian and a former producer at ESPN. Kevin had many years of working on high-profile stories, dealing with athletes who transcended sports to permeate the wider American consciousness. Doling out an interview with one of the standout players in the NFL was routine for him. But the words rocked my world.

I had less than one hour to decide a line of questioning with a player known across the entire league. I knew enough at that stage of my career to not ask the questions that Emmitt had been asked numerous times before—even though many veteran reporters still use this flawed approach.

What could I ask him that would be new to *him*?

I knew his collegiate and professional progression. (Who didn't?) Combing through the media guide, the book of information provided by the team, I focused on the first line. His birthdate. It gave me my opening line.

I hurriedly powdered my face again and accessorized my white, V-necked, polycotton shirt with a red-and-white scarf. The video would live on forever, I reminded myself. Hence, the extra sprucing up with a fresh coat of lipstick and a final look in the mirror at my hairstyle.

Two of our photographers prepared an interview-type set in a corner of the university dining hall. I took my place with my back to the camera, something I had done many times while working in Memphis, Tennessee, and in Seattle, Washington.

Emmitt arrived and said hello to everyone. The thirty-year-old MVP of the 1993 Super Bowl exhibited familiar ease with my co-workers. They had covered him when the Cowboys won three Super Bowls in the 1990s (Super Bowls XXVII, XXVIII, and XXX). Before that moment, he and I had not spoken to each other but had shared only nods of hello in passing. He must have realized that I had some sports moxie to be there with the Fox affiliate. While the photographers made some final camera adjustments, Emmitt seemed patient and intent on listening to whatever questions might come out of the mouth of the unknown entity sitting across from him.

I told him that our families came from the same geographical location. His childhood in the western part of Pensacola, Florida, linked him to my father's home on North J Street and the neighborhood where I had spent some summers.

A good start.

Camera rolling, I engaged him by mentioning another thing we had in common, our birthdays—May 15 for him, May 7 for me. "We're both Taurus," I pointed out.

When Emmitt's face showed confusion about the importance of this fact, I explained, "It means that we set goals." (Goal-setting is an astrological personality trait of Taurus people.)

Emmitt's confusion melted away. "Exactly," he agreed.

And I added, "I was eight when I decided I wanted to cover the Cowboys."

Emmitt picked up the comparison game, saying, "I was about seven when I told my father I would play for the Dallas Cowboys one day. And it happened," he declared.

We nodded with understanding.

"And you have to speak your goals, don't you?" I added.

"Oh, yes. What you say will come true," the three-time Super Bowl winner readily agreed.

I found Emmitt to be an open, positive, and relaxed subject. At the time that I interviewed him, he had been an NFL player for nine years. The league's Rookie of the Year in 1990 had become accustomed to handling reporters. But, I connected with him on a human level. From there, Emmitt took over the conversation, easily sharing his thoughts with me. He discussed what he'd had to do to reach the apex of his career. He talked about having to make the right moves when not on the field, as well as exploiting the open spaces created by the offensive line in the games. I led him into a discussion about his possibly breaking the record for rushing yards in the NFL.[63]

Toward the end of the interview, Emmitt shared a thought that I knew viewers would like. "I learn from the valleys and I learn from the peaks," he said. "The valleys allow you to recognize who you are and to go inside yourself to come out on the other side."

"Are those valleys professional or personal?" I inquired.

"Both," answered Emmitt, who would play eleven years as Cowboys running back before signing for two years with Arizona.

The entire interview went along with ease and candor.

Quite a training-camp coup for a thirty-five-year-old *intern*.

---

63. Taken No. 17 in the 1990 draft, Emmitt Smith set many league and franchise records. For the Cowboys, he established the record for rushing yards (17,162) and total points (986). Smith was inducted into the Dallas Cowboys Ring of Honor in 2005, along with quarterback Troy Aikman and wide receiver Michael Irvin, in a trio that became known as "the Triplets." Smith, an inductee into the Pro Football Hall of Fame in 2010, owns the record for NFL career rushing yards (18,355), NFL career rushing touchdowns (164), and career 100+ rushing yards games (78). See emmittsmith.com.

CHAPTER 26

"Have You Seen My Super Bowl Trophies?"

My rookie season in Dallas, 1999, Cowboys owner Jerry Jones approached me as I watched the team practice at the lauded Valley Ranch training facility.

For some reporters, the regular-season practices were tedious and uninteresting. For me, quite the opposite was the case. I would watch, with a scrutinizing eye, which players tackled hard and ran hard. I would watch who talked to whom or who took water breaks with whom—my effort to discern the friendships that might be developing beyond the field. Studying this interaction would signal to me which players to interview in a life-off-the-field personality profile. I would observe also which coaches applauded which players. I would make eye contact with coaches and make comments to them about—*whatever*, but always something related to the day's work.

One such day and in the absence of other television reporters, Jerry rewarded my steadfastness with an enticing question.

"Have you seen my Super Bowl trophies?" he asked with the broad and welcoming smile of a Texan, even one transplanted from Arkansas. "I have five in my office," he added.

"No, I haven't seen your Super Bowl trophies," I replied playfully.

He sweetened the offer to tour the office. "And I have a photo with Elizabeth Taylor to show you," added Jerry, who was fifty-eight years old at the time.

"I would like to see your office. Maybe I can shoot video and interview you," I suggested.

"Sure. Just tell Rich that I said that we'd do this." Rich Dalrymple was media director for the Cowboys.

"Great," I said, trying to mute my excitement.

Jerry instructed me to lock in the time with Rich, and he walked off. As practice continued, I found Rich on the sidelines.

"Jerry said that I can come and see the Super Bowl trophies and interview him in his office," I said, excited beyond belief. "He told me to find a time with you."

Rich, an angularly built and youthful-looking white male with bangs and salt-and-pepper hair, resented something I had done— either my approach or some other inadvertent breach of protocol. Whatever it was made him testy.

"I'm the one who's going to tell *you* how it's going to be," he answered me.

I hesitated, taken aback, not sure what had released the bee in Rich's bonnet. But all I said in response was a curious, "OK." I did not want Rich the Gatekeeper to construct a roadblock in front of me in this new setting. Good thing, too, because Rich did come through with an appointment time, allowing a three-person KDFW team to enter the private office of Jerry Jones to work the story.

I succeeded in the report, interacting one-on-one, on camera, with the most high-profile owner-GM in America's top sports league. And this, even though I had been on the job in Dallas only a few months! My photography colleague Fred Church[64] told me that he had never been inside Jerry's office, despite having worked nearly a decade in Dallas-Fort Worth.

Jerry Justice

Because working in sports journalism in a pro sports city carries a load of responsibility, I developed a way to ensure that viewers talked about my stories even if games and teams did not interest them. I continued to evolve my particular way of humanizing the

---

64. The name has been changed.

sports figures I interviewed, treating them as people, not as perfect gods or indefatigable superheroes who feel no pain.

Several of my family-related interview extracts have reappeared on Fox 4 since my departure from Dallas; TV stations often reuse unique material. Another Jerry Jones interview lives on in replays because of an endearing quip its subject delivered on screen.

In a personality profile, I asked Jerry to share his three keys to staying married for so long—thirty-seven years, at the time. He responded with a freshness in his voice and a memorable statement:

"An understanding wife, an understanding wife, and ..." (He paused for emphasis and continued with smiling eyes.) "...an understanding wife."

CHAPTER 27

Inclusiveness and Bob Hayes: Roger That

I scored aces because of my dad's love of sports; it wonderfully colored my life and helped me in my Dallas reporting. For example, I knew the name Bob Hayes at an early age. The "World's Fastest Human" established himself in the Tokyo Olympics in 1964, a few months after I was born. Dad, who was twenty-seven years old at the time, reveled in Bob's Olympic conquest because of Bob's American nationality and Jacksonville, Florida, birthplace. My father grew up in Pensacola, Florida, and followed exploits of the state's athletes and teams.

A sports trailblazer, Bob became the first person in history to win an Olympic gold medal (actually, two) and a Super Bowl title. The Dallas Cowboys drafted Bob the same year that he pulled off his history-making feat. The precision touch of quarterbacks "Dandy" Don Meredith and Roger Staubach, who threw to Bob, forced NFL defenses to rewrite their schemes to counter the high-octane offense.[65]

When the Cowboys announced Bob Hayes' addition to the Ring of Honor at Texas Stadium in 2001, I started mining my contacts

---

65. Bob Hayes played eight seasons in Dallas and set 22 receiving records along the way. ESPN's Ralph Wiley wrote: "One year, 1970, [Bob] averaged 26.1 yards per catch. The next year, he averaged 24.0 per catch. That's a quarter of the length of the field, every time he touched it." In 132 NFL games, he scored 71 touchdowns. He caught 371 passes for 7,414 yards—leading to a career average of 20 yards per catch. Bob played his final season, in 1975, for San Francisco. He emphasized in an interview with the author that, in addition to being the world's fastest man, he had demonstrated extraordinary football skills even while at Florida A & M University. See pro-football-reference.com.

to arrange an interview with this athlete of mythic proportions. I found out from a contact when Bob would arrive from Florida to accept the franchise's ultimate honor. The installation ceremony would take place on a later date, so Bob would visit two times, and two times I would have the chance to report about him. A teammate of Bob's shared his itinerary with me—though the details were not supposed to be publicly released. My sports director scheduled a photographer to work with me for Bob's fly-in and forty-eight-hour turnaround to fly out.

My photographer Shannon Bales and I went to the private hangar of Love Field Airport and staked out the scene. We saw other retired Cowboys players, so we knew we had received the correct tip. There were no other television stations represented, which was remarkable because of the significance of the story to the Dallas-Fort Worth viewers. Cowboys news typically grabbed a high slot in the news—if not the lead. A Ring of Honor addition, even more so. At that time, Bob became only the eleventh person selected for the Ring of Honor in the team's first forty-one years.[66] If other reporters had tracked down the flight information, I believe they would have been standing around with us.

After a wait of maybe an hour, the private plane of Cowboys owner Jerry Jones touched down. The stairs folded out; Bob Hayes and his son and sister, among other people, descended. Some of the former teammates greeted the group on the tarmac.

Bob, fifty-eight years old, six feet tall, and gaunt, showed the ravages of prostate cancer and liver disease. Seeing him, lean but walking under his own power, reassured everyone that he was winning the battle over his illnesses on that day. However, he would move around in a wheelchair for part of the weekend visit.

When Bob finally reached me, I extended my hand to shake his and to welcome him. I kept thinking, *Say something to make sure he remembers me.*

---

66. Cowboys owner and general manager Jerry Jones added coach Tom Landry to the Ring of Honor on November 7, 1993. Therefore, Bob Hayes would become the 10th *player* inducted.

"I have known your name all my life," I said warmly.

It worked. Despite looking frail, Bob Hayes turned on the charm with a bright smile and gentle voice. "How is it you have known my name your whole life?" he asked.

"My dad talked about you and the Olympics from the earliest days I can remember," I answered.

We would have continued our pleasantries, but I said, "Let's talk again after you say hello to everyone." He agreed, so we parted.

It was sealed. Bob Hayes would remember me. And our warm first exchange would later pull us back together.

It's "Dandy" to See You Again

Bob invited the KDFW photographer and me to ride with him in the shuttle van from the airport to the hotel. I declined because someone needed to drive our news car to the other locations. I drove the car, freeing our photographer to ride in the van and shoot exclusive video of Bob's candid musings about seeing Dallas after twenty years of being away. The photographer and I later developed our up-close-and-personal footage into a weekend-with-Bob Hayes exclusive.

Before the team dinner honoring Bob that night, the guest of honor reunited with his first Cowboys quarterback, Don Meredith.[67] Don and Bob played fifty-two games together between 1965 and 1968, at a time when the Cowboys franchise was the new kid on the block—and so were the men. Don rarely returned to Dallas, but celebrating Bob's addition to the Ring of Honor had roped Meredith back into the team fold, if only for a day.

The two former partners arrived at the banquet hall at the same time—something they had not planned. Like the quarterback-to-receiver timing they had shared in the past, their movements through space were synchronized on that banquet day, which created the chance meeting outside the hall. It was a spectacularly memorable

---

67. Don Meredith retired from the Cowboys and the NFL after the 1968 season. He played a total of 132 NFL games—all for Dallas—from the team's first season, in 1960, until 1968.

moment; the two men had not been together since their playing days forty years earlier.

The encounter began when Hayes dipped his shoulder toward me and, in a lowered but excited voice, said, "There's my quarterback, there's my quarterback!" He trained his eyes on Meredith, who was still at a distance but was approaching on the sidewalk. I imagined Bob had trained his eyes on Meredith's spiraling passes on the football field in the same way. He waited for "Dandy" Don to recognize him.

When the moment came, Don broke into a smile and the men came together. They clutched hands but quickly shoved aside formality and moved into a bear hug with bursts of youthful laughter. My photographer captured video of a moment that followers of the Hayes-Meredith Cowboys era would consider sacred.

Among sports journalists, Don Meredith had a reputation for shunning reporters. My colleagues in the KDFW office had even warned me about this. However, the reclusive Meredith consented to an interview with me. (So much for the warning. I had long before stopped listening to the unnecessary caution of others.) I believe Don agreed to comment on camera with me largely because he sensed the closeness between Bob and me. Meredith trusted that closeness. He granted me a precious reporter's score—probably the only Hayes-Meredith joint interview of the weekend.

"He looks good. It's great to see him," said Meredith, who added that Hayes richly deserved the honor in Dallas.

What the men had lost in time apart, they made up for in physical proximity during those precious reunion moments. At one point while explaining to me what they meant to each other, Hayes and Meredith stood so close that no inch of the fading daylight pierced the space where their bodies met.

Despite my having only two years on the Cowboys beat by that time in 2001, my insider coverage of Bob Hayes' weekend stood shoulder-to-shoulder with what the longtime reporters in the market put on the air. By any objective measure, my reporting on Fox 4 won the weekend for followers of the team. My package included the behind-the-scenes footage with Hayes, his embrace with Meredith, and their joint on-camera interview with me. That last aspect, the tender comments the men shared about each other, may be the last ones ever recorded.

One month later, on September 23, 2001, a black curtain fell away from a plaque at Texas Stadium to reveal to a capacity crowd the words *Bob Hayes 1965 – 1974*. The sixty-five thousand fans attending the Dallas vs. San Diego game cheered upon seeing the plaque, and they screamed with appreciation at seeing Hayes in the flesh. All the living members of the Ring of Honor, except Don Meredith, appeared at the on-field induction ceremony. (Meredith's absence sealed for KDFW the irreplaceable nature of the interview I had scored a month earlier.)

As everyone else was leaving the field to make way for the second half of the game, Bob remained on the field.

"Where is Nita? Where is Nita?" Bob asked anyone standing nearby.

When meeting Bob one month earlier, I had asked him if he would agree to meet my father. "I'd be happy to meet your dad," he had answered warmly. Now, Bob was trying to make that happen. He had suggested I bring my father to Jerry Jones' private stadium suite after half-time. I needed to connect with Bob on the field to gain entry to the suite.

Finishing my interview duties related to the ceremony, I spied Bob near the far-away end zone. He had exited the artificial grass surface and started walking up the ramp to the ring road under the stadium. I had to run more than fifty yards along the sidelines to catch up to the former speedster. Because he was struggling to make the climb, I caught him before he disappeared into the bowels of the stadium.

Bob leaned lightly on me and we walked together to the top of the fifty-foot ramp. At just the right time, a stadium employee arrived, driving a cart. Bob and I got on. The driver knew to deposit Bob at the elevator to the Jones family suite.

"Go and get your dad," Bob said to me.

I bounded off the cart, happy to find my father in the seats.

He Deserves Fame, Not Shame

In a series of interviews that examined the possibility of the Pro Football Hall of Fame's honoring Bob, Dallas quarterback Roger Staubach urged the voters to install Bob in the pantheon of football greats. Staubach, who entered the Hall in 1985, was a squeaky-clean pro athlete, Heisman Trophy winner, Naval Academy graduate, "proud" Viet Nam veteran (as he told me), two-time Super Bowl winner, and father of five. During the campaign by Bob's loyal fans, extended family, and football family, Roger simply summed up his view.

"I'm more for inclusion than exclusion," Staubach told me in an interview.

The statement lifted Roger to a plateau higher than the elevated place he already held in my view. He was supporting a teammate and a person he valued, though some corners of the football community criticized Bob about his drug use and ten-month prison sentence, which stemmed from his involvement with drugs.

Few athletes will ever have a ledger of sports accomplishments as rich as Roger Staubach's. He told me that after retiring from the NFL, he became far more successful in business than he had been in college and professional ball. He could have used his success to set up barriers—to discount the people around him as being unworthy of recognition and deficient in value, but he did not do that.

From his lofty threshold in the sanctuary of American success, Staubach did not smugly block the door of opportunity for others. He did not rest on the laurels that his skills had secured for him in the powerful industries of sports and business. Instead, on numerous occasions, Roger voiced support for Bob Hayes. Staubach did not believe others should block the game-changer Hayes from entering the doors of the Hall of Fame.

"I'm more for inclusion than exclusion," Roger had said.

A Bullet Falls

In the months after Hayes' return to Dallas, people in his circle maintained their contact with me because they appreciated the reverent treatment I gave their beloved Bob in my reports. One of those contacts called to tell me when Bob's health took a serious downturn.

Because of the news value of the information, I immediately told assistant news director Kingsley Smith. He asked whether the sports department had a video tribute ready to air. I told him that we did not and that I was holding onto the possibility of a medical recovery. When I had introduced my dad to Bob in Jerry Jones' private suite, the two Florida men had hit it off. Bob asked my dad, the man who had idolized him for forty-five years, to be his friend. I did not want to think about the loss of my father's new friend.

But Kingsley gave me a touching reply—exactly what I needed to hear to get on with the task.

"Who better than you to write about Bob Hayes?"

Thus charged, I wrote a tribute to the man. I had known, my entire life, what the person of Bob Hayes meant to people who tracked his career. I was able to write something that focused on what he meant beyond the running track and the football field. I wrote the script my father would need to hear at the passing of the person he most admired, his cherished friend.

"Bullet Bob" Hayes died in September 2002—nearly one year after his induction into Dallas' Ring of Honor. Seven years would pass before the senior committee of the Pro Football Hall of Fame approved him, finally, for induction into its hallowed halls.

At the Hall of Fame ceremony held August 8, 2009, in the HOF headquarters in Canton, Ohio, Staubach said that Bob "truly gave a darn about someone other than himself and was loved by his teammates." Roger also said, "So, it's a real privilege...it's a real privilege for me to say, 'Thank you, Canton. Thank you, NFL. Thank you to the Football Hall of Fame for making sure that this great athlete that had an impact on the NFL is in the Hall of Fame.' "[68]

Inclusion.

Roger that!

---

68. Transcribed by the author from Pro Football Hall of Fame speech, August 8, 2009. See profootballhof.com.

CHAPTER 28

Robbed by Dennis Miller on *MNF*

The letters *MNF* used to prompt the American public to get ready for a weekly must-see, prime-time TV event broadcast live from a pulsating NFL city. Howard Cosell's loud and nasally New Yorker's voice would blare out the names of the football teams slated to do battle. A lawyer by training, Cosell's wit and intellect extended the reach of the game to various segments of the 1970s audiences. *Monday Night Football*, or *MNF*, even entertained people who did not follow sports.

The show climbed to iconic status. Play-by-play announcers Keith ("Whoa, Nellie!") Jackson and former Dallas quarterback Don Meredith offered levity and information, which complemented Howard's high-brow role. Former NFL player Fred "Black Caesar" Williamson became the first black presenter. He worked in 1974, but only in the preseason. The first woman, a white woman, Lesley Visser, appeared in the 1998-1999 season. She delivered her information from the sidelines, not from the booth where the men worked. Lesley told me in a candid conversation that in her earliest days of covering the NFL, the press credential from the league expressly stated that there were to be "no women and no children in the locker room." To get her job done, she conducted her postgame interviews in the parking lot as players left the stadium.

My Moment on *MNF*'s Mt. Olympus—Almost

From the 1990s to the early 2000s, an audience of fifty million people watched *Monday Night Football* every week.[69]

I made it to *MNF* during that heyday—or, at least, my *words* made it.

Viewers did not know that it was I—a black, female journalist— who had given them something intelligent to talk about at the office water cooler the next morning.

Comedian Dennis Miller, an *MNF* booth broadcaster in 2000 and 2001, heavily cited a report I aired on KDFW Fox 4 on Sunday, October 14, 2001. He heavily cited me—but did not attribute to me the information he had appropriated from our ten-thirty p.m. *Sports Sunday on Fox* program.

As a teenager, I appreciated the schtick of Pittsburgh-born Miller, who was a member of the cast of the comedy variety show *Saturday Night Live*. During the mid-1980s, Miller convincingly read the fake news on the show's hilarious "Weekend Update" segment. His dark, wavy hair, coiffed in a sporty TV newsman's 'do, his dark suit jacket, and his well-timed delivery enabled him to perfectly pull off the fake. Some years later, he would pull off a similar fake—except that it was in real life, and he was using my reporting. Miller's actor's acumen allowed him to relay the lines as if he had sourced the information.

I realize it's no small matter to accuse a high-profile TV star of using my material. (Miller won two Emmys in the 1990s for his *Dennis Miller Show* on HBO, a platform that added to his stardom.) I could easily trace the information's chain of custody, though.

In *Monday Night Football*'s thirty-second year and its thirteenth edition of Dallas vs. Washington, I began scratching for something fresh in the weeks before the game. I found it. A story angle that no TV journalist had shown the audience. I did all the researching and interviewing, so the information stayed within the Fox 4 sports department until airtime. I produced a package about the unveiling of a nine-foot-tall, larger-than-life bronze statue of legendary Dallas

---

69. Figure provided by ESPN's website, 2003.

coach Tom Landry. The statue was to be installed in front of Gate One at Texas Stadium in Irving, Texas, the week of the *MNF* game.

That season, 2001, *MNF* was many seasons removed from Mr. Cosell's bombastic and appealing personality. Even high-profile athletes Don Meredith, O.J. Simpson, and Joe Namath were long gone as color commentators. There sat Miller, a non-football person. As an on-air personality with a rich contract, he faced heat consistently over not meshing well with the dominant football flavor of *MNF.*

My material was what the show needed and what Dennis Miller needed. My story married esoteric tastes—the artistic crowd that Miller was supposed to stoke—to football lore, such as the fabled Hall of Fame coach Landry.

I applauded what Dennis Miller did away from *MNF*—his humorous acidic rants—and I wanted to tell him so. In that spirit, I walked over to him in the end zone before the game. My hand extended, I planned to congratulate him for facing down the criticism, for inventing a place for himself on the mega-successful *MNF* franchise. That's what I did at every big-time event; I would sincerely compliment the visiting journalists on something they did well.

Seeing me approach him, Miller painted an Evander Holyfield-type snarl on his face. He abruptly pivoted and walked quickly in the other direction. At five-foot-eight, he easily disappeared in the mass of reporters and other dignitaries in town for the *MNF* broadcast. Later I remarked to another Dallas-based reporter that Miller had bolted when I tried to speak to him.

"He must have seen your report last night. Everything you said in your report about Tom Landry's statue, he said on TV today."

"You're kidding!" I replied, surprised and displeased. I prided myself on the contacts I had cultivated within the Cowboys organization. I always sought to inform the nation about the team in a way no one else had. But now, someone was taking a shortcut on the footwork and getting the airtime to share my information.

"He described the statue, how Coach Landry was holding a game plan from a New York Giants game because he loved to strategize to play the Giants," the reporter continued. "He [Miller] probably recognized you."

I processed what I was hearing and kept listening.

"And he talked about the fedora and the coaching shoes," my colleague continued, referring to personal effects I had mentioned in my report.

Finally, I found my words. "The sculptor told me that he has to have some personal items from the subject to get a feel of the person," I said.

"Dennis Miller said that, too."

I fully understood. In a flash, I remembered the time I fed in-depth details about the 1995 Seattle Mariners to a *Baseball America* magazine writer. He published a well-crafted story based on my information, but he failed to make any mention of me. It left me feeling robbed. Admittedly, not receiving credit for my baseball insights was my fault because I talked freely and had not asked for attribution. I had assumed the writer would credit a fellow professional.

This time was different. I had conducted honest research and presented an exclusive story; journalistic etiquette dictated that anyone who borrowed from my report needed to attribute it. Dennis Miller obviously had not done that. (He is no Cheryl Miller. See Chapter 38.)

As my fellow Dallas journalist and I parted ways, I thanked him for sharing what he knew. As he walked away, he said, "I thought you did a good job on the story, by the way."

I appreciated his compliment, but I mulled over the sobering news. Dennis Miller had recounted on the October 15, 2001, broadcast of *Monday Night Football* the details of my exclusive interview with renowned sculptor Robert Summers. The artist had been commissioned to create the statue of Tom Landry and had welcomed me into his studio in Glen Rose, Texas. He showed me the fedora, the coaching shoes, and the game-day chart that widow Alicia Landry loaned him for the successful completion of the project.

I understood Mr. Summers' need to create while in the presence of Coach Landry's personal effects. When I was in the artist's space, I also felt the aura of Landry, someone I had never met but began watching on TV when I was six. I appreciated the sculptor-painter Summers, also. His desire to create a permanent tribute to a great sports figure like Landry moved me. I felt proud to spread Mr. Summers' thoughts about immortalizing the pillar of the Cowboys franchise. I painstakingly communicated the sentiments of the native Texas artist about one of the state's own. Our *Sports Sunday on Fox* viewers heard those sentiments, unadulterated and sincere, from my own mouth.

However, without permission, the statements that Robert Summers said on tape *only to me* were shared with the *MNF* audience by Dennis Miller.

Some fifty million viewers never knew the role I had played in that information game.

And that is simply not fair.

CHAPTER 29

Earnhardt

NASCAR lost its tower of strength on February 18, 2001, when forty-nine-year-old Dale Earnhardt died in a crash on the track in the Daytona 500.

I was not on duty in Florida covering the race when the great loss occurred. Three other members of the KDFW sports team worked the story at the legendary track that day. To distract myself from the disappointment of not winning the assignment, I entertained myself in Dallas. I spent the day with my friend Theresa Hunter, someone who liked auto racing and with whom I could talk about the sport. However, she did not mention the Daytona 500, NASCAR's Super Bowl of racing, while hanging out with me that day. She knew I felt in the Dumpster, professionally.

The station's long-serving white female general manager, Kathy Saunders, had preferred sending white sports anchor-reporter John Discepolo to the race. She made this decision even though I was KDFW Fox 4's undisputed NASCAR specialist—and I was the one who had recommended we attend the Daytona 500.

Kevin Morrell, my direct supervisor, broke the news to me with an explanation.

"Kathy says he'll look like Tom Cruise."

Kathy meant that, on camera, Discepolo would look like a Hollywood star while reporting from the track. No denying that. John, one of my solid work friends, could really rock the sunglasses. Wearing them, he drew legitimate comparisons to the publicity shots the actor Tom Cruise made for his aviator movie *Top Gun*.

But John brought more to the news team than dark coiffed hair and Ken-doll good looks. He had a rich knowledge of the National Hockey League (NHL) and other specialties that were not NASCAR. In fact, John, a New Yorker, did not care for the racing circuit born in the American South. Partly for this last reason, John and I agreed that we were perfectly paired colleagues. I preferred Cowboys football, NASCAR, boxing, cycling, and absolutely no involvement in the coverage of college sports. I also preferred being on the scene with the spectators and athletes. In absolute contrast, John wanted to be in the climate-controlled conditions of the studio. And his true love in sports? Hockey.

So, with John as an on-air co-worker, I gleefully dropped hockey into his breadbasket. In exchange, he ceded NASCAR to me—at least, until the GM gave the order otherwise.

John wasn't happy about the Daytona assignment because it would be a workday not spent in the studio. Little did he know that the racing tragedy of the year—of the decade and beyond, actually—would also fall into his breadbasket.

Once back at home on that Daytona 500 Sunday, I flipped on the television to the sports channel ESPN and saw archive video of Earnhardt, the seven-time Winston Cup champion and *living* legend, I thought at the time. I passively looked in the direction of the screen as I moved through my apartment, organizing for the coming workweek. I noticed the nonstop playing of videos featuring Earnhardt. It clicked in my mind that in the midst of this retrospective of the sport's marquee driver, not one report mentioned the winner of the season-opening race.

A pall swept over me.

Having watched NASCAR since age four or five, I understood the reason that a driver's career history would be playing on a loop. "What type of injury has sent ol' Earnhardt to the emergency room?" I wondered. Maybe he's being treated at the on-site medical center, I thought. "How soon will the crusty old guy return?" I said, mocking his hard-charging style, the grittiness that always put him in the midst of the on-track shenanigans, the rivalries real and manufactured.

The possibility of having lost Dale Earnhardt on the track that day never entered my mind. I drifted back in time to another Winston Cup season, one in which the focus was on a favored driver and his serious injuries.

In 1992, the beloved Davey Allison, though smashed up severely in a race at the Pocono track, climbed back into the cockpit the next weekend. Allison's bloodshot eyes served as an exclamation mark for the pain that wracked the rest of his body: cracked ribs, a broken right arm, and the invisible damage of a concussion.

The rules dictated that Allison (or any driver) must at least start the following race to maintain his position in the chase for the Winston championship. In one particularly memorable image of him, Allison smiles for the curious and hopeful supporters while seated in his No. 28 Havoline Ford on the second row of the starting grid. He yielded after two laps to replacement driver Bobby Hillin Jr., as planned.

I anchored the sports that day in July '92 for Augusta's WRDW-TV. Because I edited my own video for the show, I saw, over and over, the extent of Allison's facial injuries as I strung together a minute-long montage. I felt haunted by his eyes, including the purple and blue lacerations he showed everyone when he removed his sunglasses before the race. Injured, but recovered. I felt a personal relief because of this recovery. I know I shared my relief with Allison's legions of followers who were among my viewers. Getting roughed up in a car crash could not knock our Davey out of his pursuit of points.[70]

I broke from my NASCAR flashback to sit on the couch to find out about Earnhardt's injuries.

Text that crawled across the bottom of the television screen jarred me.

---

70. Davey Allison died in a helicopter crash nearly one year later, at age 32.

Dale Earnhardt . . .
. . . died from injuries in a last-lap crash . . .

The words sent a piercing alarm through my senses. I had never been so deeply jolted by the death of a sports personality—even though I felt, at that time, emotionally close to many sports figures. Not only did I absorb textbook knowledge about their achievements, I watched on TV (and sometimes in person) the most glorious and the most agonizing moments of their lives. I walked the path of their careers with them and helped tell their stories when I wrote my scripts.

This desire to share their stories crossed the boundaries of the sports world, so that I cared as much for the Olympic sprinter as I did the boxer and the tackler—and the race-car driver. Alongside sprinter-turned-football player Bob Hayes' name, the racing dynasties of NASCAR were part of my conscious, waking moments from 1970 forward.

Hardly believable, then, that I learned about the passing of Dale Earnhardt from an impersonal string of slow-moving letters on TV.

Big E and Little E

After I was blasted into disbelief on the day of his death, I learned that Earnhardt's car had slammed into the wall in turn four on the last lap of the Daytona 500.

I had watched the Earnhardt name ascend for more than twenty years, so his death meant I would never be the same in covering NASCAR. He carved out his following as Richard Petty gave way to Kyle Petty, as Bobby Allison handed off to Davey, and as Bill Elliott, "Red," my Georgia-born driver, ran with all of them.

I was already entrenched in the sport when Earnhardt's brand took off. I became especially interested in Earnhardt because he won. His name headlined the NASCAR articles in *The Augusta Chronicle* and *Augusta Herald*, the daily newspapers I read growing up. Imagine a six-year-old black girl who followed the Southern race-car circuit with its white-only drivers and owners, and with Confederate flags[71] ever-present at its venues.

Later, as a mature woman and journalist in Dallas, Big E stirred me because of how he behaved as a father with his red-haired son. "Why am I 'senior' now? I'm not that old," he once teased a journalist, referring to the new "Sr." appendage on his name. Joking, but not really.

The elder Earnhardt valued his role as father—and reminded me of my own relationship with my dad. Evidence of Earnhardt's fatherly affection is on display in a poignant video clip of events that took place after a race in Fort Worth, Texas. The scene plays in my mind even to this day.

It is the year 2000, and Dale Jr. has just won the DirecTV 500 by a five-second margin over Jeff Burton. As the custom goes, the pit crew runs out to retrieve the winning car to push it into Victory Lane. Interviews and celebrations await the victor.

The senior Earnhardt, in the crisp white race jumpsuit of his GM Goodwrench Service team, leaves his Chevy and, while running to join the winners, replaces his own No. 3 baseball cap with the No. 8 of Junior's Budweiser team.

As the car owner and proud dad, Earnhardt Senior aims a wide mustachioed grin at his son when Senior reaches the revelers. Junior, a newcomer to this type of party, starts answering the questions of a television interviewer while still seated in the car. Media-savvy Earnhardt Sr. glides his hand into the window. Senior yanks the shoulder of the red Budweiser race suit to let Junior know to get out of the car. (The better to show the sponsors' logos.)

The younger Earnhardt wraps up his sentence while climbing onto the roof of the Chevrolet. Confetti floats down over the scene. Dad stands back and watches, letting the situation breathe. He ignores

---

71. During the American Civil War, the Confederacy fought to keep the institution of slavery. Thus, some people consider the Confederate flag, or variations of it, a symbol of white racism. Others say that the flag has historical significance and commemorates Southern courage and pride, as well as the thousands of Southern lives lost during the war.

a question from a journalist and focuses on his twenty-five-year-old son, now half-standing and half-crouching on the roof of the car. Junior seems perplexed about how to get down from the perch.

"Come on, come on!" coaxes the older Earnhardt as Junior steps onto the open window and nearly rests his butt on the roof of the car.

Dad Earnhardt extends both arms and wraps them around the waist of his son. Junior unhesitatingly releases into his dad's steady arms. Big E adjusts his son's baseball cap. The scene resembles a moment in which a father helps his five-year-old down from a dangerous height.

Junior, the conqueror of the man-sized 500-mile race, with an average speed of 131.152 mph, welcomes the embrace even in front of the cameras.

"I tell you, he's something else," Earnhardt Sr. says to a reporter.

The Earnhardt vignette illustrates what drew me to NASCAR as a reporter: the interactions among the people, the bloodlines, the cohesion, the teamwork. These are the qualities I began admiring as a child, when I watched sports on TV or in person with my father. I watched his world, the world of sports, of competition, with fair play being a significant part of it all and scoreboard results determining the winner. I knew that when I grew up, I wanted to be a part of that world.

As Earnhardt Jr. had done, I followed the interests of my father. My dad's passion for sports prepared me, though he did not force me in that direction. And as Earnhardt Sr. did in Fort Worth, my dad stood back at a safe distance once I graduated beyond my training wheels, but he always let me know he was only an arm's length away.

"I'm so proud of you I can hardly stand it," Dad told me back in 2007. I knew Earnhardt Sr. felt that same emotion on the Fort Worth track.

Racing Fans Matter

On the day Earnhardt died, I found myself on the receiving end of a phone call from the KDFW crew that was more than one thousand miles away in Florida. The producer on the trip needed to ask me a few questions.

I never considered pouting about the injustice of losing an assignment I had earned. I did not say, as some might have said, "If the station had done the smart and fair thing and sent me on the assignment, instead of someone less qualified for the task, you would already have all the answers you need to run the story." The professional in me, the fan in me, and the daughter in me had suffered a bruised heart with Earnhardt's death. The most important goal for me on that day was to help KDFW deliver credible, respectful reporting to the NASCAR Nation. Millions in that group needed to be informed and consoled.

I offered information freely.

Two months later, the NASCAR show roared into Fort Worth— without Dale Earnhardt Sr. Kevin Harvick drove Richard Childress' Chevy (which Earnhardt had driven), but with a new number, 29, to show respect for the Earnhardt legacy.

In an interview, I asked Junior about the pre-race tributes race tracks were giving to his father. As a daughter, I imagined the flood of emotions I would feel if I were about to face a grueling competition but had just watched a stirring recap of my father's life. I wanted to know how he dealt with his emotions in the cockpit in the moments before the green flag. Engines are revving, people are cheering, and he is remembering special sketches of time with Dad. Dad's voice. Dad's steady hands when he needed them.

Junior told me that the tributes took him out of his race-ready mind. He said he was struggling each time on the starting grid. "You're waiting to do what you need to do—and then you're thinking back," he said. He added that sometimes the Earnhardt name weighed heavily on his shoulders.

Because of Junior's admissions, Eddie Gossage, general manager of Texas Motor Speedway, toned down the Big Bang tribute it had planned for Big E. Gossage had told me on many occasions about his close friendship with Senior, so he would naturally want to present something truly memorable. But out of respect for the feelings that Junior shared on camera with me, Gossage amended the program.

A few other track managers at upcoming races also backed away from the massive retrospectives they had planned. No one in the race game wanted to deepen Junior's pain or keep him from doing more to make Dad proud.

My interaction with Dale Earnhardt Jr. over the years allowed me to produce, in April 2004, a story unlike the others being done the week of NASCAR's Fort Worth weekend. I searched for and developed a creative angle. Junior would turn thirty that year, on October 10. My story looked at Dale Earnhardt's little boy who was now a man. The beauty of the story for the NASCAR Nation was that The Intimidator's little redhead belonged to all of us—because Dale Senior belonged to all of us.

In the one-on-one interview, Junior spoke openly with me. He gave reflective answers about being a young man (for twenty-five years under the tutelage of his skilled father) and about being a thirty-year-old man who had learned much on his own in the five years since his father's passing. I tried to make the report a sensitive and humanizing story for the audience. With Junior's willingness to share his thoughts, I received the material I needed to succeed.[72]

---

72. The author became a voting member of the Texas Motorsports Hall of Fame during her reporting career in Dallas-Fort Worth, the first person representing KDFW-TV with the honor.

CHAPTER 30

A Woman's Racquet

Despite overlooking me for the NASCAR assignment in 2001, KDFW's general manager Kathy Saunders proved to be an integral part of my career advancement. She and news director Maria Barrs agreed to hire me as a sports reporter in June 1999. That had to be some kind of record, two women in non-traditional TV-executive roles hiring me in a non-traditional reporting role. The three of us never discussed that aspect of the business together; we just kept our heads in the game and worked hard.

There are still many television stations in the United States that have never hired women for on-air sports jobs, let alone as news directors and general managers. Kathy, a former account executive, served nearly twenty years as GM for KDFW, a great money-making engine for the Fox group. In chatter amongst my co-workers in the early 2000s, I heard estimations of earnings topping twelve million dollars a year for the Dallas-Fort Worth operation. Published reports years earlier put the financial figures even higher, at more than twenty million dollars annually. I float the financial figures to emphasize the responsibility that fell to all of us on the team, starting with GM Kathy.

To validate in the minds of my managers that I was doing something with my grand opportunity, I wrote an extensive self-evaluation in October 2004. It includes descriptions of unique and in-depth stories involving the current starting quarterback of the Cowboys, a NASCAR superstar, a Hall of Fame Cowboy, a soon-to-be-inducted

Hall of Fame Cowboy, and a world-class cycling champion. I also mention a story I broke about the family of the highest-paid player in major league baseball. All during one annual evaluation.

October 2004:

> Just like last year, the timing is right for me to write an evaluation of myself. Within hours of getting the assignment, I had two conversations with the mother of the newest Cowboys player, Quincy Morgan. She and other family members will talk to us for our show this week. I developed a relationship with her at least three years ago. This is further evidence that my Cowboys contacts are unparalleled on the sports reporting staff.

> Quincy Carter appeared for the entire thirty-minute *Sports Sunday* show during the February ratings book because of the relationship he and I have established. Tony Dorsett appeared on Sports Sunday in November. In saying yes to the invitation, he said, "Because you are asking, I'll do it."

> I had a satellite interview with Darrell Waltrip. Everyone on staff felt that I could conduct the best interview because of the subject matter. Waltrip and I discussed unique topics, including the possible reversal of a decision Dale Earnhardt made shortly before his death. (Anything regarding Big-E is big for the NASCAR Nation, and that's a huge audience.) No one on staff even knew of the Earnhardt angle.

Le Tour de France:

2004 was our most extensive coverage of the Tour de France and it should have been. Lance Armstrong achieved what no one in one hundred-plus years of the event had done. I returned from France to air a *Sports Sunday* feature package, a Thursday night package (both with stand-ups in France) and then an "Open Mike" segment with my opinions about the competition, Lance's chances, and behind-the-scenes photos I took.

Anchoring:

I have improved as an anchor. The evidence is on the tape.

In the same evaluation, under a section I called "Sharing the Wealth," I wrote:

I had a lot to offer the shows. I had been compiling interviews with high-profile fathers since the spring. Also, Alex Rodriguez brought up the topic of parenting and fatherhood with me—in the spring. Because I have known him since 1993, I continued the discussion with him on tape for the station's benefit.

A-Rod's wife was pregnant by the time the show aired. No one in the market had A-Rod talking about fatherhood.

Pro Football Hall of Fame:

Every evaluation gives me a chance to lay out how I've become the go-to reporter for Cowboys of the past. Future Hall of Fame inductee Rayfield

> Wright (...) told me that whatever I ask, he will do
> in the way of sports coverage.
>
> He promises to do it "First on Fox."

For these unique reports, KDFW-TV had rewarded me hand-somely with two contract renewals from 1999 to 2004. My first three-year contract, secured in July 1999, paid seventy thousand dollars a year, with programmed raises of three thousand dollars each year. In July 2004, I accepted the station's new offer, which had jumped to ninety thousand dollars a year.

Slow and steady, I felt, in regards to my increasing pay. For the next contract, I was scheduled to earn ninety-four thousand dollars a year. An equitable exchange, in my view, for all the formerly untold stories I had captured for our viewers.

A Little Mo in Tennis

While representing KDFW at a Girls Inc. empowerment luncheon in 2001, I introduced myself and started a conversation with a woman seated next to me. Playfully following up on a suggestion from one of the program's speakers, I asked her to share a recent success in her life. I expected nothing more than a pleasant exchange of words covering light subjects. However, my nibble at politeness would lead me into an intimate encounter with sports history.

The beaming and vibrant woman told me she was releasing a book, a long-running project, about the positive messages she had received from her mother. (File this exclusive story under You Never Know What You'll Discover During Polite Table Talk with a Stranger.) "My mother was Little Mo," the woman began to explain. "She was— "

I cut her off excitedly, unable to believe my ears. "I know Little Mo! I know that she won the Grand Slam as a teenager! I know—"

The woman interrupted me, hopping onto my enthusiastic response. "I have the Wimbledon trophies at home! I have all my mom's trophies!"

The woman turned out to be Cindy Brinker Simmons, president of a public-relations firm and daughter of a tennis legend.

My heart pounded, and in that instant I felt as breathless at the white-linen luncheon as I had felt when absorbing the unbelievable baseball comebacks in Seattle.

Maureen Connolly conquered women's tennis from 1951 to 1954—while she was in her teens. She won her first Wimbledon championship at age seventeen. Fortunately for the sport, she played with urgency. She compiled a lengthy string of wins in her three years of top-level tennis.[73]

All this I knew, so I asked Cindy if I could do a story about the book she was releasing, *Little Mo's Legacy: A Mother's Lessons, A Daughter's Story.*[74] We would air the story Mother's Day weekend.

Cindy agreed.

I entered Cindy's sunlit Dallas home on the day of the interview. She opened the massive front door, displaying a radiant smile. As I absorbed the warmth of her greeting, I inhaled the sweet smell of fresh-cut flowers. I spotted the gorgeous bouquet overflowing with color and fragrance and told Cindy how lovely it was.

She led me through the foyer. As we turned into the kitchen/family-room area, I spotted another impressive floral arrangement. She and I had interrupted each other's sentences at the luncheon; we seemed to have the same thoughts to blurt. At her home, it happened again. As I cycled through a creative way to compliment her home, including the second display of flowers, Cindy seemed to read my mind. She explained, "Mom always had fresh flowers around. She always wanted us to have joy in our home."

Cindy motioned to the solid dark wood shelf behind me and to the right of the entrance through which I had come. I looked back.

---

73. In 1953, Maureen Connolly won four international tournaments known as the Grand Slam of tennis. She secured the wins within one calendar year, an accomplishment later achieved by only two other female players, Margaret Court and Steffi Graf. Not only was Connolly honored by the Associated Press as Female Athlete of the Year in 1951, 1952, and 1953, she was the number-one ranked female tennis player in the world in 1952, 1953, and 1954. See espn.com. Though dominant against their competition, Martina Navratilova and Serena Williams each needed one more Grand Slam title, in 1984 and 2015, respectively, to achieve a Grand Slam of tennis, also known as a Calendar Slam. See espn.com.

74. Cindy Brinker Simmons with Robert Darden, *Little Mo's Legacy: A Mother's Lessons, A Daughter's Story* (Irving, Texas: Tapestry Press, 2001).

Was it the aroma of flowers or the sparkling silver images? I'm not sure, but one of those things made my belly flinch with happy excitement.

Three Wimbledon platters!

We have all seen Steffi, or Serena and Venus, or Martina and Chris, or Billie Jean raising the Rosewater Dish triumphantly overhead.[75] Wimbledon presents to the women's singles winner the ornately decorated platter. Its motif includes Roman mythological figures such as Minerva and Temperance. The ovolo molding adds African and Islamic art to the design.

And now, there they were, three of these precious platters, three silver goddesses of triumph, looking back at me.

I studied them from a distance. Cindy urged me to move closer.

"You can touch them," I heard her say.

So, I did.

I carefully placed my hands where surely the champion herself had once placed her triumphant young hands.

Measuring eighteen inches in diameter, each Rosewater Dish by itself leaves an impression. But here were three, dating back to the 1950s. They were more than home accessories. Each was the precious payoff earned by a diminutive yet dominant teenaged athlete I had long admired.

I was not born when five-foot-four Little Mo was competing. I learned of her as I schooled myself about historic sports performances. No internet at the time, so I used books, magazine articles, and TV sports programs to learn about her. Thus, I had always known her story and always felt a fire of kinship with her. Just as I had done, she determined at a young age to pursue a goal—and reached it.

Now, I stood in her daughter's home, in the presence of the storied trophies that represented part of Mo's career. I had touched the proof of her greatness. Being there, for me, ranks second only to the sensory fulfillment I received from Rosa Parks' maternal embrace.

---

75. Steffi Graf, sisters Serena Williams and Venus Williams, Martina Navratilova, Chris Evert, and Billie Jean King are all Wimbledon winners and among the most famous athletes of all time.

Connolly's competitive days ended just weeks after her 1954 Wimbledon trophy. She broke her leg in a horseback-riding accident. Retirement, marriage to pioneering restaurateur Norman Brinker,[76] a move to Dallas, Texas, and the births of two children followed. The retired star had adapted joyfully to the life she was creating when a diagnosis of ovarian cancer interrupted her new game plan.

When Maureen Connolly Brinker passed away at age thirty-four after two years of illness, Cindy, the older of Maureen's daughters, was twelve. Though she lost her mother at so young an age, she fought to fan the flames of blessedness her mother had instilled in her. Thirty years after Little Mo's passing, I saw evidence of that joy in the warmth coming from forty-two-year-old Cindy. She explained to me that life must be *lived*, in whatever form and for whatever length of time. Her book outlines that lesson as part of a list of seven that she learned from her famous racquet-swinging mother.

For my broadcast package of Cindy's story, I edited in the lovely Nat King Cole and Natalie Cole duet "Unforgettable." I alternated my narrated voice track with the smooth vocals of the world-famous father-daughter singers. The story of Maureen Connolly's daughter, another exclusive in the Dallas-Fort Worth TV market, prominently featured video of the Wimbledon trophies and shots of the sunny home that Cindy Brinker Simmons built for her family. She suggested we shoot the grave of Little Mo in a nearby cemetery. We did.

Maureen Connolly's nickname comes from the American battleship the *USS Missouri*. The abbreviation for the state of Missouri is "MO." A battleship is not an easy thing to stop even when it has been hit by a bomb. The same was true of Connolly, whether facing groundstrokes returned at bruising speeds or the explosive hit of cancer.

---

76. Cindy Brinker's father, Norman Brinker, made casual dining mainstream in America with his Steak & Ale and Bennigan's chains, as well as his acquisition and expansion of other brands, including Chili's. He is credited with making the concept of the restaurant salad bar a national custom. See William Grimes, "Norman Brinker, Casual Dining Innovator, Dies at 78," *The New York Times*, June 9, 2009.

On the Medal Podium

I touched sporting supremacy another time in 2001, with a beloved Olympic champion. The Women's Business Council-Southwest of Arlington, Texas, made me an offer that put me on the podium with Jackie Joyner-Kersee. The group needed someone to introduce the American three-time Olympic gold medalist, who had agreed to be the keynote speaker at its upcoming luncheon. The executive director called me at Fox 4.

"When we landed Jackie Joyner-Kersee, the members of our group all asked, 'Who should we get to introduce her?' You were the unanimous choice," the group's director informed me. Could I find time in my sportscaster schedule, she continued, to attend the event and introduce the retired champion-turned-humanitarian and author?

I needed no convincing; as soon as I heard the words "Jackie Joyner-Kersee is on the program," I knew I would arrange my plans so that I could see the track-and-field queen for a second time.

On the day of the luncheon, before my gratifying moment of sharing a podium with sports royalty, JJK and I had a private exchange. She told me that it pleased her to see me again and that she had found our discussion in Seattle in 1996 to be meaningful and memorable.

Wow. JJK had remembered me! Along with the numerous international reporters she had to have met while competing in four Olympic Games from 1984 to 1996,[77] she filed away her basketball postgame interview with me.

The knowledge that Jackie had remembered me meant more than she could know. At the time, at least one of my bosses had written, in my annual employee review, that I was repeatedly failing to make an impact.

Well—the great Olympian Jackie Joyner-Kersee told me something different.

---

77. Jackie Joyner-Kersee (she married her coach, Bob Kersee, in 1986) competed for the United States and earned Olympic medals in Los Angeles (1984); Seoul, South Korea ('88); Barcelona ('92); and Atlanta ('96). She dominated the Olympic heptathlon and long-jump events throughout her career. Despite advancements in technology and training used by athletes around the world over the last three decades, Joyner-Kersee still held, at the time of this book's second printing in 2021, the World Heptathlon Record she set at the 1988 Games in Seoul. See jackiejoynerkersee.com.

CHAPTER 31

Introducing America's Quarterbacks

The bread-and-butter stories in Dallas-Fort Worth came from the hot news associated with the Cowboys players. My years in the television market intersected with one such hot ticket.

Quincy Carter arrived in Dallas in 2001 and won a preeminent sports position as starting quarterback.[78] As two natives of Georgia living in Texas, our shared place of upbringing gave us an immediate connection during our first meeting. This feeling of closeness with Quincy put me in a supreme position, professionally. To gain access to the starting quarterback, I did not need approval from Cowboys media director Rich Dalrymple's office. I could dispense with protocol because the quarterback trusted me. I enjoyed the privilege.

Of course, I did not share commonalities only with black athletes from Georgia. When quarterback Drew Bledsoe[79] arrived in Dallas in 2005 after his playing days with the Seattle Seahawks, I made sure I let him know that we had two things in common.

"I saw the article with you and your son on your motorcycle," I said to him one day in the Dallas locker room.

Drew looked sheepish. "Yeah, I know I'm supposed to wear a helmet," he admitted.

---

78. The Decatur, Georgia, native played 31 regular-season games and one playoff game for Dallas from 2001 to January 2004.

79. Drew Bledsoe, a native of Ellensburg, Washington, played 22 games for the Cowboys in 2005 and 2006. He replaced Quincy Carter. Bledsoe played 14 seasons in the NFL. During his college career, he was quarterback for the Washington State Cougars, a team the author of this book covered from 1995 to 1997.

We laughed quietly as if one of us were confessing to eating the last chocolate-chip cookie. I realized he had misunderstood my motive. He thought my remark had been a scolding.

"I was thinking about something *else*," I clarified. "I was going to say that I enjoyed riding my motorcycle, too, when I lived in Seattle."

We laughed again. Drew relaxed. Though his motorcycle riding later became fodder for other journalists, in me, Bledsoe found a person who also had lived in beautiful Seattle and embraced the freedom of traveling on two wheels through its scenic landscape.

It was usually a challenge to get in private words with the star players during the open locker-room period. Still, I always made it my mission to have a hushed conversation with an athlete. I wanted each one to get used to interacting with me personally and, thus, return my questions with personal reflections. The Cowboys locker room wasn't designed for that. Reporters had to routinely step around one another and invade another's personal space while pointing cameras and boom microphones at Emmitt Smith, Troy Aikman, Terrell Owens, and Joey Galloway—some of the interview magnets.

NFL rules set the roster limit at fifty-three men for the regular season, so at least that many players could be in the locker room at the same time. The rectangular room had eighty or so lockers. The lockers of the high-profile players were positioned at points relatively far from one another. This was supposed to provide plenty of gathering room around each popular player. Still, more often than not, I found myself shoulder-to-shoulder in the cluster of journalists surrounding a superstar. In that atmosphere, we reporters got to know one another—and one another's work—well. A player's clever answer to one reporter's well-researched question ended up in everybody's sportscast, or in everybody's newspaper story.

The arrival of Quincy Carter changed that for me during my early days in Dallas. Buoyed by the stories I got from inside the Carter camp and away from the locker room, I was able to separate myself from the crowd.

For three seasons, I cultivated a super relationship not only with Quincy, but also with his mother, Sherry Carter-Embree. A cheerful woman and supportive parent, Sherry wore lovely cowboy hats adorned with sequins and Quincy's No. 17. She and I chatted together before games, at the team's charitable events held in Dallas, even in those luxury hotels the journalists and players shared during weekend road trips.

Mrs. Carter-Embree made my Dallas years more fulfilling because she offered me a feminine outlet in the midst of football, football, and more football. My many female friends followed the team, so they would want to talk about the Cowboys with me. With Sherry, we tackled every topic under the sun; we could back-burner football.

Thanks to Sherry, I knew most of Quincy's comings and goings. Nothing too personal, but if a journalist could transform it into something newsworthy, Sherry would tell me first. For example, during a road trip to Atlanta, the family's home base, Sherry clued me in to a private gathering in which Gene and Jerry Jones were to meet Quincy's high school coach and his Atlanta-area support system.

My photographer and I covered the meetup. We broadcast the video and the interviews no other reporter had uncovered during my weekend coverage of the NFL team. It was unparalleled.

TV gold.

Sharing the Fortune

Before one of the regular-season games, Quincy hosted a barbecue at his home, his mother informed me. The offensive linemen were the guests, she said, because Quincy wanted to show them how much he appreciated their keeping the defensive players away from him.

I went on television with that morsel of information during the pregame show. I reinforced it with statistics showing how infrequently Quincy had been sacked during play. Sports fans like to hear these types of tales. They want to know about the relationships that exist among athletes off the playing field. Because of this, I always worked the angles within the team, honestly and professionally. At the right time, I shared the fruits of my field research.

One of those years, to capitalize on the hype of the season-opener for the Cowboys, my KDFW-TV boss Kevin Morrell asked me to deliver the starting quarterback for an interview.

No, Kevin informed me, *I* was not going to conduct the interview; it was to be done live by the sports anchor from our studio.

No problem. I'm a team player, I told myself. Because I grew up a Cowboys fan outside of Texas, it thrilled me to facilitate getting the top-of-the-line interview on television for the sake of the viewers who did not live in Texas. I wanted to provide a service to others who felt about the team the way I had felt when I was growing up. So, I asked Quincy to do the exclusive with Fox 4—though not with me.

Quincy agreed. Sports anchor and white male colleague Marc Fein got the plum assignment.

"A live interview with the quarterback of America's Team!" Marc marveled, gazing at me with what looked like disbelief and appreciation. He knew it was unusual for a contacts-rich reporter to not balk at setting up for another journalist such a prestigious assignment.

He was right. No matter what story I developed and kept for myself that day, it would find secondary status, or lower, behind the sweet Quincy story I had gleefully handed off to Marc.

The following season, I secured the Quincy season-opening live assignment for Marc a second time. He was just as excited as he had been the first time. To be the person in the chair for an interview that carried with it the gravitas of a national story—what anchor wouldn't get excited?

And Marc wasn't the only colleague with whom I shared some of these treasures. One of the three times that Quincy opened the season as starting QB for America's Team, lead sports anchor Mike Doocy benefited from my fieldwork and interviewed Quincy live from the studio. Viewers could not see that I was at Quincy's house, off camera. Yet, another white male colleague appeared on TV with the quarterback after I made it possible.

When the station asked me to set up the interview, I could have easily said that Quincy was not available. But I didn't. I never shortchanged the sports team or the viewers who expected Fox 4 to show them something a cut above the rest.

In addition to assignments that put my sports-anchor colleagues in a good light, I used my relationship with Quincy to do an unusual favor for my boss. Kevin wanted me to arrange a visit by the starting quarterback of the Cowboys to his son's school. I willingly took on the task, though I was not sure if Quincy would find it a valuable use of his free time. I told Quincy how over the moon his young followers would be to meet him—and that the gesture would keep my sports boss in my corner.

He agreed to the visit.

I finalized everything, provided Quincy with the address of the school, and told him the best time to arrive during the school assembly.

Just as he repeatedly did on the field, Quincy delivered on his end of our deal. He showed up on cue, igniting cheers and joyful shrieks from the kids. We shot a story, one that the other stations missed.

Dismissal of the Mighty Quin

The Carter era in Dallas fell apart at the start of the training camp in Oxnard, California, in 2004—what would have been Quincy's fourth year in the NFL and with the franchise.

A telephone call came in to me at my KDFW desk from our California reporting crew, which included anchor Mike, executive sports producer Kevin, probably another male producer, and the photographers.

"Do you have a phone number for Quincy?" one of my colleagues asked. I do not recall which frantic male voice I heard.

"Of course," I answered.

"Well, he left camp! We need to talk to him!"

Before that phone call, I had not heard that the morning's practice had started without Quincy. He was expected to begin the year as the returning starting quarterback.

"Quincy's been cut! We need to know where he is," my colleague informed me.

Shock and disappointment hit me like a one-two combination.

I felt the sting for Quincy. I also knew that if his departure were a finality, I would be losing my direct line to accurate information about the most important team in our TV market.

"I'll call him and I'll get back to you," I replied.

No answer on Quincy's phone. Naturally.

Kevin, the sports boss, called me while I was waiting for a call-back from the message I had left on Quincy's cell phone. I told Kevin that I called every contact I had for Quincy: mom, coach from high school. No one answered, I explained.

Our crew in California was cut off from the information, cut off from Quincy. If I had been sent on the assignment I legitimately earned, I would have had a better grip on what happened and on how to get some reaction from the missing quarterback. Quincy's closest personal connections present in California might even have talked with me on camera.

Unfortunately, because the station had decided that Quincy's media confidante did not deserve the assignment, I was one thousand four hundred miles away from the scene. The staffing decisions by KDFW left the station ill-equipped to lead the Dallas market—and, indeed, the entire country—with that story. It could have been different.

Quincy left the team's camp that day in August 2004. The fallen star remained interesting to Dallas viewers long after the thirty-two games he played for the city. No one was better positioned than I to tell his story as it developed.

Interestingly, with Quincy's departure came a drop in positive feedback in my job evaluations. Did the flawed thinking of previous news manager Bill Cummings trail me from West Virginia to the top-five market of Dallas? Was I incapable of reporting reliably if my interview subjects and subject matter were not linked to my race? In other words: The black quarterback is out, so we cannot expect black reporter Nita to generate up-close stories on other sports personalities.

I hope not. That would be a sweeping and disparaging indictment of my former employer, if not of the entire broadcasting industry. I want to believe in sensible, reflective, smart personnel decisions based on training, experiences, and demonstrated merit.

Besides, I had more than proven myself capable of handling athletes and stories that had culturally diverse appeal. I intentionally and wisely built bonds with numerous team leaders. In addition to the up-close story angles about Quincy, I created an unparalleled dossier of reports on another Dallas-area athlete, someone with national appeal that I began following to Europe for reports as early as 2001. I played up my international work by writing the following in my self-evaluation in October 2004:

> This is the year I will cover the Tour de France for the fourth time and provide the market's most in-depth reports of Lance Armstrong[80] and the phenomenon of American pro cycling.

> I've completed nearly two years of college-level study of the French language. I am the only sports staff member who speaks a language that was not endemic to his/her birthplace.

> This demonstrates my consistent willingness to enhance my skills to benefit my station. (October 2004)

In addition to the thrill I got from reporting beside journalists from around the world at the Tour de France, the glimpses I got

---

80. Born in Plano, Texas, in 1971, Lance Armstrong survived testicular cancer as well as tumors that spread to his abdomen, lungs, lymph nodes, and brain. As a professional cyclist, he won the Tour de France seven times between 1999 and 2007. In 2012, the U.S. Anti-Doping Agency stripped Armstrong of all wins from 1998 forward due to evidence of performance-enhancing drug use. During an exclusive interview with Oprah Winfrey in January 2013, Lance admitted to doping. (This information is compiled from the author's interview with Linda Armstrong, mother of the cyclist, in 1999; the cyclist's 2013 Oprah interview; and livestrong.org, previously the official website for Lance Armstrong information.)

of European living began to catch my interest. Here I was, a child who had grown up not dreaming of foreign travels or being curious about what else there could be for me in the wide-open world. After a day-long visit to France's Louvre Museum in January 2001 and my barrier-breaking reports on the Tour, I began to wonder whether listening to my inner child had limited my adult possibilities.

My inner child had always screamed for Dallas, but suddenly I had to ask myself, *Why am I so drawn to Dallas?* Of course, I knew the answer: the marvelous Cowboys. But now I was forced to ponder a new question: Why had I never thought to dream *beyond* Dallas?

CHAPTER 32

Uprooted

Quincy Carter confessed to me in one of our post-Cowboys exclusive interviews that he gave away his job. Handed over the reins of the hottest job in pro sports, he said, because of his self-sabotage and faulty decision-making. He said he alone put himself in position to fail. When on camera with me, he admitted marijuana use. Tremendous social pressures accompanied his walk of fame, his lead-athlete status, and he had succumbed.

I understood Quincy's pressure-cooker existence, most likely in a way few people do. Or, more accurately, few people would readily admit being in a crucible, if they understood that they were. During the final years of my career in television, I was one who would not admit it, even though I was headed toward my own melting point.

Daily in the mid-2000s, I battled internally to reassure myself that I still had control over the events of my career, control over something. The troubled feeling reawakened in me the turbulent times I faced with my news directors in Huntington and Augusta—and, to a lesser extent, with my sports director in Seattle.

Intractable and unseen forces in the Dallas workplace were defeating my personal cheerleading. The television overlords were selecting other journalists for prime assignments that my expertise should have brought to me: the 2001 Daytona 500, which proved to be an unparalleled racing tragedy with the death of Dale Earnhardt, and the opening week of the 2004 Cowboys training camp in which Quincy Carter lost his job. In both cases, I had the inside edge, the training,

222 Civil Rights Baby

and the specialization. I could have performed the best work for the employer and the viewers. Despite this, other journalists received the assignments. I received their long-distance phone calls looking for guidance on the stories.

Would I forever face such insults? Would I never experience the sweetness of exerting myself in a workplace where no one kept doors of opportunity pressed shut in my face? Where I received roles and assignments for no other reason except that I was qualified?

I felt trapped. On one side were my own standards of professional integrity. On the other side were the expectations and demands of my employers and colleagues. When the latter requested that I share with them my valuable contacts, I did so. The station was a team, after all, and a good teammate takes actions in support of the team.

But my sharing often benefited my colleagues more than it did my reporting portfolio.

Still, life for me was not bad in Dallas. I had valuable experience—no one could erase that. I had the trust of my contacts. I had pleasant, professional interactions with many of my colleagues. Plus, I had a salary of more than ninety thousand dollars a year.

That high pay might have contributed to my problem.

Negative evaluations of my job performance started after July 2005, when my pay increased to ninety-four thousand dollars, as stipulated in the previous year's two-year contract. Under the *comments/goals* section in an evaluation I received at that time, I was instructed to improve my storytelling and use my contacts to "develop hard-hitting stories. Nita needs to be breaking news with her contacts," wrote Maria Barrs, news director.

Turning up the pressure for me to get it together, Maria scheduled me for another employee review, a mere three months later, instead of a full year later. In the ninety days between my two evaluations, Fox 4 had developed a harsher performance-evaluation document called the Performance Appraisal.

I received a 2 out of a possible high score of 5.

The alarming words "probation," "disciplinary action," and "discharge," for anyone who received a "1" or "unsatisfactory," stared back at me when I read the new document. The follow-up evaluation repeated the stern words from three months earlier: "Nita needs to be breaking news with her contacts."

I *was* breaking stories, though the managers were not reflecting it on the evaluations. My sports boss Kevin once asked, with admiration in his eyes, "How do you find these stories?" He saluted the family football-drama story I had produced for a segment of Fox 4's family-oriented Cotton Bowl game preview show for January 1, 2005. My unique story replaced Kevin's idea to rehash the waffling by a college quarterback over his choice of a school.

My exclusive story relived the successful gender-equality campaign launched by the wife of University of Tennessee Coach Phil Fulmer. Vicky Fulmer fought for the right of the Fulmer daughters to assist their father on the sidelines during college games. The sons of coaches already had the privilege of doing so. The practice was roundly applauded throughout the Southeastern Conference (a league of university sports).

During the interview, Vicky Fulmer vowed that she was not going to let any boys engage in any activity in support of an SEC football team—as long as her girls were barred from engaging in the same activity. I interviewed two of the Fulmer daughters, most likely the youngest two, Brittany and Allison, who beamed proudly when they spoke of the stand their mother took.

The story made prominent the issues of social and gender justice, and it evoked strong emotions in the woman at its center. As she spoke to me for the camera, Vicky Fulmer lowered her voice and set her face in a resolute expression to punctuate her immovability over the cause. She was clearly determined to defeat any would-be obstructionists.

I needed Vicky Fulmer's determination; I had become an easy target for non-renewal of contract.

TV stations seek to make money and to cut costs—no surprise in that. To help achieve this goal, the budget scalpel exorcises the older female journalists quicker than it does the males. Signs of aging and even extra pounds are not factors that automatically send a male TV journalist's career rushing toward the grave. Many experienced male reporters in my age range earned the same attractive salary that I did, a salary that signaled success, but they did so without incident.

A woman? Better to inject some youth into the on-air staff. It's the *un*-secret secret of the industry. Everyone in the business knows this.

Oh, and better create a paper file to support your ouster campaign.

The imbalance of control in the TV newsrooms is the same dynamic that the Me Too movement exposed in the entertainment business. Complaints of abusive actions toward women, marked by unchecked sexual misconduct, including rape, gained force after 2017 and flipped the table on some of the aggressors.[81] [82]

As a teenager, I suspected my television career would have an early expiration date. Too many female journalists faced limited TV lifespans. The example of 37-year-old co-anchor Christine Craft underscores this fact. Hired in 1981 by KMBC-TV in Kansas City, Missouri (Metromedia, Inc.), Craft said in her 1983 discrimination lawsuit that she was shifted from the studio to reporting duties because management felt she looked too old for the role of female anchor. These events overlapped the beginning of my university studies in pursuit of a communications degree in 1982.

Two decades later, it looked as if I were to follow in Craft's footsteps and down the road known to many capable female broadcasters. In this round of my employment clash, ageism, not necessarily sexism and racism, presented itself as my foe. I fully expected the July 2005

81. By late 2020, a conservative count would show 200 men who lost their positions of influence in film, TV and entertainment, and university sports in the U.S. Movie producer Harvey Weinstein was convicted of third-degree rape and sexual assaults, and other charges against him are pending in 2021.

82. Julie Burton, president of the Women's Media Center, says: "With Me Too exposing horrible individual and institutional practices, we see an opportunity for a new transparency and permanent changes aimed at greater equality and power for women." Gloria Steinem, co-founder of the Women's Media Center, says, "Naming sexualized violence makes it visible and subject to prosecution."
Source: https://womensmediacenter.com/reports/media-and-metoo-how-a-movement-affected-press-coverage-of-sexual-assault. Both quotes from Women's Media Center website, accessed May 10, 2021.

contract to be my last one. It was not, but it was the last time KDFW showed on paper a positive appraisal of my work. The subsequent contract—the one offered by KDFW in July 2006—would reveal the truth. If there were no pay increase, there would be no future for me at the station.

My Lonely State

I had some outlets to release the emotional steam building inside of me. Frolicking with my dog Pepper, practicing hatha and restorative yoga, riding my bike at White Rock Lake, and landscaping the corner lot of my Dallas home helped, but they were not enough for me to recover from the arrows of resistance that regularly stung me at KDFW.

What made the Dallas days particularly difficult is that I had not cultivated emotional intimacy. I had not provided it to anyone on a sustained level, and I had not earned it from anyone. The way I vacantly failed the people in the significant relationships in my private life came back to haunt me. My dad knew about my travails, but I chose not to unload the entire miserable burden on him. Professionally, I could not tell just anybody about my struggle. Confiding in someone would be the equivalent of handing over dangerous ammunition to someone who might possibly be an enemy. Besides, no one in television wants to latch onto a colleague who is obviously on the manager's short list for the chopping block.

For these reasons, I did not bare my soul to anyone.

Over the years, I had developed friendships within the television industry with other women, some black, but not all. When I would have meals or go clubbing or shopping with the women, we would leave behind conversations about work. We were living the same experiences, by and large, so there was no need to disclose anything in conversation.

Even those in the more traditional role of newswoman suffered some form of beatdown. One day, a friend who was an anchorwoman stopped me in the hallway of our TV station. Normally a composed woman, that day her face was flushed. The newsroom managers had just told her—as they had repeatedly done—that to keep her job as a studio newsreader, she would have to straighten her hair. They wanted her to consistently wear a smooth, flat hairstyle.

My colleague was neither black nor white; her gorgeous face and expressive almond-shaped eyes resulted from mixed ancestry—from her mother's Pacific Island ethnicity and from several European countries on her father's side. Her hair was a beautiful dark mane of curly tresses. But the hair had suffered. She pushed back her bangs and the hair at the temple to show me the damage. I saw patches where strands had broken because she had hot-combed her hair or applied chemical relaxers.

How ridiculous that a talented journalist with a college degree has to endure this to hold on to a job.

Despite my friend's warm delivery and polished work in the anchor chair, the station did not renew her contract. However, she resurfaced as a national studio newsreader on one of America's twenty-four-hour channels. I smiled happily when I saw her sable-colored, shoulder-skimming tendrils hanging loosely. The dark ringlets she had inherited from her mother accentuated her beaming face. To me, they represented a victory—a rejection of the nonsensical demands of our local TV bosses.

She may not have won completely, though. A few times, I tuned in and saw that her ethnic beauty was again disguised with a straightened or flat-ironed hairstyle.

Deflating stories like hers—what she endured when we were workmates—were the reason none of us female journalists wanted to talk about the job during our off hours. To escape reminders of the job, I mostly chose friends who were not broadcasters. This included a self-employed accountant and a flight attendant, while I was in Seattle, and a tech-industry headhunter, when I was in Dallas. As for my platonic male friends, none of whom were journalists, we fell into watching sports events—so, conversation not necessary.

I did not confess my career worries to anyone. I kept my disappointment at such a low simmer that many of my Dallas colleagues thought all was superb in my sphere. By the time I landed in Dallas, I had stopped seeking new female friends in the industry, so I did not hang out with the women in the KDFW newsroom.

Most of my colleagues realized that my time away from the office meant an unplugging from them, as well. My private life became such a curiosity that one co-worker I liked a lot, a respected, black, live-truck engineer named Rodney Kyle, playfully asked:

"What is it that makes Nita Wiggins happy?"

He posed the question in the manner of a reporter, using my first and last names. He paused after the question, an expectant expression on his face. I imagine he had seen me use that technique during interviews.

"Travel," I responded simply, and I smiled.

I traveled much during my Dallas decade. Having the money, plus the patience to endure a ten-hour flight, I found flying to Europe a strong fix. Even more, flying across the Atlantic Ocean provided some elixir for my troubles. I yearned to put many miles between me and the smothering negative web of the workplace. After my maiden voyage to Paris in 2001, I returned home to jump into French-immersion classes. Learning the foreign language and culture effectively diverted some of my energy away from my workplace battles.

Despite my coping strategies, I reached my mental basement by late 2005. I speculated often about the reasons the managers fabricated a false paper file of my journalistic failures. I never solved the question with any certainty, but I continued to fight for survival. I defended myself in every self-evaluation, but I knew—Don't we all know?—that employees never win against ouster campaigns.

Is my career really ending? I would ask myself. *And where could I thrive as an over-the-hill, former TV journalist?*

To be proactive, I began exploring ways I could rescue myself professionally. From the outset of the negative evaluations, I floated a personal trial balloon, one that carried considerable emotional pain. *Where could I live happily, if not in Dallas? Could I really muster the courage to move to a foreign country?* I had always been one who runs *to* something, not from something. I was not going to change that successful pattern in my forties. So, I started looking for something alluring.

A Malicious Church

I was uncontrollably aiding in my exit from TV because my body was beginning to misbehave. My waistline was expanding with no fewer than three fibroid tumors below the belt. The largest of the tumors grew to the size of a grapefruit.

I could not disguise it every day. Having a belly the size of a four-month pregnancy would not be the worst thing in the world—if I were pregnant. Not being so gave the appearance of a lack of attention to fitness or an affection for undisciplined living. In the minds of television managers, the look, regardless of the reason, was out of synch with the atmosphere of sports, athleticism, competition, and the expectations of a woman's look on TV. Additionally, stress lines creased my face and showed too often in my stand-ups.

That is why one of the unseen forces torpedoing me at work, my photographer colleague Fred Church, became a critical factor in my battle to stay afloat. I needed to have the most flattering camerawork, but Fred had repeatedly given me the opposite. His videos of me displayed a variety of technical problems: harsh overhead shadows or uneven lighting; insufficient lighting; and the use of the gold side of the reflector, which gave me a shiny face. The silver side of the reflector would have filled shadows with a cool hue, not one that left a sweat-soaked appearance.

If a video-production teacher were grading the videos, he would have flunked the shooter. Our KDFW boss Kevin also had seen enough of Fred's poor-quality video of me.

"You need to use a plug-in light," Kevin instructed Fred during the plum assignment of following the Cowboys at their training camp at the Alamodome in San Antonio, Texas.

To ensure that I would look unflattering in the video, Fred had chosen to do bad work on that all-important road assignment. To me, this audacity indicated Fred's belief that he was untouchable. (At some stations—in Paris, France, for example—the names of the videographer and others who work on a report appear on screen at the end of the video package. If KDFW had identified team members on stories, Fred could have been held accountable for the bad-quality video because his name would have been regularly linked with the images.)

Kevin told Fred to use an electric light because the battery-powered light did not have enough juice to make a real difference on brown skin in tough lighting conditions. Fred did not need this advice; he already knew which lighting he should use for me. In the No. 4 Nielsen market, a photographer has enough experience and the requisite equipment to do a quality job. Failure to perform appropriately is a choice.

Immediately after our boss gave him the directive, Fred obeyed; he used the electric light for a period of time. But his practice of using inconsistent lighting for my reports would rear up time and again during my nine years in Dallas.

Why Fred did what he did might not be clear, but that he did what he did *on purpose* is indisputable. He inadvertently left evidence on tape.

He and I were shooting a story inside the basketball arena at Southern Methodist University. As our boss had ordered, we carried an electric light with us, along with the camera and tripod. We located a place in the upper seats for the stand-up. I had learned my lines and told him I was ready to go.

He pressed the *record* button on the camera. The tape rolling, I began, "Three, two, one..."—counting down to the beginning of my statements. I was barely three words into the text when Fred interrupted me with the words, "No, I don't like the shot. Let's try it outside."

OK, I thought. I had no problem doing extra work to make a shot look good.

Having lugged the equipment into the seats, we packed everything and headed down to the exit. Outside, we set up once again. I modified my statements to reflect being outside.

Later, I saw the results. The results Fred wanted.

He shot the stand-up with the camera pointed up at me, showing the basketball arena in the backdrop. Though the lighting was not horrible, the angle he selected distorted my face and body. Shooting up rarely looks fantastic. So, while I thought we had done extra work to make the shot look good, under Fred's prompting we had worked extra to make the shot look *bad*.

He made the shooting mistake on purpose, but his other mistake made clear what he had been doing for years. He left on tape the few seconds of stand-up we had shot inside the arena. The person I saw on that brief clip looked attractive and engaging—a woman stylishly dressed in well-fitting clothes, someone male and female viewers would want to see on their TV screens again and again. The electric light gave a smooth coating, and the illuminated basketball court behind me nicely illustrated our topic.

No, I don't like the shot, Fred had said. *Let's try it outside.*

No, he did not like the shot. Because everyone else would have.

In addition to damaging my career, Fred's bad photography work was interfering with the goal of building viewer loyalty for the station. On occasions when I introduced myself to members of our public, they would say: "You look better in person. I didn't even know that was you." Or they would say, "I'm sorry to say, but somebody's not shooting you right." Another viewer said: "I don't know who shoots you, but they're not doing a good job." Or, still: "I don't know how to say this, but in person you don't look like the same person I've seen on TV."

Colleagues from competing news organizations asked me several times about my working relationship with Fred. They realized something was out of order. They had seen my flawed stand-ups after they had seen me in person, attractively dressed and beautifully made up to greet the workday and the camera. All admitted that I looked much better in person than I did on TV.

One of these sympathetic competitors, a veteran in the business, speculated that Fred might have found it difficult, because of being a native of Oklahoma, to give full effort to a black female co-worker, especially one who was in a higher position and was self-willed and outspoken.

The words from the veteran journalist sounded like an unfair profiling of Fred—ascribing an attitude to him because of his birthplace. He made the statement because white resistance against black people and their progress is a prominent part of Oklahoma history.[83] I do not accept it when someone makes assumptions about my beliefs based on my Georgia birthplace, so I did not want to accept the suggestion that a well-paid, college-trained television professional had dragged old attitudes of race-based economic jealousy into our workplace. But it was the second time a long-serving Dallas media member hinted at the minefield of sabotage I might face.

I felt frustrated. Had journalism's cornerstones of honesty, fair play, decency, and merit failed to override good ol' boy exclusionary thinking and economic lynching?

To avoid Fred Church's pattern of shooting bad video of me in the field, I began incorporating in-studio stand-ups into my packages. However, having the studio cameraman shoot for my story did not always provide a remedy. Fox was experimenting with using head-to-toe shots for in-studio tapings, and the full-body shot really exposed my stomach paunch. Even if it were somewhat camouflaged by the strategic color-blocking of my outfit or a well-cut dress, I did not exude confidence. I wondered how much attention my belly was grabbing each time I spoke my lines.

Three out of four women of color experience fibroid tumors, my doctor in Dallas had said.

With my condition, I fell on the wrong side of that medical statistic and did not know how to save myself.

---

83. Eyewitness accounts from three centenarians entered the horrors of the 1921 Tulsa Race Massacre and its aftermath into the U.S. Congressional Record in May 2021. Witnesses Viola Fletcher, Lessie Benningfield Randle, and Hughes Van Ellis (ages 107, 106, and 100 years old, respectively) testified that gun-toting white men raided and burned their all-black neighborhood of Greenwood, Oklahoma, located near Tulsa. At least 300 black people died in the melee. (See Endnotes.)

CHAPTER 33

A Dallas *Dog Day Afternoon*

Like many Americans, I had not yet switched from teller banking to online banking in early 2006. For my transactions, I used my bank's branch on Mockingbird Lane in the heart of Dallas.

My visit to the bank one afternoon began like every other visit.

I knew the place well. I had had regular friendly conversations with the tellers over the years, and even with the guards. That day, three tellers were on the job—all, white women and under the age of thirty. Probably college-educated and future banking executives.

I joined the end of the line to wait for one of them. Four or five other bank customers waited ahead of me.

Other than the brief, softly spoken words that passed from a teller to a customer standing at her counter, the spacious room of the bank was silent, with limited actions and movements from those inside. On another day, I might have found the air-conditioned stillness peaceful, but on this day, I found the precise climate control oppressive.

I knew I would have several minutes to stand in line, so I mulled over my life, pondering the current state of my career. I thought about my relationship with my bosses at work, the silent efforts of a colleague to take me down, and how both parties were winning. I was losing all I had fought to attain during my adult years—and everything I had desired since the age of eight.

How can I shake myself out of this career spiral? my own voice asked in my head.

I had contemplated leaving Dallas, yes, but that day in the bank, a more life-altering and extremely ridiculous idea entered my mind.

What if I slip a note to a teller? What if I write, "Give me all your money"?

A customer left the line for his turn at the teller's window. I moved up. A step closer to taking action.

Deep in reflection, I continued the dastardly plan in my head.

I don't have any kind of weapon on me, nor in my car, so no one will think it's a serious demand. It's not as if anyone could prove intent or premeditation. I'll just pass the note and then say, "Psych!" The tellers, the managers, the guard, I'm sure they know what *psych* means. "I'm just kidding. Just psyching you out, fooling around because I'm not in control of my life the way I'd like to be." Yeah. I'll be able to explain it that way.

The three remaining bank customers and I moved up as another one took his turn with a teller.

They all know me here. They know where I work, that I don't really need the money. They talk to me about my sports reports and my international trips. So what if I pass a note? It'll be laughed away.

I tried to recall what was in my purse. I definitely had my reporter's notebook and a pen. I could write a note.

I thought about *Dog Day Afternoon*, the 1975 Warner Bros. classic. The Hollywood film stars Al Pacino as an unlikely bank robber whose simple, nonviolent plan turns into a media circus. Maybe the same could happen to me.

A media circus might be just what I needed.

I can take the attention that comes with being arrested and shout from the treetops about the last fifteen years. I could talk of how crippling the journalism business can be for minority women. I can yell that, for me, it has been a battle to engage in the pursuit of happiness.

I had begun actively building the foundation for my Dallas days when I was still a teenager. Was I about to gut it all in one afternoon?

Again, I thought of the pen and pad in my purse. They seemed to scream for me to reach inside, grab them, and write away my life.

My breathing quickened. I think I heard my heartbeat.

And then a thought rocked me.

What would my father feel?

Not "What would he think?" but "What would he *feel*?"

Remembering how involved Daddy had been in guiding me my entire life, I instantly decided he did not deserve to endure what he would feel. Even if I flamed out under the pressure of job stress, I could not bear the thought of hurting him. The thought of doing so yanked me away from the edge of an emotional abyss.

Once rescued, I experienced another barrage of thoughts. By the time I stood on deck to see the next teller, scenes from my life had faded in and out of my consciousness.

I thought of the question I asked baseball's Cal Ripken Jr. in Seattle on August 21, 1995.

"Can you make it?"

With sixteen games to play before he might eclipse "Iron Horse" Lou Gehrig's record for consecutive games played, Cal chuckled before answering. He appreciated the simplicity and sincerity of the question. He did, indeed, go on to establish the new MLB mark.[84]

It was no laughing matter when I turned the question back on myself. Could *I* make it through this phase of my life and on to something else worthwhile?

I thought of Cowboys player Rayfield Wright and an interview I did at his home in Weatherford, Texas. The Pro Football Hall of Famer and Georgia native confided in me about how it felt to grow up fatherless, to not have a man "covering the home"—his colorful expression. Yet, Wright had persisted and played in five Super Bowls during thirteen Cowboys seasons. Known as "Big Cat," he entered the Pro Football Hall of Fame in 2006.

I thought of Jessie Tuggle, of the Atlanta Falcons, and his first Pro Bowl game. When I interviewed him at his home in Griffin, Georgia, in 1992, Jessie told me that he defied the experts who had predicted he had no chance to achieve what he went on to achieve.[85]

---

84. On September 5, 1995, Cal Ripken Jr. tied Lou Gehrig's consecutive-games streak of 2,130. Ripken homered in his history-making 2,131st consecutive game one day later, with President Bill Clinton and Vice President Al Gore in attendance. He had started his streak 13 years earlier, on May 30, 1982. It ended at 2,632 games in 1998, when Ripken asked manager Ray Miller to take him out of the starting lineup.

I thought of Oprah Winfrey, who placed her steady hand on my shoulder in 1990 and spread her Midas touch through me.

Other memories flowed back to me with such poignancy, that day at the bank, that some of them felt like pin pricks. Before that moment, I had hardened my spirit and deadened my soul to fight for my job, but the pin pricks let me know I was still alive. And I still remembered.

There was the brief "You go, girl!" from Cindy Pleasants. Illness and death claimed her before she could fulfill her dream of becoming a sports reporter, but she had encouraged me in my quest. I think, on some level, I always shared the spoils of my achievements with her.

There was Rosa Parks and her lingering hug in Tuskegee, Alabama...and Muhammad Ali, who cleared the way for my first sports anchoring on television...and my grandmother and the good-hearted people at her church in Macon, Georgia.

If I had written and passed a threatening note to the teller, I would never again be invited to speak on a panel with a Nobel Peace Prize winner, as I had done with Mairead Corrigan in Dallas in 2000. I would have become suddenly unworthy of all the support I had received from remarkable people. I would have become a pariah in the eyes of well-meaning ones I admired.

As I walked up to one of the teller's windows, I thought of colleague Fred Church and other George Wallace-type obstructionists I had known. No, they will not win this struggle! They will not defeat my father's daughter. They will not score a collective takedown of someone who set out, from her earliest days, to do right—and to do right by others.

Roosevelt Wiggins raised me to exceed expectations—mine, and the limiting expectations of others.

So: No note requesting money. Instead, I politely and pleasantly conducted my legal banking business for the day—and departed.

---

85. Jessie Tuggle played 14 NFL seasons at linebacker and performed in five Pro Bowls (1992, '94, '95, '97, and '98) despite being considered too small, at five-foot-eleven, 230 pounds.

CHAPTER 34

Unassisted Triple Play: Three Top Stories in Forty-Eight Hours

It was crunch time in my career. My KDFW future hung in the balance. Biting words from news director Maria Barrs affirmed it in my July 2006 evaluation. Showing no letup in the harsh evaluations, she said, in part, that with my long tenure in the market, "[Nita] should be a stronger player than she is now."

And:

"Nita needs to understand what makes a good story and why."

I did not really believe I was not a strong player in the market. My story file proved the contrary. Still, like the athletes whose stories I covered, I felt the pressure to perform.

On the weekend of December 15-16, 2006, I hit pay dirt. My hard-earned contacts came through as at no other time. The result: I was the leading information source on the three top stories during that weekend, demonstrating my value to the sports team and to my employer—and re-establishing the fact that I was a strong player in the market.

Game On

Sports manager Kevin Morrell selected me to fly on the Cowboys' team plane with the press corps to Atlanta, Georgia, for a game against the Falcons. Traveling for the NFL games provided me with a platform and visibility. It was the highest reward of my sports career.

In that role for nine years in Dallas, I reported from twenty-seven of the league's thirty-two cities. I saw all thirty-two teams of my era, if not at their stadiums, then at Texas Stadium. I took to heart my responsibility of linking the Cowboys players and coaches to the team's loyal followers in the U.S. and around the world.

I felt an emotional charge from giving the team's devotees information that moved and informed them. Throughout my service in Dallas, I remained confident that I was not failing the trade of journalism. I believed I was serving well the people who witnessed me in the fullness of my career.

Despite subsequent job evaluations, which ignored the significance of my reports, that December 2006 weekend reinforced my self-confidence in my work. In the Sunday-morning pregame broadcast, I reported live on several aspects of the matchup from ground level at the Georgia Dome. After the game, I worked the locker room and team press conference for interviews. That's a solid enough workday, meeting quality expectations in writing and editing, and in interviewing playing-field warriors.

In addition to the big game in Atlanta, two other lead stories were coming my way. Those stories would relegate the Cowboys' victory in Georgia to secondary status, I am sure, in the minds of viewers.

Marijuana, Again

Two years after Quincy Carter's abrupt departure from the Cowboys, his hopes of returning to the NFL unraveled even more—specifically, on Friday, December 14, 2006.

In the wake of a smattering of media reports about an overnight marijuana-related arrest of Quincy, my boss Kevin called me on the morning of December 15. He asked me to find out the facts of the story.

I thought, "It's up to me to work *this* story, too?"—not with annoyance but with pleasure. I would have my finger on two hot spots at the same time. I was eager to scratch for information about the Quincy arrest because I knew I would treat him fairly, when some others might not.

I held the keys to contacting Quincy, which would be part of a two-pronged lead story in the sportscast. I dialed Quincy's cell. No response.

His mom? His coach from Northwest DeKalb High School? I followed the same run-down of phone numbers I used after Quincy's unexpected release from the team.

Nothing.

I thought it was futile, but I honestly worked the phones; my efforts would make KDFW Quincy's outlet on which to speak, if he cared to do so. Eventually, however, I had to tell Kevin that I came up empty. We both assumed Quincy had his own timeframe in which he planned to talk to reporters.

We were not concerned that we would be beaten by other television reporters. I had Quincy's trust. Our professional history shows I treated him right 100 percent of the time. We therefore expected that when he was ready to talk, he would contact me—representing KDFW—first.

Dorsett's Bubbles and the Eternally Hopeful Springs

So, there I was, in mid-December 2006, enjoying a deliciously hectic moment in my career. I had my thumb on two breaking stories. I could not have predicted that a third story, an exclusive I was nurturing on retired player Ron Springs, would become urgent within that frenzied forty-eight-hour span.

Because of my longtime affection for the Dallas team, I knew the contributions Ron made from 1979 to 1985. And before I met him face-to-face in 2005, I learned more. But this was saddening, private news that had changed Ron's life.

I was talking with Ring of Honor running back and Pro Football Hall of Famer Tony Dorsett one afternoon after a football-related event in mid-2005. We lingered together after the event ended. I had interviewed Dorsett at his home during my first year in Dallas in 1999. The Heisman Trophy he had earned in 1976 at the University of Pittsburgh[86] was the first I had ever seen with my own eyes. During that first encounter with him, I pointed out to Tony another distinction he held for me.

"I liked your Ebony photos," I said, referring to a photo spread in the popular niche magazine for black consumers.

Smiling, he asked, "Which ones?" He already knew the answer.

"The one with the bubbles."

"Yeah. I keep hearing about that, even now," said Tony, still smiling.

At the time that we spoke about the bubbles, Tony was forty-six years old and handsome, just under six feet tall, broad-shouldered, pecan-complexioned, square-jawed, with an electric smile. *Ebony* magazine had published the revealing photographs twenty years earlier, not long after Tony's arrival to the NFL in 1977. The photo that I clipped from the magazine featured Mr. Football in his physical prime at age twenty-five, stepping out of a bathtub, wearing shorts. Bubbles cuddled up to the muscles of his biceps, triceps, pectorals, thighs, and calves. Chiseled to perfection everywhere the eye could see.

But it wasn't my schoolgirl appreciation for Tony's looks that evoked our mutual admiration. I respected Tony for his football successes. He, in turn, recognized my appreciation for the forebears of the current league and my serious approach to journalism.

Now, six years later in 2005, Tony and I stood in a hotel lobby (most likely Hotel Intercontinental in Addison, Texas, where the Cowboys held many events). While chatting, Tony received a call on his cell phone. Ron Springs' battle with diabetes had taken a terrible turn, the caller informed Tony.

---

86. Tony Dorsett established the NCAA's all-time career rushing record with 6,082 yards, a mark that stood for 22 years. He was the first major college running back to compile four 1,000-yard seasons. Selected by Dallas in the first round of the 1977 NFL Draft, Dorsett played 11 seasons for the Cowboys (1977-87) and his final year with the Denver Broncos (1988). He retired as the second all-time leading rusher in NFL history (12,739). Dorsett received his pro and college Hall of Fame inductions in 1994. See heisman.com.

"Ron just had his foot amputated," Tony turned to me and said. A moment later, Tony clicked off the call. A strained expression clouded his handsome face.

A football player absorbs massive shocks to the body over a career of hard-hitting practices and bone-cracking game-day battles. Tony Dorsett endured the collisions over eleven NFL seasons and four college seasons. But football titans can be doubled over by blows of another kind. I witnessed that second kind of assault when it happened to Tony. His stoic expression had crumbled into a grimace of emotional pain when the voice on the other end of his cell phone told him that Ron Springs' lower right leg had been amputated.

As I absorbed the pain he was feeling, Tony added, "Nita, that's not for the news. That's just you and me talking."

"OK, of course," I said, at a loss to say anything more. The news about the amputation felt like a swift kick in the gut. Ron Springs, one of the invincible Cowboys—one who helped build the mythology of the America's Team of my youth—wasn't invincible, after all. That solemn reality stunned me.

As Tony and I reeled from the news of Ron's amputation, we realized we had better get on with the obligations we both faced that day. Tony's close-knit friendship with Ron demanded that Tony check in with his friend and the people close to them both. For me, duty called. I went back to work—but I had a serious professional decision to make.

It was no accident that Tony Dorsett and I lingered after an event to talk; it *was* an accident that I happened to be with Dorsett when he received what turned out to be confidential news. What was I to do with such a coincidence?

I had been challenged in my job evaluations to break stories.

Breaking news is food to a journalist. This is especially true of news that reveals the misfortunes of others. It's even more true of news that reveals the misfortunes of famous people. But because I was born with journalism in my blood, I knew it would be unethical to discuss the confidential information the legendary player had shared with me. No news organization deserved to know what the cadre of Cowboys from the 1970s and 1980s asked me not to broadcast.

Despite what other journalists under pressure to save their jobs might have done, I did not share Ron's personal news. I did not run to my television station to produce a story. I was not mining my contacts that day. I would receive Ron's permission one year later to report on his health. It was part of my three-pronged blockbuster weekend.

Faithfulness Rewarded

The day came, in mid-December 2006, when Ron and Tony and another key member of the equation rewarded me for keeping the Dallas media out of their closed ranks. Of course, I was "Dallas media," too, but some of the Cowboys allowed me inside their circle. I believed the universe was rewarding me for thirty years of interviewing people and telling their stories with integrity and sensitivity. For thirty years of trying to do my best work even when it seemed a few co-workers might not have had my best interests at heart.

In the months following the amputation, Ron made a public appearance in his wheelchair. He spoke with interviewer Norm Hitzges, of Dallas' Sportsradio 1310 (KTCK, The Ticket), about his battles to reclaim his health. During the interview, Ron admitted that he needed a kidney transplant, due, in part, to diabetes.

While listening to the interview on my car radio, I knew what I had to do. I called Tony's cell phone to ask him to introduce me to Ron. I had known the news about the amputation, but I had not yet met the man. Ron's condition warranted a story and he had begun to do interviews about it.

Eyeing the multipronged objectives, my report would increase public awareness about organ donation, inform the fans about the struggle of a beloved Cowboy, and maintain my position as an insider concerning Cowboys news. I would try to share Ron's human drama with the appropriate delicacy. The husband of Adriane and father of three (Shawn, Ayra, and Ashley) created a solid family life alongside his success in the NFL.[87] I needed to air the story of the family, the man, and what lay ahead.

Tony agreed to my request. He called Ron and arranged for me to drop in after Ron's radio segment. When I arrived, Ron and I locked eyes. We said hello and quickly fell into a comfortable association. I asked to do an interview at his home. He signed on to the idea.

In the report, Ron tried to put the amputation in perspective. "I can lose my foot because I don't have to try out anymore or run any forties [40-yard dashes] or do any blocking. So, I said I would lose my foot before I lose my life, because I got a lot to finish."

I landed interviews with two other Cowboys legends to round out my first story on Ron. Tony Dorsett said on camera, "I cried for Ron. I prayed for Ron." Their quarterback, Roger Staubach, met with me to call Ron a "tough, courageous guy" who was facing a tough disease.

There is no way Ron and I could have known what road we would travel together over the next two years.

---

87. Ron Springs played 112 games over eight seasons in the NFL, from 1979 to 1986; he gained 2,519 rushing yards and scored 28 touchdowns, with 2,259 receiving yards and 10 touchdowns. He played his last two pro seasons with Tampa Bay. See nfl.com.

CHAPTER 35

For the Love of Ron Springs

Ron Springs believed his failing kidneys and requisite dialysis would lead to a powerful testimony about unwavering faith and eventual recovery. All the while, he waited on the national kidney-transplant list.

A Dallas-area transplant specialist named Pamela Silvestri, the person working with the Springs family, told me it was standard practice for the person in need *not* to ask his close connections to serve as donors. Immeasurable pressure, she explained to me. No one wants to feel coerced into donating an organ in an attempt to save someone's life, she said.

Ron's son Shawn Springs, the decorated cornerback on the Washington NFL team, did offer to donate one of his kidneys, but Ron refused. He wanted Shawn, thirty years old at the time and in his ninth NFL season, to remain healthy enough to continue his professional success.

During the three years of waiting, a member of Ron's tight Cowboys circle quietly got tested and found himself to be a match for Ron's type O blood. Initially, Ron did not know that Everson Walls[88] had voluntarily checked their compatibility. Walls, at forty-seven and three years younger than Ron, had grown tired of watching Ron wait for a gift that might never come. Everson eventually told

---

88. Everson Walls, an NFL cornerback for 13 seasons with three different teams, played with Ron Springs in Dallas from 1981 to 1986. Walls played 186 games and made 57 interceptions, putting him 10th on the NFL's all-time list in the category.

Ron and several other people that he was going to donate one of his healthy kidneys.

Ron told me about Everson's generous pledge when I was visiting Ron on a non-work day. The information was not for publication, Ron told me. He knew that I would protect the secret. Though I recognized the magnitude of the story on a national, human-interest level, I held on to the glorious news. I kept it within our Cowboys group, as I had done with the news about Ron's amputation.

But Ron's son Shawn, while doing an interview with a reporter in Washington, D.C., slipped up and revealed the news about Everson's pledge. The date of Wednesday, December 13, 2006, happened to be an off day for me because I was going to Atlanta with the Cowboys the upcoming weekend. I was enjoying a quiet day of gardening and hanging out with my dog when Jeff Crilley, a white male colleague with whom I always had a good working relationship, rang me up on my cell phone.

"We need to interview Ron Springs. Kevin gave me your number and asked me to get Ron's info," Jeff said, referring to our sports director, Kevin. Apparently, the news staff had tried internet searches to reach anyone connected with the Springs family. No one was answering the phones, or perhaps the numbers were not the right ones.

Jeff explained that Shawn Springs, in an article in *The Washington Post* online, had shared the news about Everson's planned donation of a kidney.

"I'll give Kevin a call," I assured Jeff, realizing that the serenity at my central-city Dallas home had ended for the day. Later, when I spoke to Kevin, his reply shook me.

"Let the news people handle this. They want to keep it in news," he said, explaining that the news division was big-footing us, or pulling rank. I kept quiet and listened to my boss. What he said next was even more biting.

"We need you to call Ron."

I immediately understood. While the station continued to demand that I break stories, on this day the managers wanted my *contacts* but not my reporting on this national story. Since I was in the throes of being called out about my skills, why wouldn't the managers let me run with the breaking news?

"OK," I replied to Kevin's command. I clicked off the phone. I then dialed the home and cell numbers that I had for Ron. No response for me, either. Good. I reported the no-response results to my boss, mulling the fact that the news division was grabbing a story that clearly belonged to sports and to me. "Super. Good luck," I thought.

Ron did not answer calls from anyone. When he and I finally talked the next day, he explained that he had been at a doctor's appointment when his son broke the news about Everson's transplant gift. From that point on, Ron said, it was too overwhelming to listen to the phone messages that were coming from everywhere.

Ron also shared with me the news that Jeff Crilley and a photographer drove to the Springs family home and parked. When Ron arrived, Jeff approached him—professionally, I am sure; Jeff's style has always been correct. Jeff introduced himself as a KDFW Fox 4 reporter and asked for an interview. According to Ron, he said to Jeff, "You work at Fox 4 with Nita Wiggins?"

"Yes," answered Jeff.

"Well, tell them at Fox I will only talk with Nita," Ron insisted.

Because the words had come from a man waiting for an organ transplant, who could deny him his request?

Everson's Brotherly Gift

Fox 4 immediately aired something, even though it was not the story the producers had sent Jeff to get. The station repeated the news that other outlets had been playing all day across the country about the kidney match and the forthcoming passing of the gift between two well-known Dallas Cowboys. However, for the *exclusive*, the interview with the selfless kidney donor and the grateful recipient sitting on the living-room couch, everyone would have to wait for me.

In fact, everyone would have to wait for the weekend of December 15-16. During the forty-eight hours, I owned the top three stories on television in Dallas, Texas, the No. 4 market in the U.S. The stories included the latest arrest of the former Dallas quarterback, the road-trip coverage of the Cowboys game in Atlanta, and the first television interview between former NFL teammates who were going to be linked through one's donation of a kidney to the other.

During the same phone call in which Ron told me he had talked to my colleague in his driveway, he promised that he and Everson would do interviews with me—first. "We're not talking to anyone before you," he said. He also explained that his son spoke out of turn about the transplant but had done so out of a sense of relief.

Excitedly, I thanked Ron for holding out for me. I told him that because of my assignment in Atlanta, it would be a few days before we could get together.

"We'll wait for you," Ron promised.

Days later, I produced the first joint interview of the transplant patient and his teammate donor. It is actually the first time in history that NFL teammates were involved in a shared organ transplant. When one speaks of football family, the story of Ron and Everson proves that among the players, deep brotherly love does exist. Together, the men created the Ron Springs-Everson Walls Gift for Life Foundation with the purpose of increasing organ donation.

A quick four months later, I confidently wrote on page two of my list of accomplishments in my April 2007 performance evaluation:

> Funny to have listed all these successes that are the direct result of my contacts and work without mentioning the Ron Springs-Everson Walls kidney transplant until now [the sixth section of the self-evaluation]. I knew the plan for Everson to make the donation but had to sit on it for six months because both former Cowboys asked me to do it (and because organ donation protocol calls for privacy). I alerted Kevin, Kingsley [assistant news director Kingsley Smith], and [health reporter John] Hammarley about the info I had and what to do about delaying the story.

Ron's at-home exclusive with me occurred on the eve of the press conference he held for everyone else. He then followed through with another exclusive at-home interview—post-operation, with Everson. At the time my job contract ended, Fox 4 was the only station to have both men together post-op, at home.

How did the breaking stories and exclusives impact my future at KDFW? Not in the way I expected. In the evaluation that followed my having the top three stories on TV for that forty-eight-hour period in December, my KDFW supervisors stubbornly wrote in April 2007, under the Career Growth Recommendations heading:

> Nita needs to take her off-air reporting skills, such as the information she gets from her many contacts, and learn to translate that into on-air reporting and anchoring that makes an impact. Considering her time in the market, Nita should be making more of an impact with viewers.

Under a section of short-term objectives:

> She needs to break more stories. She must improve her work performance. Failure to make required improvements will result in disciplinary action up to and including termination.

I believe everyone at Fox 4 was tasked with breaking stories. But I don't know whether such an expectation was written in threatening terms in the evaluations of my peers. Still, I welcomed the challenge and I met the challenge.

I delivered an array of stories, some of which focused on important players who kept low profiles around reporters. One such was Flozell "the Hotel" Adams, a starter on the offensive line of the Cowboys. A Fox 4 sports colleague remarked that he had never heard Adams' voice. Yet, I was inside Flozell's home, in his game room. I spurred him to talk about the team and to satisfy the curiosity of viewers about his relatively unknown life.

I found and reported two exclusive stories that connected the attacks on September 11, 2001, with the Cowboys. Nose guard Brandon Noble described shielding his wife from all televisions at the hospital for the delivery of their baby, their first, that morning. Receiver Reggie Swinton revealed that he spent part of that day fearing for the safety of his son's mother, a flight attendant for American Airlines.

Early on in Dallas, I produced a story featuring the city's biggest hockey star, Stanley Cup winner Mike Modano, and his mother. It was a Mother's Day story, so my angle concentrated on the difficulties of raising an athlete and how heart-wrenching it was to watch teenaged Mike pack his duffle bag and leave home for hockey camp. Stories at home with defensive stars Roy Williams and George Teague, receivers Joey Galloway and "Rocket" Ismail, and with hard-tackling Keith Davis in his hospital room are also part of my dossier of up close reports.

I was leading with top-line sports interviews when I arrived in Dallas. I continued this throughout my time at the station. The stories mentioned here don't constitute a complete list, by any means, but a blind man could see that the jig was up.

In retrospect, I believe that even if I could have resurrected and interviewed Joe Louis, Knute Rockne, and Babe Ruth, KDFW managers would still have declared me a weak reporter worthy of dismissal.

꧁꧂

The powerhouse weekend of reports I delivered in December 2006 did not cool the hot water in which I was swimming. Over three-plus years, from July 2005 to January 2009, my salary reflected a paltry increase of only fifteen hundred dollars—less than four hundred dollars per year. By the close of my tenure at Fox 4 in January 2009, my salary had inched to ninety-five thousand five hundred dollars.

I am not dismissing the fact that the figure is high; it paid for a pleasurable lifestyle for a household of one. I am saying that it did not take a veteran reporter to detect what was coming. During each agonizing month and with each workday insult coming from the unprofessional work of my photography colleague—and accepted by my managers—I smelled the end.

Nevertheless, I focused on improving the other aspect of television work, my on-camera appearance. I paid handsome salon prices to professionally lighten my hair color and to bleach my eyebrows. "You're Tina Turner!" exclaimed my shocked friend Edouard when he saw the change. I had tried to strip the richness of my natural sable or ash-brown hair color and imitate the sexy singer's flirty, flaxen, honey shade. Edouard's tone indicated I had failed. The drastic color change could be described as burnt orange or cantaloupe. I was not comfortable with the cycle of chemicals needed to maintain the color, but I wanted to hold on to my career.

To fight the weight gain that accompanied my fibroids, I maintained an active lifestyle. Fred's footage had not captured my real appearance, as colleagues and viewers had let me know, but I wanted to make sure I was not doing anything to contribute to his unflattering presentation of me.

Despite these efforts, the paper trail was developing. What value, then, were the exclusive stories I had secured from some of the most outstanding athletes in Dallas-Fort Worth? The at-home interviews that no other reporter had delivered?

CHAPTER 36

Heavyweight Support from Leonard Davis

In 2007, I secured the city's first exclusive at-home television interview with a new Dallas Cowboys starter, Leonard Davis. Six unsatisfying years with the Arizona Cardinals had freed Davis to return home to Texas and become a richly paid free-agent guard.

My story detailed Leonard's climb to the top rung of sports salaries—the kind of rags-to-riches, homegrown-talent-makes-good tale that people love. In securing the exclusive, I was fulfilling my KDFW supervisors' demands that I break stories.

I met the six-foot-six, three-hundred-fifty-four-pound Davis on his first day in the Cowboys locker room.[89] The carefree smile he flashed me, a stranger, told me immediately that his Southern gentlemanliness had survived his Arizona stopover. His size and deep brown complexion reminded me of a sculpture cut out of massive granite stone. I accepted the smiling exchange with him as an invitation for me to introduce myself.

At one point during our many conversations, the blue-chip signee told me proudly, but not boastfully, that he had reached an unexpected financial level in sports. A player typically shies away from discussing money with outsiders, especially those whose earnings don't approach the player's. However, Leonard told me that his new

---

89. Leonard Davis' height was 198 cm; his weight was 170 kg.

financial standing exceeded everything he had dreamed of while growing up in dire circumstances in dusty, rural Wortham, Texas.

"Did you see my name on the Forbes list?" he asked, reeling from the turnaround of fortunes.

No, I had not seen it.

"I'm the number-one NFL player on the Forbes list," he said. "Ahead of Brett Favre and Peyton Manning," he added.[90] (Favre is a retired Super Bowl-winning quarterback and former National Football Conference MVP; Manning is a retired Super Bowl-winning quarterback and former American Football Conference MVP.)

"Really? Well, congratulations on that!" I said brightly.

Leonard grew up in a family of origin that had to consistently stretch its meager resources to survive. For him to break the bank and lead all NFL players in pay in 2007 warranted a story. Having Leonard candidly reveal his feelings about his turn of financial fortune could draw in business-minded non-football people.

To tell the story in an unusual way, I would have to visit Davis' home. This would illustrate for viewers his luxurious quality of life in Texas, the place where he had started so precariously. Leonard said he would talk with his wife Amanda before confirming with me the interview at their home.

While Davis worked on the details at home, I brainstormed about my approach. Quite humorously, I had once tripped over one of Leonard's gigantic rubber flip-flops on the floor of the Cowboys locker room. I backed up over it while talking with him. It would have been credited with a tackle if I had fallen. When I discussed with him my plans to shoot video inside his closet, it was because of my comical stumble. He assured me that the dangerous flip-flop would be in its proper place.

So, inside the closet at the Davis home it would have to be.

For such a big *get*, an at-home feature on a Cowboys star who was expected to help revive past greatness, I needed flawless video

---

90. New England's Tom Brady also lagged behind Leonard's salary, with Brady's six-year, $57.3 million contract signed in May 2005.

support. With all the right visual elements, including an attractive clip of me in the report, I believed I could move my next evaluation in a positive direction.

I asked Kevin Morrell to assign me to work with someone other than videographer Fred Church. But first, I prepared for the fight.

I went into the station's video library and clipped off several of my stand-ups shot by Fred. I selected about six stand-ups that showed mistakes so basic that either the camera operator was a rookie or was intentionally performing badly. (Fred was no rookie; he boasted that he had covered a significant national event eleven years earlier.) I also selected one stand-up shot by a different photographer. The clip displayed correct lighting and the other components of professional work.

Thus armed, I went into battle.

Fighting for Survival

I thought I understood all the moving pieces that would save my Dallas career. By sticking to a disciplined exercise, beauty, and eating plan, and in putting together heartwarming exclusives, I was swimming as fast as I could. Maybe the Davis report would help me stay on top of the written warnings about my incompetency.

I suspected, however, that it was actually not my stories that the station brass disapproved. It was the expense of keeping me aboard. Of course, none of my evaluators would admit such a thing on paper, but it is common practice for businesses to get rid of high-price employees.

Approaching twenty years in the industry, I had become such an employee. What better way to justify cutting me than to attack my skill? And if my on-air appearance were not appealing to viewers because of bad camera angles and lighting, that made the decision to get rid of me seem even more justified.

So, I lobbied hard not to work with Fred on the Davis story. If I could do an exceptional job, and look good on camera while doing so, it would be difficult for the station to continue to slam my stories and to ultimately usher me to the door.

I told sports director Kevin, in no uncertain terms, that I did not want Fred on the Davis exclusive. In the days leading up to the interview, I repeatedly pleaded with Kevin to grant my demand. "I'm tired of looking bad in video," I said.

Kevin was normally an understanding leader, but he balked at pulling Fred off the assignment.

I showed Kevin the montage I edited of my on-location stand-ups. He grimaced and winced several times as the poorly shot video rolled in front of his eyes. Before Dallas, Kevin had worked at ESPN Network, for decades the worldwide leader in sports broadcasting. He knew good work; he knew bad work. And he knew I worked hard every day to strengthen his sports department and to build my reputation.

Finally, in the montage Kevin was viewing, one particular stand-up appeared. "It's not so bad," he remarked.

"Fred didn't shoot it," I said, pleased that Kevin had taken the bait I presented. "This is the reason I want to work with someone other than Fred on the Leonard Davis exclusive."

"We can't just take him off the story," Kevin replied.

I argued on. "Well, it's not right that I go out and get the stories that no one else has, and then I'm ashamed to look at them later. This happens a lot, you see."

I searched for and then froze the video player on one of the embarrassingly bad videos. I continued to plead my case. I felt embarrassed to encounter viewers face-to-face (at games, for instance) after some of the really ugly images, I told Kevin.

Kevin dug in his heels.

I would not take no for an answer.

"Go and talk to Bob," he said.

Bob Hawman was the chief photographer, another white male, and Fred's boss in the video department. I opened with the same script, saying to Bob that I did not want to work with Fred because of the *years* of unflattering video. "It's all about the video," I argued. I repeated the drill of showing the clips of my ugly on-camera appearances.

Bob grimaced as he watched the bad videos. He, too, fell into my video-evidence trap.

"This one is not so bad," he said, pausing the tape on the one stand-up not shot by Fred Church.

"That one was not shot by Fred," I informed him.

Bob was caught—burned by embarrassment and mixed emotions. How could he possibly defend the work done by one of his photographers when the quality discrepancy was staring him in the face? Bob's facial expressions revealed what he refused to honestly admit.

I said imploringly, "I talked to Kevin and I'm talking to you because I do not want Fred to shoot my exclusive story at Leonard Davis' house."

"We can't just take him off the story. It depends on who will be working that day," Bob said.

"I don't care what the schedule says!" I replied. "It's a big story. No one else knows the story because it is Leonard who told me about it. He says we can go to his house. I've done my part to get the interview. Now we need to make sure the photographer does a good job."

The conversation ended with a promise from Bob. "I'll talk to Fred."

I ejected the tape and lost professional respect for Bob in that moment. No true leader would minimize the damaging effect of poor-quality footage. He would never try to defend indefensible work. And my superiors' hesitancy in dealing with Fred baffled me. Fred's lousy work shortchanged the station as much as it did my stories. KDFW paid photographers between fifty thousand and sixty-five thousand dollars a year in the early 2000s. What fair return was the station getting by accepting his bad video?

As I left Bob's office, I recalled the time, some seventeen years earlier, when I had gone to the general manager of WSAZ in Huntington. The GM sided with me. Now, I left Bob's workspace with a similar intent. I entered the hallway and instead of returning to the sports office, I hooked a turn to the left, seeking KDFW's news director, Maria Barrs.

I repeated the drill with Maria, who, like the two managers under her, brightened when she saw the one video not shot by Fred. I appealed to her sense of fairness.

In her reassuring voice, Maria said that she would talk with Bob about Fred. "I promise you, you won't have this problem anymore," she said.

There was nothing left for me to do except to believe in Maria. As the TV exec who had hired me for my dream job, she had an investment in my success. But she had also signed off, along with Kevin, on my failing job appraisals.

I could only hope Maria would examine the facts and make a fair and long-overdue decision in my favor.

PART IV

Taking Off

CHAPTER 37

Shame on the Shooter or Shame on Me?

I was not lucky in the draw. Despite my battle to prevent him from doing so, Fred Church shot the video of my exclusive at-home interview with Leonard Davis. His camera captured a slice of the big man's home life and his incredibly large walk-in closet. Large, for I estimate it was easily 40 x 30 feet. The living space of the multi-level home was maybe ten thousand square feet, but with the triple garage and swimming pool, the whole thing might have approached twice that size on official real-estate rolls. (I hope I am not laughably underestimating.)

Leonard played to the camera with his broad smile, laid-back Texas accent, and body language that displayed his comfort with me and the line of questions. At one point while in the closet, he pulled a hanger off the rack. On it hung a pair of railroad-conductor overalls made of light-blue pinstriped denim. A huge piece of cloth, for much was needed to cover Leonard's three-hundred-fifty-four-pound, six-foot-six frame. We laughed together on tape about the overalls and the array of over-sized shoes. He pointed out the dastardly flip-flop that had tripped me in the Cowboys locker room. Such was the fun side of the giant man.

A poignant moment colored the interchange when I asked Leonard about his father, a lifelong Cowboys fan who died before his son ever wore the fabled star-logo helmet and No. 70 jersey. He said his success would have meant the most to his dad.

I tried to portray the fullness of Leonard's character and life. Viewers later told me that they liked the tour of the closet and the honest answers Davis gave me. As for Fred Church—well, while he adequately shot the story, I still did not get a résumé-quality clip of me. Therefore, I once again produced an exclusive story with a likeable subject, but it could not help me in my battle to retain my position or to secure a comparable one.

CHAPTER 38

Great Stories, Bad Reporter?

My performance evaluations proved that KDFW did not believe in me anymore. More than once, I would think, with disbelief, "At what point in my career did I become such a substandard journalist? Was it before or *after* someone decided I was good enough to earn ninety thousand dollars a year?"

Not one evaluation talked about what I thought was really at issue: how I looked in the reports. I felt that my managers had to manufacture something critical about my performance to avoid another hike in pay, like the one from seventy-six thousand dollars in my July 2001 contract to ninety thousand dollars in July 2004. Rather than rectify the problem of how Fred Church chose to photograph me, the managers left themselves with two options. They could 1) criticize the on-camera look of a black female journalist over the age of forty and possibly risk the appearance of racism, sexism, and ageism. (This was the legally precarious option to take, not to mention a potential public-relations nightmare.) Or they could 2) complain about the inability of a journalist to construct a story or avoid other flaws of the trade. (This represented the easier option.) Of course, the station took the easier route, which was to pretend I was suddenly an irreparably incompetent reporter and broadcaster.

In this vein, supervisors found a new complaint to cite in my July 2006 evaluation: my sound.

"Her delivery comes across as tentative rather than credible and self-assured. These issues were outlined in her last evaluation and have not significantly improved since. We need to see growth." Also in my permanent file were these words about my voice: "[W]hile pleasant, it tends to rise."

My file also included the concern that I should "be more creative in writing and storytelling." The April 2007 evaluation stated: "Nita needs a great deal of work. Too often the writing is choppy and has no flow."

Horrible!

The bad reviews just did not make sense to me. And they got worse. By 2008, the pitch in my voice was "too high to the point of being annoying," said the appraisal signed by Kevin and Maria, usually my two champions at the station. The "annoying" comment still puzzles me. My voice rings clear and strong and, with crisp articulation, defies an easily identifiable regional accent.

If I had an "annoying" voice, history has shown that this is not necessarily a career ender. Two superlatives in American TV journalism achieved more than their contemporaries despite some people's incessant criticism about their "annoying" voices. Television's first one-million-dollar newswoman, Barbara Walters, became famous even though she could not clearly pronounce the "r" sound. And sports trendsetter Howard Cosell never dropped his staccato, nasal New York sound on the way to rewriting broadcasting standards. They both reached into living rooms across the country with at-home, sit-down interviews with newsmakers. They covered hot-button issues with the most influential people of the period. For decades, they outperformed their contemporaries and influenced me in my early television viewing.

As a journalist, I believed I was working in the mold of Walters and Cosell—but without the vocal handicaps each possessed. I imagined the kind of stories the two would produce for Dallas-Fort Worth if they were in my position. I made it my mission to secure such stories.

As Walters and Cosell would have done, I crashed geographic and cultural barriers to find stories, going to Senegal, West Africa; Dusseldorf, Germany; and various locales in France. Getting on an airplane shows the people in the audience a journalist's commitment. My efforts in this quest are reflected in the self-evaluation portion of my July 2006 evaluation. In it, I wrote:

Further Pace-Setting Since January (2006)

Drew Henson:

I was the only broadcast reporter (from Dallas) to travel to Europe for specialized sports coverage. Fortunately for Fox 4 and for me, Cowboys quarterback Drew Henson played for NFL Europe this spring. I went to Germany to do an exclusive interview.

From the trip, I produced a *Sports Sunday on Fox* report and a lengthier *Insights* [a public affairs program] piece dealing with the worldly view American athletes will develop from their European exposure. No other Dallas station, as of this writing, has endeavored to match what I have been doing with our local sports figures in Europe.

BTW Europe:

By the way, an ESPN-based producer [Leah Siegel] told me she had to sell the "worldwide leader in sports" on going to cover the Tour de France after she saw my Dallas exclusives for three years. I covered it four times during Lance's run. (July 2006)

As the only Dallas-based reporter covering Texan Lance Armstrong at the Tour de France, I was relieved to see him consistently finish ahead of the field. His successes gave legs to my stories and I became recognizable in the media rooms of the Tour. I liked the warm greetings from the event's beat reporters, year after year. I basked in their compliments for my progress in speaking French.

Unfortunately, Lance's remarkable results steered some cycling specialists, particularly those from the sport's hotbeds of Italy and Belgium, to approach me with negative comments. Because he finished in first place seven times, between 1997 and 2005, many European journalists pressed me, not aggressively but repeatedly, saying things like, "You know he's cheating, don't you?" Or: "Everybody in Europe knows he's doping. Why don't you Americans report it?"

Often, I would see a sheepish or apologetic expression on the face of an inquiring journalist. Each knew I was not linked to the cycling team and should not be targeted by such interrogations. But there was no one better to question about the issue. I was, after all, the American reporter from the cradle of Lance's support.

Finally, I crafted a diplomatic response, a variation of the following statement:

"I haven't seen any proof. Lance has not failed a drug test, so how am I going to say he's a cheater? I'm a reporter. Like you, I will report that when it happens, if it happens."

It happened.

In October 2012, the International Cycling Union stripped Armstrong of all seven Tour titles. The U.S. Anti-Doping Agency had found irrefutable evidence of doping nearly eight years after Armstrong's domination of the two-thousand-mile race. Caught and exposed, Armstrong confessed in an exclusive with Oprah that he had used banned substances and doped his blood to perform at a maximum level.

My overseas reporting did not end with Armstrong's fall from grace. As my job evaluations show, I kept bolstering my employee value by securing other foreign assignments.

SUNDAY August 3 / FIRST REPORT FROM AFRICA (April 2007)

Only reporter to travel from Dallas to Senegal, Africa, to cover the two-day basketball camp held by Mavs starter Sagana Diop.[91] Coach Avery Johnson was there. I shot, edited and aired 3 three packages on what was going on.

Interviews included the player and coach, Diop's father, Senegalese kids at the camp, business leaders, an oncologist. I conducted four of the interviews in French and wrote translation for two people to voice.

Diop donated money to the children's cancer hospital—an aspect I included in my exclusive reports.

Along with covering Diop's story overseas, I broke stories with other NBA players on the Dallas Mavericks basketball team.

Exclusive Mavericks:

In previous evals, I have been urged to work angles with the other teams. The Mavs' Jason Terry is an example of that.... The relationship that I developed with his mother led to a story that even NBA TV and TNT, the regular basketball outlets, did not know. I know that because Cheryl Miller, their correspondent, asked me whether they could use the info and credit me on air! (July 2006)

I also continued to deliver unique stories about the football team. About one such fact-grabber, I wrote:

Gunshot injury of Cowboys' Keith Davis

Only broadcast reporter to talk face-to-face with Davis. He spent twenty minutes, actually maybe

---

91. Senegal-born NBA player DeSagana Diop played for the Mavericks from 2005 to May 2009, overlapping the author's last three years at KDFW. He welcomed her as a one-woman band to cover his return to Dakar in 2006, a trip they took accompanied by Mavericks coach Avery Johnson.

more, talking to me about what he went through, showing me the gunshot wounds, demonstrating that he could do football drills.

While other stations reported that he had undergone surgery and that he had left the hospital, my direct contact with him led to factual info. (April 2007)

Finally, we as a sports team have consistently increased our ratings in the time I have been here. I arrived in 1999, when WFAA was untouchable on Sunday nights.

We're in the [ratings] game every week and have won our share. (April 2007)

I was flippant in the earliest evaluations because I felt I was running against others who were fast-walking, at best, in getting memorable stories on the air. Whether sitting on family couches with Dallas sports figures, or viewing Wimbledon championship platters on a family bookcase, I had the impression I was offering something meaningful to the KDFW Fox 4 viewers. I remained confident that I could win over the decision-makers, believing that the arc would bend toward job justice for me.

Drowning, Despite My Best Efforts

My own gleaming words did not sway my supervisors. At the same time, KDFW did notice some of my on-the-job positives in June 2008. Maria Barrs wrote:

Nita was the first reporter offered the chance to attend the (NASCAR) drivers meeting the morning of the race and had the rare access to many events because Tony Stewart said, "I love Nita's passion for the sport."

I turned the extremely rare five-hour behind-the-scenes shoot with racing megastar Tony Stewart into a full-length piece.[92] Stewart, with Jeff Gordon and Dale Earnhardt Jr., were the top three NASCAR brands at the time.

Additionally, NASCAR had muscled basketball and baseball aside to place itself second behind only the NFL in the battle for weekly ratings. One in three Americans was a NASCAR fan.[93] Nielsen Media Research from 2003 showed that female viewers preferred NASCAR over the NFL and major league baseball. Our own Fox channel profited from the seven-hundred-and fifty million-dollar sponsorship deal NASCAR signed with Sprint Nextel Corporation in 2004 for a period of ten years. The 2007 TV deal (for eight years) paid five hundred and sixty million dollars a year. The bottom line is that a great deal of money was being made in my second reporting specialty.

In the midst of all that, I get Tony Stewart's sweet invitation to ride with him on a flatbed truck and wave at two hundred thousand spectators before the start of the Samsung-Radio Shack 500 race in Texas.

What more could a reporter do to represent the station and serve the interests of the viewers? I was vexed by my tenuous hold on my job. KDFW supervisors consistently noted my "cheerful attitude and personality" and said, "Nita seeks feedback on her stories and handles constructive criticism well."

I knew that the station saw the future without me in it. Truth be told, I was churning on the inside even while supervisors applauded my "cheerfulness." But I faithfully went to work every day and remained diligent, truth-seeking, and earnest. I put on my makeup—and then my "helmet" (thick-skinned endurance), as my first agent, San Francisco-based David Crane, had instructed me to do. Still, I knew I could not forever keep the dam in Dallas from bursting. I felt burned by negative appraisals and caught in a net that was supposed to pull me down.

Or in a noose that was supposed to snatch me up.

---

92. Tony Stewart won NASCAR's Rookie of the Year award in 1999 and followed with championship titles in 2002, 2005, and 2011.
93. Steve Odland, "NASCAR's Back!" *Forbes*, Feb. 27, 2012.

Confronting the Meanness

At some point in 2006, I questioned the chief obstructionist in my way at KDFW, photographer Fred Church. I was two years into the spiral of negative job evaluations and had nothing to lose. Plus, I truly wanted an answer. I wanted to know why Fred had continuously torpedoed my work with poor-quality lighting and unflattering angles.

We were setting out on a two-hour drive, so my timing was purposeful. I thought having Fred as a captive audience might force him to discuss the matter with me. I broached the topic by trying to appeal to his sense of empathy. I knew he was the father of two young daughters, so I asked:

"How would you feel if one of your daughters told you that someone on her job treated her as you treat me?"

Fred had turned to me to listen to my question. When I was done, he turned back to watch the road.

I waited, but there came no response. Not even a murmur.

I had braced to hear that *I* had created the toxic situation. I would have accepted that, knowing that improving any bad situation starts with understanding the root. Receiving no response, I closed my eyes and slept for the long drive.

We arrived in silence at our destination. After I awakened, I wondered if Fred had tried to picture his daughters under the thumb of an uncooperative co-worker. I hoped he had reflected on his inappropriate actions that had led me to ask my question.

I have since learned about an intriguing aspect of women's health—something that might make a man like Fred, the father of daughters, rethink carrying out microaggressions against a female co-worker. At a conference I attended in 2017, I heard these words:

"Discrimination can cause fibroid tumors."

This was the assertion of Dr. Deborah K. Witt, a Philadelphia family practitioner and a panel speaker at the event.[94]

---

94. Dr. Deborah Witt spoke at the Literary Bliss National Book Club Conference on a panel discussion titled "A Conversation About Black Women's Health in the Trump Era." It was held in July 2017 in Atlanta, Georgia.

The news astounded me—as it did my table companions, who were all women. Every one of us reacted with a startled expression. I shook my head, marveling in disbelief over the explosive medical information.

Another panelist, a specialist in public health, supported Dr. Witt's conclusion. "It has been found that experiences of racial discrimination cause uterine fibroid tumors in black women," said Linda Goler Blount, president and CEO of the Black Women's Health Imperative.

Until I heard respected medical professionals say it that day, I'd had no idea that years of receiving unjust treatment on the job could create fibroid tumors.

Had my chosen career compromised my health? Likely. I could not identify another culprit. My family medical history revealed no causes for alarm. Additionally, throughout my life, I had made healthy and prudent choices with diet and exercise. But medical research shows that sustained exposure to stress—such as one might experience when constantly faced with obstructive prejudices—can knock a body out of balance and put health at risk.[95]

While the medical profession had long claimed that three out of four women of color experience fibroids, Dr. Witt's updated 2017 statistics had moved the number to *eight out of every ten* women of color in the U.S. Most of us at the conference were women of color. Many of us had long ago encountered our own tumors—and, if not our own, we had each had a close connection with a woman whose body had carried the growths. Despite this high occurrence, we would all have been told the same grim fact: that medical research had simply found no explanation for something that touched such a high percentage of us.

I approached Drs. Witt and Blount and panel moderator Jemea Dorsey, president and CEO of the Atlanta-based Center for Black

---

95. A study carried out in the U.S. with randomly selected women between the ages of 35 and 49 (who were screened by self-report, medical record, and sonography) showed that the incidence of uterine fibroids by age 35 was 60 percent among African-American women, increasing to greater than 80 percent by age 50, whereas Caucasian women showed an incidence of 40 percent by age 35, and almost 70 percent by age 50. Accessed Sept. 3, 2017, at https://www.ncbi.nlm.nih.gov/pmc/articles/PMC3787340/.

Women's Wellness. Dorsey affirmed the doctors' statements. Before that day, I had not known that there were medical professionals who were seriously studying a problem that heavily affected women of color. I had never forgotten the vague answers my personal doctor and imaging technician had given me during my own diagnosis a decade earlier in Dallas. But now, I stood with three experts who revealed to me that someone had cared enough to dig for answers. I no longer felt like a throwaway patient. I felt acknowledged and validated.

Grateful, I asked for and received from Drs. Witt and Blount, and from Dorsey, permission to cite their statements in this book.

This is the knowledge I did not have when I questioned Fred Church that day in the news vehicle. It may not have mattered to him that his opposition could have created a medical hardship for me. Maybe he would have been moved by the knowledge that fibroids affect white women, too. Medical professionals report that four out of ten white women develop the growths by age thirty-five. Would it have mattered to Fred that his two daughters could grow up and work with someone whose behavior mirrored his?

⁓

Since Fred and I were virtually the same age and enjoyed sports and the same generation of rock-and-roll classic songs, we had a few things upon which to build a positive work relationship. I admired that he often buried his nose in a thick book as we waited for interviews. He probably encountered some interesting concepts in those books. I never talked to him about what he was reading. Never established that common ground, or any other.

I wonder why I failed to make the connection with him. I enjoyed friendly interactions with the station's other photographers, black and white and Hispanic, including Shannon Bales, Kevin Bell, Bill George, Guy Hernandez, Rodney Horton, Marc Kaminer, Rick Larsen, Cody Marcom, Norvis Nance, John Thompson, Jorge Villarreal, and Dwayne Watkins. And there was sports photographer

Larry Rodriguez, second in workplace friendship to my buddy Jim Backus in West Virginia.

But with Fred, I could never achieve anything but coolness even though I treated him with respect and had shown kindness to his daughters. Several times, one of his girls had to go to a sports shoot with us, possibly because of a disruption in babysitting arrangements. I don't know the details, but each time, I felt fine having the little one along.

"She has a ten-day contract with us," I quipped to Mavericks Coach Avery Johnson on one of the days when Fred's daughter arrived with us at basketball practice. (NBA clubs can offer a ten-day contract to a player to stem an emergency shortage of players.) Coach Johnson, a former NBA player, laughed warmly at my explanation. I imagine he had wondered why a little white girl seemed to have accompanied me to the morning practice.

I am child-free by choice but never minded being Mother Hen in a pinch. I divided my attention between the happenings on the basketball court and the whereabouts of Fred's daughter. I wanted to prevent her from feeling out of place in the company of so many adults and sweaty pro athletes. I also wanted her to develop a respect for people of color—by remembering my kindness.

The same thoughts had guided me in the 1990s when I warned my coercive and prejudiced West Virginia boss that racial sensitivity starts at home. I hoped that the sons of WSAZ-TV news director Bill Cummings would be taught to deal more evenhandedly with the "other" than their father had done with me. I hoped the fruit—in their case and in the case of Fred Church—fell far from the tree.

A Silent Victory

I had failed to draw Fred into an honest, off-camera conversation about our working conflict, but I had no problem drawing other people into on-camera conversations. During my last two years at the station in Dallas, I was still securing big-time exclusive interviews for Dallas-Fort Worth television viewers.

In an at-home exclusive with Michelle and Jason Witten, my story introduced to the public the first baby of the celebrated Cowboys tight end. The 2007 Father's Day piece showed cute shots of Jason and baby Christopher Joseph, or CJ, sprawled on a blanket designed by a fan. The blanket prominently displayed Jason's No. 82.

The report cemented Jason's Captain America image, the post-2000 version of a sports hero and family man that Roger Staubach had represented decades earlier. Among other things, Jason explained his five-point plan for changing CJ's diapers. The plan included making sure the "business" was done before going for a fresh diaper and covering up the front "zone" while cleaning the backside.

On a serious note, Jason talked about his turbulent childhood and his aim to give CJ freedom from fear in the family home. He let me probe his relationship with the Cowboys' marquee player and quarterback, his best friend, Tony Romo. In 2007, Romo had accompanied singer Carrie Underwood to the Academy of Country Music Awards and served as a celebrity judge for the Miss Universe beauty pageant. His movements ignited discussions beyond the sports shows. Romo and his first-time-father friend could not have been more different.

"You and Tony are like Staubach and Namath, aren't you? But at the same time, you're best friends?" I questioned, trying to emulate Phyllis George's ironic style of inquiry. She posed such a question in the 1970s to contrast the lifestyles between family man Roger Staubach and playboy man-about-town Joe Namath.

Answering practically in unison, Michelle and Jason Witten said that people evolve at different times, guided by their own personal calendars.

A fun celebrity story for the audience.

Earlier in 2007, a special Dallas resident opened the door for me to interview defensive star DeMarcus Ware at his home. Carolyn Price was known throughout the city and in the minds of the team's international fan base as the Cowboys' number-one fan. Ms. Price, as most people affectionately called her, telephoned DeMarcus' wife and sang my praises as a reporter. She asked Mrs. Ware to allow me in with a camera crew. Because of this, the husband and wife welcomed me for a poolside chat, an exclusive.

We discussed the origins of their relationship—their teenaged years. DeMarcus said that he would have followed his then-girlfriend Taniqua into the military had football not developed into something solid. He said he worked so hard at the sport (as defensive lineman and linebacker) because he was inspired to take care of her—and of them, as a couple.

Their memories conjured up for viewers the high schooler DeMarcus spending his limited gas money and driving forty-five minutes to see Taniqua on a military base. At the time of our at-home interview, DeMarcus was the team's top defensive player.

Quarterback Romo, tight end Witten, and defensive playmaker Ware were the most adored Cowboys on the field during the closing years of my Dallas Decade. I appreciated the interview time they gave me. This does not diminish any of the special history created by Troy Aikman, Michael Irvin, and Emmitt Smith—the Triplets—but the latter three were wrapping up their careers as I arrived in 1999.

Before his departure, Irvin added to my timeline of TV exclusives. The career of the franchise's ultimate playmaker, who was nicknamed "The Playmaker," ended during my first Dallas season. Fortunately for me, his admiration for Jerry Jones, and Jerry's for him, kept Irvin at the Valley Ranch team complex. Michael and I had met years earlier in Tennessee at a fundraising celebrity basketball game in which he was a player and I was a celebrity referee. During our first conversation in Dallas, he and I laughed about that Memphis game. We talked many times, on and off camera. This friendly relationship worked to my advantage.

When Michael got approved for induction into the Pro Football Hall of Fame, every journalist looked for a way to make his story stand apart. I found out where Michael would be on the final weekend before being immortalized in Canton, Ohio, at the August 2007 ceremony. Following the tip from a contact, I arrived at the semi-private event held in Michael's honor. When The Playmaker saw me, he feigned agitation and said, "Who called the media?"

No one had called the media; my hard-earned and invaluable contacts list had come through for me again. Despite the unexpectedness of my arrival, Michael and I both knew that he was going to do a sit-down interview with me. We had done so before.

I was the reporter in Cowboys training camp in 1999 to whom Michael admitted he had been playing basketball with injured team-mate Deion Sanders. How could the team's important and expensive defensive star Sanders play basketball if he were supposed to be rehabilitating an injury? When Michael slipped up and revealed the secret on camera, he laughed and shook his head with acceptance. The news was out there and not going back.

I broke the story—always a good thing, but even more impressive because it occurred during my first training camp.

In the one-on-one interview before the HOF induction, I asked Michael to whom he would give credit first during his acceptance speech. He thoughtfully paused, swallowed hard, lowered his head. When he looked up at me to begin, his face showed that he had paused more to contain his feelings than to find an answer. Michael already knew the answer. He had known it ever since he devoted himself to purposefully and consistently outdoing all others at football practice. The answer was Walter Irvin, Michael's late father.

As he spoke of his hard-working roofer father, Michael's brown eyes filled with tears. (Sports director Kevin Morrell did not hide the fact that my interview impressed him. I was present in his office when Kevin called in different members of the KDFW staff to play them the clip.) Michael said his gains in football came from watching, with his young eyes, his daddy's take-your-lunch-pail-to-work example. When Michael was seventeen, he lost his father, but he carried the irrepressible Walter Irvin tradition forward by working hard at football for another twenty years.[96]

---

96. Receiver Michael Irvin caught 750 passes for 11,904 yards and 65 touchdowns from 1988 to 1999. His quarterbacks were Troy Aikman (1989 until 1999) and Steve Pelleur, in Irvin's rookie season of 1988. Irvin played on Coach Tom Landry's last team in 1988, a year in which the Cowboys finished 3-13. Under the ownership of Jerry Jones, Dallas won Super Bowl XXVII in 1993 (over Buffalo), SB XXVIII in 1994 (over Buffalo), and SB XXX in 1996 (over Pittsburgh). See nfl.com. Irvin also won a college national championship with the Miami Hurricanes.

The Playmaker looked handsome in his acorn-squash-colored HOF blazer at the induction that I attended with Ms. Price. He repeated the statements he had made on camera to me, and added to them:

"Before my father made his journey to heaven, he sat with me. His final words to me were, 'Take care of your mother.'"

Suddenly it was all clear. Michael had chosen football to keep his oath to his father, resulting in three Super Bowl wins in four years with Dallas. Those of us who loved the city and its team and the way he played experienced many joyful tears with him.

CHAPTER 39

Two Faces of Fox

I worked many days with KDFW-TV photographer Fred Church—from 1999 to 2009. More times than not, he created video of me that was professional enough to pass for a newscast but so unflattering it was unusable for a video résumé that would take me to a higher level. During what should have been the pinnacle of my American career, I did not garner the creative weapons I needed to compete for better positions. Even when I complained to KDFW superiors about Fred's undermining tactics, I received no lasting remedy.

Though *I* no longer need a remedy, I am setting my eye on the people after me who desire their fair shot in the TV industry. I want fairness for those who currently are held voiceless in the face of unending mistreatment. I want to help them sidestep the economic lynching that my career suffered. I am convinced that my story mirrors the agonizing predicament of many idealistic people whose names I will never know. But I do personally know at least nine African American television reporters from my era, all women, who endured unnecessary resistance and suppressive acts at their places of work. I mentioned them early in my story, in the introduction of this book. Four of them working together at one station were so under the gun at the hands of their white male news director that their menstrual periods shut down. A fifth woman on that reporting team took the prescription drug Zoloft to fight depression.

I argue that those women and I suffered under a modern-day manifestation of the same racial hatred and economic jealousy that drove some Americans in the past. Such "implicit bias"[97] still threatens not only the professional positions but also the health of many talented black people and their families—or the families they would like to raise.

A woman suffering from unnatural menstrual cessation, amenorrhea, cannot get pregnant because her body's systems have triggered a physiological defense mechanism. Another way to look at it: A woman's reproductive processes shut down when her body senses that she is in a situation too dangerous to carry a pregnancy to term.

How awful that a work environment could become just such a harmful incubator.

Bad Deeds Get Paid Off at Fox Headquarters

As my managers were failing to secure a fair and balanced work ethic from Fred Church, Fox's parent office in New York was shielding another white male employee, the top network draw, Bill O'Reilly. *The O'Reilly Factor*, his primetime show, earned an estimated sixty million dollars a year for the Fox conglomerate. In October 2004, a former producer of O'Reilly's show filed a harassment lawsuit in the Supreme Court of the State of New York. Plaintiff Andrea Mackris claimed, under section 24, that she faced:

> *...sexual harassment at the hands of her immediate supervisor, Defendant BILL O'REILLY, and a sexually hostile work environment, perpetrated by Defendant BILL O'Reilly, and other supervisors, managers, officers, employees and/or agents of Defendant FOX.*

---

97. "Recent social cognition research—a mixture of social psychology, cognitive psychology, and cognitive neuroscience—has provided stunning results that...reveal that most of us have implicit biases in the form of negative beliefs (stereotypes) and attitudes (prejudice) against racial minorities. This is notwithstanding sincere self-reports to the contrary," writes Jerry Kang, in "Trojan Horses of Race," *Harvard Law Review* 118:5 (February 2005).

And:

> *Within Defendants FOX and WESTWOOD ONE,*
> *a permissive and encouraging environment for*
> *gender discrimination and sexual harassment*
> *reigns among supervisors, managers and employ-*
> *ees of the companies.*

Under Section 27, Mackris contended that the defendants created and "maintained a virulently hostile work environment through explicit, rampant, pervasive and continued sex discrimination" against the plaintiff and other female employees that was so "offensive and severe that it detrimentally altered the terms and conditions of Plaintiff's employment."[98]

O'Reilly, with Fox's knowledge, paid a settlement to sweep away the nasty deeds the lawsuit alleged he had carried out. Mackris accepted the money, which likely numbered in the millions. With that, she is prohibited from publicly confirming the details.

O'Reilly was fired in 2017.

The New York Times calls the harassment saga at Big Fox a pattern in which an influential newsroom figure holds the cards. The newspaper adds that the vile misconduct that forced out Fox chairman Roger Ailes in 2016, one year ahead of O'Reilly, suggests "a broader workplace problem."

That is putting it mildly.

A "nightmare factory" of "sexual harassment and psychological torture" is how Tessa Stuart describes the Fox problem in an article for *Rolling Stone* magazine. (The article asserts that "some of the allegations against the newly ousted *The O'Reilly Factor* host date back to the early 2000s.")[99]

---

98. The author viewed the lawsuit at thesmokinggun.com.
99. Tessa Stuart, "A Timeline of Bill O'Reilly's Vileness," *Rolling Stone*, April 19, 2017. Accessed Nov. 3, 2017, at http://www.rollingstone.com/politics/features/a-timeline-of-bill-oreillys-vileness-w477663.

What is the link between Fox in New York and Fox in Dallas in the early 2000s? Easy: Money and the treatment of women. One operation condoned seven-figure hush-money payouts to hide heavy-handed, misogynistic behavior. The other sanctioned a sabotage of a woman's work, an undermining of her health, and an ouster campaign that accused her of failing to meet standards. It was a maneuver that forced her out of her job as she approached the six-figure mark in salary.

CHAPTER 40

Tears in My Manager's Eyes

In October 2008, my female news director in Dallas, Texas, told me that my contract would not be renewed.

Maria Barrs, a woman of Filipino heritage and perhaps ten years older than the forty-four years I carried at the time, called me at home on my day off.

"Are you available to meet me for coffee?" she asked.

My mind raced over the possible purpose of the meeting. Maria had made the request in her normal, reassuring voice (I never heard her being cross or inappropriate), but still I knew something out of the ordinary was up. She and I did not do coffee. On top of that, her tone of formal friendliness did not lead me to believe she was organizing a celebration.

"I'd like to talk with you away from the station," Maria continued.

We agreed on a rendezvous at Starbucks.

As soon as the call ended, I telephoned my agent, Peter Goldberg, with the powerful N.S. Bienstock agency in New York City.

"She's going to tell you that they are not renewing your contract," he said gently. The ninety-day window to opt out of an automatic extension was opening. Either the employee or the television station could exercise the option, he clarified.

I had been represented by Peter since 1992. Back then he worked for IMG, the leading agency in management of television journalists. He had heard about me, as I worked in Augusta, Georgia, so he traveled down from New York City to meet me. He conducted a dinner interview at The Snug restaurant in Martinez, Georgia. I confided to him my long-range goal of covering the Dallas Cowboys in their home city. He made it his goal to place me there.

For more than sixteen years thereafter, I trusted Peter's advice every step of the way. "The best agent in the world," I crowed to many a news director during the interviews Peter set up for me.

"Stay calm. Just listen," he advised on the morning of the Starbucks meeting with Maria. He added it was a definitive decision on the part of the station due to the economic condition of the broadcasting industry and the cost of keeping me, a twenty-one-year television veteran.

Peter had negotiated my most recent contract with KDFW, one that would have paid ninety-seven thousand dollars a year unless the station opted out for contract year 2009. He knew it would hurt me to have a paycheck of that great sum disappear.

I felt a jolt of foreboding about my career. Naturally. But no time to linger over it. I needed to prepare to see Maria.

She arrived first at the Starbucks and, seated, waved me over to the table. After brief hellos, we got in line to order coffee. Even though we both knew the reason for the mid-morning meeting, we still had to play the role of customers.

I valued Maria's sensitivity in giving me the boot away from two hundred colleagues inside the news building. With tears in her eyes, she heaved a heavy breath and began.

"We're not renewing your contract."

In a broken string of sentences, but with clear meaning and definitely with no turning back, she explained.

"We have to make cuts. We're starting in sports."

Since 2002, the broadcast industry had been reducing its workforce across the U.S. Even the largest markets braced for the repercussions. The economic spiral in 2002 had become the 2008 crisis. The decline in advertising dollars at TV stations meant positions such as sports reporters were being cut first. Anchors who worked in-studio were safe, but I had not pursued anchoring jobs. At KDFW, I held the position I had always coveted—sports reporter on location at games, in the locker room, at news conferences, at home with sports personalities. But I always knew my beloved position held a vulnerable place on the employee tree.

Still, I made it my calling card to report accurate information to viewers before other reporters had gotten a sniff. I had also refined the skill of getting the cell and home phone numbers of sports people. And I was inside the homes of our area stars before Tweets and Facebook posts opened personal information for public consumption.

Among the stars I interviewed were top-line Dallas Cowboys such as Troy Aikman, Darren Woodson, and George Teague, who all called me by name and watched my reports. Roger Staubach gave me a nickname. He pronounced it *Neets* and used it during the numerous times I interviewed him in his office. My friend Ray de Beasley once wondered aloud whether Roger spelled it *Niits* or *Nitz*.

So flattering.

But now, I was being fired.

I kept my emotions contained as I looked across the table at my soon-to-be-former news director.

"I admire you and the work you have done," Maria said that morning. She knew how much I had contributed to the sports division from July 1999 until that life-changing coffee break in October 2008. She knew about the lack of cooperation I'd had with the videographer who consistently failed to do his job with quality, which often made my job hard to perform.

"I admire how you handled it," she finished.

I wasn't sure what she meant by "it." Was it the work I had performed or the resistance I had endured?

As it settled upon me that my Dallas days would be over in ninety days, my skin began to tingle with anticipation. Why? Because I knew my life was going to monumentally change, and I gladly received it. I was exhausted physically and emotionally. I needed to restore balance. And in that instant, I knew I could focus on the serious fibroids surgery I had delayed.

Waiting any longer could pose a risk. Prolonged inaction can allow fibroids to worsen, which can trigger other health concerns—for example, heart disease, the number-one cause of death for U.S. women. Knowing the ending date for my service in Dallas (and the end of my full-coverage medical insurance), I pinpointed a date to have my fibroids removed. To avoid bearing the cost of the surgery, I would need to schedule it within the next two months.

Early in 2008, several months before I sat across from Maria Barrs in Starbucks, I had informed my supervisor Kevin Morrell that I would undergo an abdominal surgery that would keep me at home for several weeks. Looking over the sports calendar and specifically the Cowboys draft, mini-camps, summer training camp, preseason, and regular season, we settled on mid-December. My doctor saw no risk in my job-first timetable. Delaying, I thought at the time, could help me save my job. Now, after hearing Maria's news, concern for my job was off the table. The time was upon me to focus on my health.

It was a five-hour surgery with no complications. The doctor removed the tumors through three one-inch-long incisions cut into my midsection. I spent one night in the hospital to sleep off the painkillers. A slow safe ride on a cloud of pillows in a friend's big Texas four-wheel-drive vehicle delivered me back to my Vickery Place home and Pepper, my shih tzu. Recuperation required weeks of bed rest, with limited movement if I got out of bed. My retired father (who traveled from Augusta to Texas) and a Dallas friend who worked from his home took care of me.

I recovered in time to report on the 2009 Cotton Bowl, a college football game held on January 2. For Fox 4's family-oriented pregame program, I aired a story on future NFL player Michael Oher and three members of his adoptive family. What the family members shared with me in exclusive interviews in my last report on KDFW would become known to the wider public later that year in the Hollywood movie *The Blindside*.

CHAPTER 41

International Independence

Although I prepared for the inevitable and accepted it with equanimity, I would never have quit my career voluntarily. Too many pleasant occasions and people filled my years as a TV journalist. Who could argue with the beauty of having the high salary that comes from dressing up to talk to athletes and their families, and traveling at the expense of my employer? I savored the agreeable exchanges I had with people who recognized me when I encountered them on the street. And there was something exhilarating about calling someone and saying, "I'm with Fox 4 (or WTVM or WREG). May I come get your comments on camera?" The answer was hardly ever a *no*.

All of it was the manifestation of my childhood dream to succeed at sports journalism in Dallas. I had actually achieved it and lived it for nine-and-a-half years.

But in the first week of January 2009, my swan song was about to sound. Three months earlier, news director Maria Barrs had delivered the news to me at the Knox-Henderson Starbucks. She had cried; I had not.

But what had I felt?

In all honesty, a sunbeam had turned on inside me when I heard the finality of Maria's disclosure.

We're not renewing your contract.

I had heard the words in normal speed—not in slow motion, as we experience when something disastrous happens. It had been nothing like that. A physical response swept over me just the same. My face had flushed hot and then cooled. My heart rate had accelerated as I thought of the freedom that having no job would give me.

I probably said to Maria, "OK. I understand."

I had felt suddenly unburdened. I was leaving behind what had been, for me, the Wile E. Coyote's five-hundred-pound ACME weight in the Looney Tunes cartoons. Maria's words became the swing of a hatchet that untethered me.

At the same time, I had the curious thought that I had been not only the burdened Coyote but also his prey, the Road Runner. Like the latter, I had slipped out of sticky situations. Those were opposition-filled work relationships during stretches of time from 1986 until that moment in October 2008. Maria's announcement put an end to the exhausting chase.

Aware that KDFW saw the future without me in it, I had begun, as far back as 2005, to plan for a life abroad. I pitched and completed several international assignments from 2001 to 2009. After rescuing myself from the brink in the Dallas bank, I started preparing for a career of teaching my strategies of journalism in Europe. Perhaps that is why I had no tears to swallow with my coffee and my termination notice. I had packed my mental knapsack years earlier.

During the first five months after my contract ended, I routinely slept until noon on my own one-thousand-thread-count luxury bedsheets—when I was not traveling. When I did roam, I went first to Cabo San Lucas, Mexico, with nothing on my agenda except whale-watching with a friend.

June 25, 2009, became my bittersweet liberation day. My little Pepper died at our cozy home on Willis Avenue in Dallas. I had expected her death. My black-and-white shih tzu had been with me since Seattle in 1995 and was approaching the end of her breed's lifespan. Her large saucer-shaped eyes and her soft fluffy coat had provided me with tenderness whenever I rushed home from frustrating nastiness. Though a tiny dog, my Lionheart's loving force ushered me through the ugly times.

An inner-ear infection and a loss of balance took Pepper. I knew the gravity of her health before I departed for a Paris vacation that would last nearly three weeks. I would like to believe she let herself die in order to liberate me.

I would never have uprooted my little pumpkin from her fenced corner lot with the cushiony, wide-blade St. Augustine green grass that she loved to lie on. I couldn't have taken her away from the dog door that allowed her free access to our home; wouldn't have removed her from the love of Auntie Massiel, Pepper's caregiver whenever I traveled. For all Pepper had done for me to make my houses feel homey, I could not have confined her to live in a small apartment in Europe during the final stage of her life. I, though, was contemplating giving the Old Continent a try.

My French friend Sandrine helped me create a dossier in French. We selected four Paris schools that offered journalism classes. To each, we wrote a personalized cover letter to either a personnel director or a school director. On a Thursday (that must be my luckiest day of the week), I dressed in a classic navy-blue cotton wrap dress, a blue and leprechaun-green scarf, and three-inch-high, tobacco-colored ankle-strap sandals. (It is Paris, after all.) I charted the subway trains I would need to take and set out to hand-deliver my French letters and French CV.

I arrived without appointments but received welcoming responses at the first three schools. Speaking in French, I asked staff members to kindly pass my paperwork up the pipeline.

It was mentally taxing to show up at the prestigious schools and to speak French with enough proficiency to effectively sell myself. But I had studied the language for seven years and was able to deliver my pitches.

After the third school, I settled into a seat on train line 7. I was headed toward the Tolbiac stop and L'École Supérieure de Journalisme de Paris (ESJ Paris). On the journey, I thought about breaking for lunch and enjoying a Kir, a traditional Paris cocktail. I thought about calling off the day's job search entirely and resuming the next day. Cold-calling and bilingual gymnastics had exhausted me. But then I envisioned the finish line, a tantalizing prize of a good-paying, career-building position. It sobered me. A voice in my head challenged me. *You're a championship journalist, aren't you?* the voice asked.

I had always thought of myself in those terms.

So, what would a championship journalist do right now?

I answered with my actions. I organized the remaining documents in my briefcase and readied my mind to dial back into profession-al-grade French for the fourth and final stop of the day.

At ESJ Paris, I repeated the drill. From staff members, I learned that I would need to see the school's president, Guillaume Jobin, to discuss my candidacy. He was seeking a person with a particular professional background for the new sports-journalism master's program, they told me. Problem was, no one could estimate when Guillaume would return to school that day. I knew enough French to draw the director of external communications, Nathalie Bédé, into an extended conversation. A stalling tactic. She and I talked so long that I was still there when Guillaume returned.

"You need to look at her résumé," Nathalie urged Guillaume, wid-ening her eyes to show that she liked what she had read in my dossier.

Eagerness to start my pitch must have been written all over my face.

"Give me five minutes, please," said Guillaume.

I took a seat in the computer lab, where Guillaume later joined me.

I told him I had interviewed the internationally known sports people of the day, including Lance, Jordan, and Tiger. To show the variety of my work history, I mentioned my time with Muhammad Ali, Rosa Parks, and President Jimmy Carter, and my seven full-time TV jobs working for ABC, CBS, NBC, and Fox affiliates. After seven minutes, Guillaume said the most beautiful words imaginable.

"You are exactly the person we need."

Wasting no time, the president of the world's oldest journal-ism-only institution (founded in 1899) told me what the position paid and the start date for the 2009 academic year.

"I'll be back," I said in a restrained voice, though inside, the spirit that many obstructionists failed to bury was soaring. Guillaume

Jobin could not have known that offering me a teaching position validated all I had wanted to do in the September of my life. To train the next wave of journalists to find and share stories with sensitivity and care, to value the various voices that exist in a community—the way I felt journalism needed to be practiced. The time had come for me to disseminate my training pearls.

And—teaching? Forty years earlier I had felt scorn at the suggestion. Now, I saw the profession as a means to share my personal story—and a way to fight injustice.

I left Guillaume's campus full of anticipation. In a matter of months, students from around the world would be in my classroom to hear how I had endured systemic racism, sexism, and ageism—much of it covert, but nevertheless damaging—and how I had become a survivor of economic lynching. I would stress to students the importance of inclusion of all people and ideas that fall outside of the mainstream narrative. My presence would be the proof students needed to believe that they, too, could reach their potential. Along with my story, I would have an arsenal of journalistic techniques that I had created and that I would train them to use.

To augment the firsthand cultural references I already had (from Senegal, Germany, France, Mexico, and Canada), I spent thirteen days in Moscow, Russia, before the reboot of my career.

As I stepped into a new commission in front of a classroom, I accepted greater social responsibility. My crystal-clear mission in Europe became simple: to train journalists of the future to use only ethical and unbiased practices. To inspire them to become diggers for facts at a time when real facts were being crowded out by fake news, shallow researching, and lazy or nonexistent fact-checking. I would prepare the people who passed through my classroom to care as much about journalism as I had cared as a youngster and as a student.

I was born with a tidal pull toward truth seeking and truth telling. Perhaps that is why I began to wonder, during my childhood, why I saw only white men holding influential positions in broadcasting. There is a measure of diversity now, but much more is needed.

That matters because a multiplicity of views would give people useful information in exchange for the time they spend consuming news. I am not alone in seeing this as a shortcoming. On many occasions from the late-1990s until now, I have asked my father, an intelligent and perceptive man, what he has taken away from news reports we watch on mainstream television. Repeatedly, his reply has been something like: "Not one thing. There is no context given with the information." And he has said that the news "does not require me to think and it does not require me to react."

This disconnect between viewers and the reporting they receive is exactly what I address in lectures for my students. I want them to become broadcasters who create a link between the news they are sharing and the person who is watching. I train them to write with the utmost honesty and integrity about the newsmakers of their time and about the men and women who went before. To find hidden stories. I want their reports to be so gripping, engrossing, intelligent, and relevant to their audiences that they lure the next wave of the brightest people to our field.

I teach future journalists to avoid "shiny object" and "horse race" coverage of elections and to avoid being duped into following clown-like behavior of newsmakers. Other widely used, flawed approaches include giving more airtime to the results of the latest polls, while flattening voters into broad and largely inaccurate categories and, beyond that, failing to examine the issues.

The 2016 U.S. presidential election provides the best examples of the worst types of work. Journalists did not delve into topics and make prominent the viewpoints of various communities of voters. Because I did the opposite of what has become the prevailing practices, I recognized the attraction of candidate Donald Trump. I told first-year students at ESJ Paris in October 2015 that, yes, he could win the Republican nomination and, because of the malfunctioning two-party system, the U.S. presidency, as well.

I continued to talk about his popularity when, in October 2016, I appeared on a pre-election panel on France 24 television. I said, on the Paris-based program, that candidate Hillary Clinton had not yet put candidate Trump away and that "I'm not sure that she will." I also said, "For me, the 2016 election is up in the air." At the same time, mainstream American broadcasters and widely read newspapers had been repeatedly reporting a huge polling advantage for the Democratic ticket headed by Mrs. Clinton.

In my classroom, I am proudly a political Independent, which means I am neither a Democrat nor a Republican. I talk often about equal opportunity. I advise my students to provide to lesser-known people the equal opportunity to speak. My students hear my voice as one in the chorus that cries out against identity-based and biased reporting, which is reinforced when only one narrative makes it to air. It's my deepest desire for our industry that the people who produce stories and the people who hold the power to hire and promote carry out their towering tasks evenhandedly.

I have crossed the threshold of having taught one thousand two hundred university students, mostly at L'École Supérieure de Journalisme de Paris. For journalism students I am yet to meet, and for those who will never hear my lectures, I have written this book to light a fire within them.

A Grand Goodbye

Between the whirlwind of airports and foreign destinations and relocating to Paris in the summer of 2009, I settled down for two weeks in the U.S. to face an inescapable task. I had to say goodbye to one of the loves of my life. Since my childhood, I had wondered how that day would arrive and how I would find the strength to go on.

In mid-August, I left Dallas to go home to Augusta, Georgia. There, we moved my grandmother from her assisted-living residence and set her up to spend her final days in a hospital bed in the dining room of the family home. A gentle and caring hospice worker came each day to talk with us, the family, as Grandmama's transition approached. The worker wanted to know my grandmother's mental condition. Could she recognize people?

In front of the hospice attendant, I asked, "Grandmama, who is in the room with you?"

Propped up on two pillows, she answered.

"My grandbaby Nita."

Our gazes locked; affection passed between us. Her playful eyes had once been a bottomless brown. Surprisingly, at the end of her life, they had become a grayish blue.

The hospice worker had told me earlier that the remaining time I shared with my grandmother need not be dour, so I continued our fun for the worker's amusement.

"Am I the smart one?" I asked Grandmama.

"Yes, Baby."

The exchange of words made the hospice lady smile along with Grandmama and me. Of course I wasn't the only smart grandchild my grandmother had, but I wanted to show that she was mentally keen enough to acknowledge the trait. Grandmama, with her answer, was playing a private word game with me. For the two of us, being smart meant being industrious enough to learn something and then apply the training to achieve something. In this, I had followed her example.

On another evening, when Grandmama and I were alone, I repeated two questions I had spoken to her decades earlier.

"Do you know what you mean to me? Have you understood how important it has been for me to have you as my grandmother?"

"Yes, I know," she replied serenely.

She and I knew that my questions were a masked form of a goodbye—a *just in case* goodbye. I did not know how much longer Grandmama would survive. No one knew. It could be a few weeks or many months. I hoped for months because the dictates of my life demanded that I return to Dallas to get ready for my new teaching career.

I asked for her permission.

"Sure, Baby," she said, earnest and tender.

I was not surprised that she had blessed my decision. She had always wanted me to be prepared. My grandma had anticipated all my career moves with me. And I had shared with her details of my escapades in Paris and in the French countryside. By blessing my decision to leave her bedside, she was supporting my boldest move yet.

She was moving on to her post-earthly reward, something she believed would offer her peace of mind and bliss. That day, she made it clear that she wanted me to find the same while I was still alive.

Sure, Baby, she had said tenderly.

Grandmama was ninety-three years old when she died in August 2009.

CHAPTER 42

Paris and Its Parks

My eyes traveled from one person to the next as each came into view on the busy street corner. Couples, families, those walking alone on the bustling sidewalk of the fashionable rue Saint-Honoré in Paris—the procession of people eased by my tiny round outdoor table. I was pleased to while away the time. Pleased to hear the passing strangers speak in our shared language, the beautiful French language. Their presence provided me with a moment of delicious exaltation.

So did my rich peanut-butter milkshake.

My tongue rejoiced over the smooth blend—not quite a cocktail, not quite a dessert, but soothing and sweet. It satisfied my mid-afternoon palate.

I had slept until noon and awakened to a clear and mild September day. The American in me would have called it sixty-three degrees Fahrenheit. The European woman I had become knew that it was seventeen degrees Celsius. The woman in me not bound by borders just wanted to be outside in the beauty. Thus, I had ventured to a sidewalk café in the tony part of Paris.

Now, I enjoyed the sun's warmth and the wisps of breezes upon my skin. I heard the smattering of traffic sounds.

"My favorite season of the year is upon me," I thought. Would autumn also become the favorite season of my life?

A tear formed in my right eye. I used the back of my index finger to dab it away before it could roll down my cheek. A sudden and intense joy struck me. But I hid it from passersby; I kept a neutral expression.

The rush of emotion had come because, in that moment, I became acutely aware of the fact that I had won. I had won the years-long battle against career resistance and obstructionism. And had ended up neither jaded nor jailed. Like Jackie Joyner-Kersee, I had cleared the hurdles in my path. Despite a few emotional scrapes and scars, I had triumphed.

At age fifty, I wanted for nothing. I had met an array of fascinating people and had interacted with history makers and some of the world's most gifted sports figures. I had been blessed with years of good income that allowed me to reach back to create a merit-based, full-tuition scholarship in the communications department of Augusta College. I named it after my grandfathers, Walter Wiggins and James Lott, and funded it from 1995 to 2008.

I had reached my ultimate dream in Dallas, only to find a taste for the sweetness of life on another part of the planet.

Battle-tough like Little Mo, but not too hardened, I could still sense my feelings. I could still desire. I could still set a goal that I would passionately and actively and steadfastly pursue.

Sitting on that comfortable woven-rattan café chair, people-watching, I finally accepted the fact that my Paris experiment was working. Relocating to the city had presented me with professional respect, unhurried living, and creative stimulation. These essentials I had craved my entire life.

Whenever I wanted, I went to gaze upon the breathtakingly beautiful and stirring art at the Louvre and the Arab World Institute. At the Jacquemart-André Museum in 2011, I saw rare paintings by an Impressionist I particularly adore, Gustave Caillebotte. I strolled often with friends in inviting public spaces, such as the Luxembourg Gardens, created in 1612, and elegant Parc Monceau, with its Renaissance archway encircling a fountain. Under the towering trees of Parc des Buttes-Chaumont, I dined outside on a blanket on the untended lawns and watched numerous sunsets.

Yet, despite the cultural beauty at my fingertips, hesitancy had occupied a corner of my mind. From September 2009 until that moment at the sidewalk café in September 2014, I had felt the spasms of indecision. *Should I stay in Europe (somewhere) or should I go back to the country of my birth?*

News items, especially about my home country's continuous involvement in wars, nudged me to look outside the United States. Seeing the open-carry and campus-carry gun laws that Texas was considering[100] added another rupture point with Dallas, so I was not ready, at that time, to return to the city that had meant so much to me.

Something else about Dallas. I was there when I heard disturbing national news from the front lines of America's racial battlefront.

As I sat at the sidewalk table that peaceful day in Paris, I thought back six weeks earlier to the unpeaceful day of August 9. I was in Dallas preparing to sell my home in the Vickery Place neighborhood. News hit the TV airwaves about a fatal police shooting in Ferguson, Missouri, in the middle of the country. A twenty-eight-year-old white officer had killed a black teenaged boy, an eighteen-year-old. Conflicting versions of what happened filled hour upon hour of television.

The teenager's death weighed heavily on me. While in a moving truck between Dallas and Augusta, I had nine hundred twenty miles of roadway to reflect. I could not escape the discomfort of my thoughts. My mood sank as I recalled earlier videos of white law officers shooting and killing unarmed people of color and poor people—a national crisis.

The law officers had usually gone uncharged and unpunished.

The media's mistake of reporting fast and loose with the facts in the Ferguson shooting divided Americans into warring camps of opinion. I waited, along with the anxious nation, to know the truth. Was Michael Brown carrying a weapon and charging at the officer? And if there had been a confrontation between the teenager and the officer, did that justify the use of fatal force? It took six painful days before the public knew the name of the officer, Darren Wilson.

---

100. Texas legislators approved the open-carry gun laws in September 2015. In addition, they voted to allow "campus-carry" of guns at universities if the holder of the gun has concealed-weapons training. The new Texas law permits individuals who have obtained a concealed-handgun license (CHL) to carry loaded, concealed weapons in college and university buildings. See armedcampuses.org.

Across the board, news organizations failed in the basics. Journalists and their managers did not vet sources before allowing them on air. The incendiary and unsubstantiated statements that blared out on TV whipped the country into a frenzy. The power of television unleashed, it became an out-of-control squawk box that spewed boiling opinions unfettered and made a dark situation worse. Where was the reasoned middle ground?

I flew back to Paris on the last day of August 2014 without knowing the resolution in the story. The nagging open wound of the case followed me. Would there be charges? "This time, there had to be charges!" was the sentiment of many people who were inflamed by eyewitness descriptions of Brown's holding his hands in the air. *No justice, no peace* became the favored phrase in protests around the United States.[101] [102]

After recalling the disturbing U.S. events that took place in August 2014, I let the thoughts go. I allowed my analytical mind to rest. I returned to my untroubled, easy feeling on rue Saint-Honoré. As I savored the taste of ice and cream and peanut butter upon my tongue, a gentler memory fluttered through. I thought about a frank exchange I had with KDFW news director Maria Barrs.

"Do you have any questions for me?" Maria had asked during the job interview in 1999.

I detected we were talking woman-to-woman, so I replied with a question that was more personal than professional.

---

101. One hundred seven days after teenager Michael Brown died on a street in Ferguson, Missouri, a grand jury of six white men, three white women, two black women, and one black man decided not to indict the man who fired the shots. Officer Darren Wilson would not face any charges.

102. The official word on the case can be found in the *Department of Justice Report regarding the Criminal Investigation into the Shooting Death of Michael Brown by Ferguson, Missouri police officer Darren Wilson*, March 4, 2015, p. 82. It states: "The evidence establishes that the shots fired by Wilson after Brown turned around were in self-defense and thus were not objectively unreasonable under the Fourth Amendment. The physical evidence establishes that after he ran about 180 feet away from the SUV [sports utility vehicle], Brown turned and faced Wilson, then moved toward Wilson until Wilson finally shot him in the head and killed him." The report also states: "Disinterested witnesses all agree that Brown ran or charged toward Wilson and that Wilson shot at Brown only as Brown moved toward him. Although some of the witnesses stated that Brown briefly had his hands up or out at about waist-level, none of these witnesses perceived Brown to be attempting to surrender at any point when Wilson fired upon him. To the contrary, several of these witnesses stated that they would have felt threatened by Brown and would have responded in the same way Wilson did."

"What do you think of Dallas?" I asked. I hoped to gain a bit of understanding about the *person*, not the news manager, in front of me.

She sighed. "Dallas doesn't have enough parks."

Maria's answer was not one I expected. Only years later, while sitting at the Paris sidewalk café, did I realize a broader possibility for her words.

A city without parks can easily become a city without peace, for parks are the spaces in which nature pulls back from man-made encroachments. In this tranquil space, nature's beauty manifests in the gurgling stream that flows over pebbles, wearing them smooth, deepening their color. In the grass that bends under the weight of a foot, only to instantly recover, supple and unbruised. In the taller grasses that catch the wind and wave and bow to visitors who pause to observe nature's dance. In the treetops that draw the eyes skyward, elevating the perspective, making the spirit soar. In such a setting, a woman can escape the swirling madness of a city and find not only the peace in nature but that in herself.

That day on rue Saint-Honoré, I was soothed by the fact that in Paris, these spaces of peace surrounded me. "Paris has enough parks," I thought. But then the words of my former TV boss registered with me in a way she probably never intended.

Maybe Dallas, particularly KDFW and perhaps the television industry as a whole, did not have enough *Parks*—enough people with the tenacity to change a system, as Rosa Parks had done. With that possibility in mind, I decided, in that September moment at the café, to strengthen my identity as one of those dogged campaigners.

Paris has another Parks, I concluded.

The day I met seventy-five-year-old Rosa Parks in Tuskegee in 1988, she evoked in me vivid memories of my two grandmothers—sisters of her time. Mrs. Parks' light-colored coat and flapper's hat, her honey-toned skin and silky hair, her tranquil expression and close-lipped smile placed my paternal grandmother at the scene. The charming Southern accent of the icon's *Sure, baby*—her reply when I asked if I could hug her—pleased the ears of my soul. The slowly spoken words warmed me to the core, as my maternal grandmother's voice had done.

Just as a mother, full of fierce affection, might wrap arms around her child, so the Mother of the Civil Rights Movement embraced and held onto me when I met her. I am convinced that, with this gesture, this history-changing woman imbued me with some of her spirit, her iron will. Her will locked arms with my own unswerving personality. Rosa Parks never bore biological children, but when we released each other after that heart-infusing embrace, I had become a child of the movement she personified.

It took nearly thirty years to germinate, but I now know how to grow the seeds of her incalculable gift. (*We evolve in our own time*, the Witten couple in Dallas had said.) To do this, I capitalize on my platforms as classroom instructor, public speaker, essay writer, and television, podcast, and radio guest. In these places of influence, I cultivate the gift of activism that Rosa Parks delivered to me. In line with her legacy, I focus on social-justice concerns. I provide a perspective my students and other audiences in public spaces have not heard. They inform me of this; they welcome it, they say.

I feel good about this—but that was not always the case. For most of my life, I dreaded being singled out as the only black person in a setting. Now, I proudly wear the badge of everything that I represent. I emphasize in talks that *if you don't see someone who looks like you doing what you want to do, we are waiting for you.*

I salute the work that Mrs. Parks and many other activists carried out. They succeeded in blasting away some of the stones that would have blocked me in my right to self-fulfill. That is why I expose the violators who deny full freedom to others. This work of exposing is important, for abusers successfully subjugate and discriminate—and humiliate—because people are reluctant to talk about the wrongdoing.

I am not reluctant.

I cannot be silent.

With this book, with my story, I talk.

I Have a Request

How you can help:

Someone you watch on television might be enduring the pain of mistreatment from bosses and coworkers—as I did for years. If you suspect this, would you please let me know?

When I was asked about possible on-the-job abuse, I felt I could not reveal it to anyone. I fought through it alone.

But we can now speak about it, and that is the first step to ending workplace mistreatment.

Send the information to nita@nitawiggins.com. Include the name of the employee, the television station, and details about the alleged offenses. The information can be checked without revealing your name.

If you choose to speak, you might help someone get out from under a damaging and unnecessary emotional burden.

Acknowledgments

Although *thanks* is but a six-letter word, I must use it to attempt to express my appreciation to you, Daddy, Roosevelt Wiggins. Your effect on me is on virtually every page of this book and every day of my life. I have tried to pay forward some of the love, tenderness, and understanding you have bestowed on me. I learned from you to focus my efforts on what I could control.

Thanks to line editor Janet Walker, my sounding board as I searched for the appropriate tone to convey the swings from devastating disappointments to ridiculously enduring optimism. I especially thank you for recognizing my non-angry outlook and for smoothing out the texts to ensure that readers could interpret the same. And thanks for turning off the meter in counting the time over the years that you have contributed to making this project a polished, permanent record of my story.

Thanks to doctoral candidate Doria Dee Johnson, whose courageous 2014 presentation about lynching cemented the focus of this book: exposing unpunished lawlessness. She passed away before this book could come to press, but she knew of her inspiring role in it. Doria's frankness in revealing a lynching crime inflicted upon her family generations ago showed me that I needed to speak now—in real time. Perpetrators of today's injustices in American workplaces are still bruising souls and breaking the laws of the land.

To artist Marguerite Harris (in Paris), thanks for opening a cultural-awareness door by introducing me to Lorraine Hansberry's *To Be Young, Gifted and Black*. The book allows me to see a modern timeline of African American thought in the written arts and to weave myself into the fabric.

To novelist Gaëtane Selgi (in Paris), thanks for providing a cultural and political safe place to talk about truths.

Thanks to playwright Jerry Hickey (in Paris) for turning me on to Robert McKee's *Story*. Your advice adds to what I already knew about the writing process—*beginning, middle,* and *end*—yet, it gives me a deeper training in using structure and design.

Thanks to early readers Angela Shaw (in Toulouse, France), Ed Lowe (in Dallas), and Kevin Church (in Paris).

To veteran novelist and development editor Marita Golden, thank you for working on my "communal autobiography," a term I borrow from you. Thanks for giving me a concrete explanation of my mission: to put to paper a story that becomes a bridge for people to walk across to empathize with the experiences of others.

To publishing professional and marketing maven Martha Bullen, thank you for the urgency with which you jumped in to get this second edition over the last hurdles. You have been a crucial force in zipping up the edges and making this book the best it can be. Thanks for offering your guidance and expertise in all the areas where I sought your help.

To publisher, poet, and bridge builder Lucinda Clark, thank you for opening doors on the road to the book's release.

Thanks to my Paris mentor, Guillaume Jobin, who asked me to write my life story as a legitimate heroine facing a man-made obstacle course in U.S. journalism. Thanks for being my employer for eleven years at L'École Supérieure de Journalisme de Paris, where I have had the incredible opportunity to teach students from more than thirty nationalities and to determine what to write in this book to benefit them.

To the family of Wade Livingston, thank you for granting permission to use his photography on the cover of *Civil Rights Baby*. I will forever remember the care he took with me in his Dallas, Texas, studio to capture an image I would adore.

And Ludovic (in Paris). During the years of writing, rewriting, and canceling outings you suggested for entertainment, thank you for understanding that the pages of this "communal autobiography" are my timestamp that I lived. Thank you for being patient and offering encouragement until the final keystroke.

Endnotes

From the Introduction

The Johnson-Crawford family's experience demonstrates a lesser-known aspect of the losses that occurred after a lynching. Those who murdered Anthony Crawford threatened to take the life of Doria Dee Johnson's great-great-grandmother Tebby if the family removed Crawford's lifeless body from its noose. Wrote Ms. Johnson in a 1998 essay:

"The family was ordered to vacate their land, wind up business and get out of town. They did just that. His crime you might ask [sic]: cursing a white man for offering him a low price for the cotton seed he was trying to sell and being too rich for a Negro."

With an estimated wealth of $20,000 in 1916 (approximately $300,000 in 1998), Mr. Crawford was reportedly the wealthiest Negro in the Abbeville, South Carolina, area. The 56-year-old planter reportedly owned 427 acres of land, had 13 children, and helped establish a school, church, and farms in the local black community. Ms. Johnson says he loaned money even to white people. By fleeing their home to save their lives, the Crawfords and other black families who fled after lynchings forfeited their properties and other forms of accumulated wealth. Their abandoned possessions were often absorbed by neighbors or governing bodies.

In October 2016, thanks, in large part, to Doria Dee Johnson's public scrutiny of her great-great-grandfather's lynching, Anthony Crawford's life and murder received long-overdue acknowledgment from the city where his death occurred. The Community Relations Project, based in Abbeville, placed a permanent marker in the city's Jefferson Davis Park. Excerpts from the marker explain what happened after Mr. Crawford's arrest for refusing the price offered by a white customer:

> During the Jim Crow era, successful black people were conspicuous—and arguing with whites was dangerous.... 300 white men seized him from jail and dragged him behind a buggy. Finally stopping at the fairgrounds, the mob stabbed, beat, hanged, and shot Mr. Crawford over 200 times—then forbade the Crawford family to remove his hanging body from the tree. Terrorized, the well-established, multi-generational Crawford family and many other local black people realized that Abbeville was not safe for them.

Arguing with whites was dangerous—and their murderous responses unavenged. In Crawford's case:

> The gruesome public murder, though committed openly, did not lead to prosecution or conviction for any members of the mob. Days after the lynching, Abbeville's white residents "voted" to expel the Crawford family from the area and seize their property. When South Carolina's governor [Richard Irvine Manning III] declared himself powerless to protect the family from violence, most of the surviving relatives fled to destinations as distant as New York and Illinois, fragmenting the once strong and close-knit family. [Governor Manning served from 1915 to 1919, according to the National Governors Association (nga.org, accessed July 12, 2021). Also, see "Hundreds Dedicate Lynching Marker to Anthony Crawford in Abbeville, South Carolina," Equal Justice Initiative, Oct. 24, 2016. Accessed April 22, 2017.]

From Chapter 2, Noisy Neighbors, Media Icons, and Martyrs

Many years after Medgar Evers' assassination in 1963, the author was part of a small group of Huntington, West Virginia, journalists who interviewed Myrlie Evers, widow of the man who became known as the Mississippi Martyr. The interview took place during the decade of the 1990s. One of the author's colleagues asked Mrs. Evers to evaluate the progress she thought the country had experienced in the fight for civil rights. Not a bad question. The problem is that the reporter, either uninformed or simply a victim of poorly chosen words, said something like, "Dr. King's fight for civil rights"—as if the American Civil Rights Movement had belonged only to one man. The author will never forget the quality of Myrlie Evers' voice when she responded. The voice trembled as if to suppress a pain so old and deep it could only be controlled through great effort. "It was not...*Dr. King's*...fight," she earnestly corrected. Scholars recognize 37-year-old Medgar Evers as the first civil rights activist in that era to be targeted and assassinated. The murder left the 32-year-old a widow with three preschool children, making it also *her* family's fight for civil rights.

From Chapter 7, Why Did Rosa Parks Hug Me?

Browder v. Gayle, a U.S. Supreme Court case, eradicated segregation on the buses in Montgomery. Lead plaintiff Aurelia Browder (and co-plaintiffs Susie McDonald, Claudette Colvin, and Mary Louise Smith) challenged the constitutional legitimacy of the segregation laws in Montgomery and in the state of Alabama, and won. *Browder v. Gayle* named Montgomery mayor W.A. Gayle defendant. Organizers of the protest called for its end on December 20, 1956, the date the Browder court order would take effect. Protestors had taken taxis, carpooled, hitchhiked, and walked for 381 days. (See congressofracialequality.org; King Papers at King Institute, Stanford University; and Rosa Parks with Jim Haskins, *Rosa Parks: My Story* (New York: Scholastic Inc., 1994).

From Chapter 18, **And Now: Heeeere's...Failure!**

Ten U.S. senators put forth the College Athletes Bill of Rights framework on December 17, 2020. The push follows the Senate-chamber testimony of National College Players Association Executive Director Ramogi Huma, who stated that federal legislation could ease the racial inequities reinforced by the NCAA's current structure. Read more at (ncpanow.org). The group included nine Democratic senators: Richard Blumenthal and Chris Murphy of Connecticut, Cory Booker of New Jersey, Kirsten Gillibrand of New York, Kamala Harris of California, Mazie Hirono and Brian Schatz of Hawaii, Chris Van Hollen of Maryland, Ron Wyden of Oregon. Sen. Bernie Sanders, an Independent from Vermont, supported the proposal.

Ahead of the framework proposed on the national level in 2019, California governor Gavin Newsom signed his state's Senate Bill 206. It is known as the Fair Pay to Play Act. From 2023 forward, it will allow students who are athletes at California schools to earn money from their own name, image, and likeness (called NIL). By the spring of 2020, more than 30 of the 50 state legislatures had copycat proposals under discussion. Florida Governor Ron DeSantis signed a bill in June 2020 to permit students who are athletes in Florida to sign with an agent and to earn money off of their name, image, and likeness, or NIL.

These developments follow the work by the National College Players Association, whose athletes have complained that "NCAA rules leave the so-called 'full' scholarship athletes with a shortfall of $3000/year" and that the "NCAA's cap on athletic scholarships leaves players struggling to make ends meet, [while] CBS is giving the NCAA almost $11 billion over 14 years just for the TV rights to the Men's Final Four Basketball Tournament."

The athletes' organization published an 11-point mission statement, which includes a proposed CARE Plan to reduce football brain-trauma injuries. The statement also urges shifting out-of-pocket medical bills away from the athletes themselves.

Compare the foregoing with the following money trail. The NCAA listed its media deals since 1982 in response to the unsigned question, *"Is a history of NCAA media rights agreements available?"* The NCAA media contract of 1991 eclipsed one billion dollars for the first time, with the seven-year contract with the CBS network. The NCAA-provided list also included its 2010 CBS/Turner Network agreement for the men's national basketball championship as a 10.8 billion-dollar payout over 14 years. The deal runs from 2011 through 2024. "As with the current contract, approximately 96 percent of the revenue generated from this new agreement will be used to benefit student-athletes through either programs, services or direct distribution to member conferences and schools," according to ncaa.org.

Here are just a few talking points published in October 2015 by Kain Colter, former football player for Northwestern University and a co-founder of the College Athletes Players Association (CAPA). On ncpanow.org, he writes: "1) The NCAA makes over $11 billion in revenue from their TV contracts alone. 2) Coach Mike Krzyzewski of the Duke University men's basketball team earns $9.6 million/year. 3) Coach Nick Saban (University of Alabama football team) earns $6.9 million. 4) Colleges are not required to pay for any sports-related medical expenses. Not one penny. 5) Universities are free to revoke scholarships of players in good standing for any reason, even injury. 6) Perhaps most shameful is the NCAA's refusal to implement concussion reform despite the mounting evidence of severe short and long term [sic] health risks. There have been numerous tragedies where former NFL players committed suicide and were later found to be suffering from CTE, chronic traumatic encephalopathy."

From Chapter 24, Unforgettable

Vice President Harris earned a B.A. from Howard University, making her the first person from a historically black college or university (an HBCU) to reach her post. After her 1986 undergraduate degree from D.C.-based Howard, she earned a degree from the University of California's Hastings College of Law in 1989. President

Biden earned a B.A. from the University of Delaware in 1965 and followed it with a Syracuse University law degree in 1968.

Forty years before Biden-Harris, Ronald Reagan graduated from Eureka College in Illinois, but his vice president, George H. W. Bush, graduated from Harvard. Jimmy Carter and his vice president, Walter Mondale, with their Naval Academy and University of Minnesota educational backgrounds, are the most recent president and vice president who did not come from Ivy League universities.

The great leap in voting participation in 2020 across all ethnic groups stirs a clapback of voter-suppression proposals in January 2021. Insidious maneuvers to reduce access in 47 of the 50 states replace the previous targets of suppression: third-party candidates and third-party policy input. Chief among Republican-led state-houses, Georgia passes an omnibus bill that severely restricts voting hours, ballot drop locations, and early-voting dates. Governor Brian Kemp signs it.

Across the aisle, national Democrats propose remedies to extend voting access, such as the For the People Act and the John Lewis Voting Rights Advancement Act.

From Chapter 32, Uprooted

The Fourteenth and Fifteenth Amendments to the U.S. Constitution are two of the three Reconstruction Amendments and were added in 1868 and 1870, respectively. The Fourteenth, known as the equal protection amendment and the citizenship amendment, made racial discrimination illegal in employment and other areas. The Fifteenth extended voting rights to black men, expressly saying that voting could not be denied on the basis of "race, color, or previous condition of servitude." The framers of the Constitution wrote, in Article I, Section 4, that voting rights "shall be prescribed in each state by the legislature." The result: Mostly—but not exclusively—property-owning white men had the power to vote.

Shortly after the passage of the Reconstruction Amendments, some white people began to feel that black progress encroached on their lives, writes author James W. Loewen. "Whites...ached to be rid of their African Americans." (*Sundown Towns: A Hidden Dimension of American Racism*, New York: The New Press, 2005, p. 48.) Oklahoma and other states outside the traditional South created advertising to lure only white residents to move in and increase their numbers and leave behind "malaria," "mosquitoes," "Negroes," and other undesirable elements (p. 48). After 1907, Democrats in Oklahoma passed segregation laws modeled on Mississippi's. The next year, white perpetrators dynamited a black hotel that was doing brisk business in Okemah, Oklahoma (p. 82).

Some white people in the Tulsa area of Oklahoma found it objectionable that, by 1921, African Americans had developed a bustling business district in the segregated black community of Greenwood. Author Nita Wiggins transcribed the following statements from three known survivors of the 1921 Tulsa Race Massacre and its aftermath, as made to members of the House Judiciary Subcommittee on the Constitution, Civil Rights, and Civil Liberties. The hearing took place on May 19, 2021, at the U.S. Capitol. A black sister and brother, 107-year-old Viola Fletcher and 100-year-old Hughes Van Ellis, traveled to Washington, D.C., to give testimony. Another black witness, 106-year-old Lessie Benningfield Randle, entered her statements into the national record via videoconference.

The murders, assaults, looting, burning of homes and businesses, and the dropping of flaming balls of turpentine from airplanes had been concealed for more than 50 years. Historians estimate that Tulsa's deadly raid by white aggressors is one of 100 similar occurrences that took place in the United States after the end of World War I.

From 107-year-old Viola Fletcher's testimony to the subcommittee:

> On May 31, in '21 [1921], I went to bed in my family home in Greenwood. The Tulsa neighborhood I fell asleep in that night was rich, not just in wealth, but in terms of culture, humanity, heritage, and

my family had a beautiful home. I felt safe and had everything a child could need. I had a bright future ahead of me. Greenwood had given me the chance to truly make it in this country. In a few hours, all of that was gone.

The night of the massacre, I was awakened by my family. My parents and five siblings were there. I was told we had to leave, and that was it.

I will never forget the violence of the white mob when we left our home. I still see black men being shot, black bodies in the street. I still smell smoke and see fire. I hear the screams. I have lived through the massacre every day.

The three of us here today are the only ones left that we know of. The City of Tulsa and the Tulsa Chamber of Commerce are still responsible for making it right because it was they who caused the massacre and its continued harm. The chamber helped ensure that we could not rebuild after the massacre, including holding us in the internment camps.

They owe us something. They owe me something.

I have lived much of my life poor. My opportunities were taken from me and my community, North Tulsa. Black Tulsa is still messed up today.

Our country may forget this history, but I cannot. I will not. And other survivors do not. And our descendants do not. The City of Tulsa and the Chamber of Commerce told us the massacre didn't happen, like we didn't see it with our own eyes. You have me here right now.

Testimony to the subcommittee, Hughes Van Ellis, 100 years old, World War II veteran:

> You may have been taught that when something is stolen from you, you will go to the courts to be made whole. You go to the courts to get justice. This wasn't the case for us.
>
> The courts in Oklahoma wouldn't hear us. The federal courts said we were too late. We were made to feel that our struggle was unworthy of justice, that we were less valued than whites, that we weren't fully Americans. We were shown that when black voices called out for justice, no one cared. But we still had faith things would get better. I did my duty in World War II. I served in combat in the Far East (in China, Burma, and India). I fought for freedom abroad, even though it was ripped away from me at home and even after my home and my community were destroyed.
>
> When I returned home, I didn't find any of this freedom I was fighting for overseas. Unlike white servicemen, I wasn't entitled to GI Bill benefits because of the color of my skin. I came home to segregation, a separate and unequal America, but still I believed in America.
>
> We live with it every day, and the thought of what [my] Greenwood [neighborhood] was and what it could have been.
>
> We were asking for justice for a lifetime of ongoing harm, harm that was caused by the massacre. I still believe in the ideas that I fought overseas to defend. Please do not let me leave this

earth without justice, like all the other massacre survivors [who died before being heard and
compensated].

For a discussion of the long-term financial outcomes for black
World War II veterans compared to the outcomes for white con-
temporaries, see *The Color of Law: A Forgotten History of How Our
Government Segregated America*, p. 167 (Richard Rothstein, W.W.
Norton & Company, Ltd., 2017). Rothstein's Chapter 10, "Suppressed
Incomes," reveals that the GI Bill of Rights, known as the Servicemen's
Readjustment Act of 1944, gave legal cover to the racially biased
actions of Veterans Administration personnel, who in practice limited education and job-training opportunities for black veterans. The
concrete and lingering effects are lower-paying jobs, higher-interest
bank loans, redlined home purchases, and non-existent gains from
rising home values.

***Lessie Benningfield Randle, 106 years old, testimony to the
subcommittee:***

> One hundred years ago, I was 6 years old. I was
> lucky. I was a young child and I felt very safe.
> My community was beautiful. It was filled with
> successful black people. Then, everything changed;
> it was like a war. White men with guns came and
> destroyed my community. We couldn't understand
> why. What did we do to them? We didn't under-
> stand. We were just living. But they came and they
> destroyed everything.
>
> They burned houses and businesses. They just took
> what they wanted out of the building, then they
> burned the building. They murdered people.
>
> We were told they dumped the dead bodies into
> the river. I remember when I was outside of our

house, I just passed dead bodies. It wasn't a pretty sight. I still see it today in my mind, 100 years later.

I have survived 100 years of painful losses. I have survived to tell this story. Hopefully, now you all will listen to us while we are still here.

It seems like justice in America is always so slow or not possible for black people. There are always so many excuses for why justice is so slow or never happens at all. I am here today, 106 years old, looking at you all in the eye. We have waited too long, and I am tired.

We are tired.

The following text is an excerpt from JusticeForGreenwood.org, the official website for information about the events of May 31 to June 1, 1921. Accessed June 3, 2021:

TRAUMA, INTERNMENT & STOLEN WEALTH

By the time night fell, the entire community was either ablaze or reduced to rubble. Hundreds of Black residents had been murdered, while the rest had fled in terror or been arrested. According to eyewitnesses, the bodies of the dead were piled in the streets, trucked down to the Arkansas River, and thrown into the current.

By the morning of June 1, 1921, Black Wall Street, the country's greatest model of Black prosperity, ingenuity, and hard work, lay in ashes. No whites were arrested.

- 6,000 Greenwood survivors were confined for up to eight days in internment camps.
- 10,000 black Tulsans were displaced.
- 40 city blocks burned to the ground.
- Over 100 businesses bombed and destroyed.
- $100 million total property loss.

Attorney Damario Solomon-Simmons and a legal network filed a lawsuit against the City of Tulsa and six other defendants on behalf of eleven plaintiffs. The defendants are "demanding accountability and restitution for the 1921 Tulsa Race Massacre and 100 years of continued harm."

https://www.justiceforgreenwood.org/lawsuit.
Accessed June 2, 2021.

Sports Figures, Fans Together Can Improve Policing: #GCOaG

Recruiting fans and their favorite athletes to reduce the harm of police violence before it happens.

De-escalating with #GoodCopsOnlyAtGame

by Nita Wiggins

As a TV sports reporter, I saw the police presence in the 27 NFL stadiums, many NBA arenas, and major league baseball parks where I covered games. It's a necessary part of the events, but in my judgment, it is absolutely not appropriate for an officer accused of excessive force or similar types of misconduct to be on duty at the games.

I saw with my own eyes that police officers treat black athletes just fine on game day. This respectful treatment doesn't always occur on the streets. We, the ticket-buying public, can insist on a code of conduct for officers receiving game-day pay for security work. In my mind, these pieces fit together because I was in the homes of teenaged athletes who became superstars as professionals. Many of their communities resemble the communities of the victims of police violence that we have all seen in the videos. I'm trying to create a solution that lets people—the officers and civilians—know that they live interrelated lives and that the success of one relates to the success of the other.

I am inviting you, sports fans and all other stakeholders in safer policing, to lend your influence to **Good Cops Only at Game**, which incentivizes officers to de-escalate at the start of an encounter. In this way, **#GCOaG** makes possible an immediate reduction in the harm suffered through police violence.

314

This is a public campaign that can either use social media or the tried-and-true method of telephoning the team management offices. The foundation idea is simple: *We, the people, can use our voices* to insist that officers who work up close to us at events also possess clean records when it comes to brutality committed against civilians.

Here's the process:

1. Members of the public can contact athletes, teams, team owners, and arena and stadium managers on social media (or, they can telephone the teams, arenas, and their business-partner restaurants and vendors) to insist on disqualifying any officer facing brutality charges.

2. This ticket-purchasing public can insist that security assignments to protect the public at games can go only to officers not accused of or being investigated for brutality or similar misconduct.

An officer on administrative or other disciplinary restrictions related to alleged abuse is disqualified from games (or concerts or other events that the public attends). After a transparent investigation, a cleared officer can resume game-day work. (FAQ about **GoodCopsOnlyAtGame** can be accessed on www.NitaWiggins. com. Visit LinkedIn and Instagram for more information.)

#GCOaG recognizes that a law-enforcement officer is an important part of a community, just as is the civilian population. The other essential components of GCOaG are the sports contests, which enhance the quality of life by showcasing the performing athletes. The venues of competition are the meeting place.

Will *YOU* help #GCOaG?

Join the many believers in civil rights and the countless others who fight for justice. Help us **turn #CGOaG**, an online meeting place, into a real-world solution.

Next Steps
Please Share your Feedback and Reviews

Thanks so much for reading *Civil Rights Baby*.

How did you like this book?

I love hearing from readers. So, give it to me straight. Please share your thoughts with me by emailing nita@nitawiggins.com.

If you enjoyed this book, I would appreciate your writing a review on Goodreads.com, Amazon.com, or your favorite book review site.

Go for Your Success

How can I help you with these
additional resources and opportunities?

1. **Seeking an interview for your program, podcast, article, or blog.** Send me an email at nita@nitawiggins.com.

2. **Organizing panel discussions, speakers, moderators, or in-program interviewers for your event.** Does your audience want to dig into topics such as broadcasting and journalism, career strategies, women's empowerment, getting unstuck at your job, American politics, race, sports, and personal motivation? My speaking topics include:

   • Leading Does Not Mean Leaving Someone Else Behind

   • From Augusta, Georgia, to Paris: A Believable Journey that Can Help Launch Yours

   • ** *Most requested* ** Find Your Power after a "Worst Day Ever"

3. **Building your team, targeted consulting—even half-day private exchange.** Would you like to learn how to communicate better? Contact me for the tools I provide in my program, *Listen to Others as you would have them listen to you*®.

4. **Get moving on your story with my Quality Quick Start to Write Your Book.** In twelve targeted sessions, unlock the story you want to share but have delayed for too long. Reach out to me with your questions and a complimentary consultation on your project.

Please email me at nita@nitawiggins.com if you are interested in any of the above.

Do you need one-on-one help?

Visit www.nitawiggins.com to learn more about how you can benefit from my background and experiences. Reach out if you are ready to climb toward your audacious goals. I look forward to hearing from you.

About the Author

American author Nita Wiggins is an acclaimed speaker, television commentator, and journalism instructor. She lives in Paris, France, and teaches university students the research and interview strategies she developed and used during her career on U.S. television from 1986 to 2009. *Black Women in Europe*® named her to the group's 2018 Power List for her role as an educator.

Wiggins appears regularly on the Paris-based France 24 television network to discuss workplace equality, women's working lives, and media accuracy and representation, as well as U.S. life through the lens of politics, sports, and race. A sought-after voice, Wiggins has also been interviewed on Cameroon's CRTV and Senegal's TFM networks.

Civil Rights Baby: My Story of Race, Sports, and Breaking Barriers in American Journalism is her first full-length book. She previously contributed chapters to two graphic novels by Michael Teitelbaum and Lewis Helfand, *Martin Luther King Jr.: The Dream Assassinated and Martin Luther King Jr.: I Have a Dream.*

From the iconic Eiffel Tower during Global Sports Week 2021, Wiggins moderated an international panel, *Sports as a Catalyst for Social Justice.* Also in early 2021, she presented her paper, "Testimony on Economic Lynching in the United States," at the Université de

Tours conference titled *The Black Family: Representation, Identity, and Diversity*. Economic lynching is a term she coined in 2014 to express the intentionality of choking off a person's career advancement and, from a power hierarchy, enlisting others to join in the act.

Wiggins shared in a 2001 regional Emmy for Special Events Coverage for KDFW-TV Fox 4 in Dallas, Texas, and received the RTNDF's Michele Clark Fellowship while a reporter at WSAZ-TV in West Virginia in 1989.

Currently, the Macon, Georgia, native devotes much of her time to helping people write their stories to bring out empathy in others. She is also co-developer of Good Cops Only At Game, a positive-incentive campaign designed to reduce the harm of police violence before it happens.

Wiggins earned a European master's degree from ESJ Paris and a B.A. in Communications from Augusta University in Georgia. From 1995 to 2008, she supported students at her undergraduate alma mater by awarding the Walter Wiggins-James Lott Communications Scholarship. She is a member and mentor in the National Association of Black Journalists (NABJ). For more information, please visit www.nitawiggins.com.

www.ingramcontent.com/pod-product-compliance
Lightning Source LLC
Chambersburg PA
CBHW070907030426
42336CB00014BA/2325